Make the Grade.
Your Atomic Dog Online Edition.

The Atomic Dog Online Edition includes proven study tools that expand and enhance key concepts in your text. Reinforce and review the information you absolutely 'need to know' with features like:

- **Review Quizzes**
- Key term Assessments
- Interactive Animations and Simulations
- Notes and Information from Your Instructor
- Pop-up Glossary Terms
- A Full Text Search Engine

Ensure that you 'make the grade'. Follow your lectures, complete assignments, and take advantage of all your available study resources like the Atomic Dog Online Edition.

How to Access Your Online Edition

- **If you purchased this text directly from Atomic Dog ….**
  Visit atomicdog.com and enter your email address and password in the login box at the top-right corner of the page.

- **If you purchased this text NEW from another source….**
  Visit our Students' Page on atomicdog.com and enter the **activation key located below** to register and access your Online Edition.

- **If you purchased this text USED from another source….**
  Using the Book Activation key below you can access the Online Edition at a discounted rate. Visit our Students' Page on atomicdog.com and enter the **Book Activation Key in** the field provided to register and gain access to the Online Edition.

Be sure to download our *How to Use Your Online Edition* guide located on atomicdog.com to learn about additional features!

This key activates your online edition. Visit atomicdog.com to enter your Book Activation Key and start accessing your online resources. For more information, give us a call at (800) 310-5661 or send us an email at support@atomicdog.com

2179CCPSU

T0325565

PKG

*Some online Editions do not contain all features.

Business Protocol
Contemporary American Practice

BUSINESS PROTOCOL

Contemporary American Practice

Third Edition

David Robinson
University of California, Berkeley

CENGAGE
Learning™

Australia • Brazil • Japan • Korea • Mexico • Singapore • Spain • United Kingdom • United States

CENGAGE
Learning™

**Business Protocol:
Contemporary American
Practice, 3e**

David Robinson

V.P. Product Development:
Dreis Van Landuyt

Developmental Editor: Sarah Blasco

Sr. Marketing Coordinator:
Sara Mercurio

Production/Manufacturing
Manager: Donna M. Brown

Sr. Production Coordinator:
Robin Richie

Custom Production Editor:
K.A. Espy

Rights and Permissions Specialist:
Kalina Ingham Hintz

Cover Image: © Getty Images

© 2010 Cengage Learning

ALL RIGHTS RESERVED. No part of this work covered by the copyright herein may be reproduced, transmitted, stored or used in any form or by any means graphic, electronic, or mechanical, including but not limited to photocopying, recording, scanning, digitizing, taping, Web distribution, information networks, or information storage and retrieval systems, except as permitted under Section 107 or 108 of the 1976 United States Copyright Act, without the prior written permission of the publisher.

For product information and technology assistance, contact us at
Cengage Learning Customer & Sales Support, 1-800-354-9706

For permission to use material from this text or product, submit all requests online at **cengage.com/permissions**
Further permissions questions can be emailed to
permissionrequest@cengage.com

Library of Congress Control Number: 2009925252

Book ISBN-13: 978-1-424-07249-1
Book ISBN-10: 1-424-07249-2

Package ISBN-13: 978-1-424-07659-8
Package ISBN-10: 1-424-07659-5

Cengage Learning
5191 Natorp Boulevard
Mason, OH 45040
USA

Cengage Learning is a leading provider of customized learning solutions with office locations around the globe, including Singapore, the United Kingdom, Australia, Mexico, Brazil, and Japan. Locate your local office at: **international. cengage.com/region**

Cengage Learning products are represented in Canada by Nelson Education, Ltd.

Visit our corporate website at **cengage.com**.

Printed in the United States of America
1 2 3 4 5 6 7 11 10 09

CONTENTS

LIST OF BOXES

Business Protocol in Action

It's Just Different

PREFACE

Business Protocol: A Contemporary American Practice, Third Edition, is a textbook and resource aimed at two distinct audiences: first, undergraduates who have good book learning but little experience of how business operates in practice; and second, more experienced businesspeople who are new to the United States who wish to understand the American business culture.

The book takes a "middle American" approach to business protocol with a rather prescriptive tone, setting out the right thing to do in a way that would be unlikely to cause offense on either the East or the West Coast. However, the book encourages readers to observe some nuances and differences in behavior according to local custom and the culture of specific industries.

In comparison with the large number of business communications texts that are in print, this book assumes that the reader has had several college level English writing courses and does not attempt to teach vocabulary, grammar, or word usage.

NEW TO THE THIRD EDITION: AN EMPHASIS ON ELECTRONIC COMMUNICATION

The third edition of *Business Protocol* reflects the dramatic shift toward electronic communication that is seen throughout business. For more than a decade, businesspeople have talked about the virtues of a "paperless office" and e-mail has been firmly entrenched. It has been like watching a wave approaching the shore, knowing that it will crash at some point. Well, the collapse of letter-writing has arrived. Even the most formal business transactions are routinely conducted by e-mail. Within firms, Instant Messenger and texting between members of a work group are entirely commonplace.

The text now includes a longer discussion about message planning—thinking ahead about the purpose of each communication. E-mail has a new prominence as the primary form of business communication. Compared with previous versions of the book, the third edition has a little less information on day-to-day personal behavior. This reflects that people new to U.S. business have increasing exposure to the culture through movies and TV even before they arrive in the country.

■ INSTRUCTIONAL FEATURES OF THE THIRD EDITION

In this edition, we are taking advantage of the Atomic Dog hybrid model by moving the end-of-chapter multiple choice questions to the online edition. This allows us to keep the printed form of the book a reasonable length, and many students much prefer to take practice quizzes online. However, the "Put This Chapter into Practice" exercises remain in the book, as instructors may wish to assign them as part of coursework.

Each chapter includes three text boxes that contain narratives of specific applications of business protocol.

> *Business Protocol in Action:* These boxes contain brief examples of the concepts in practice.

> *Doing the Right Thing:* This sequence concerns ethical best practices in business.

> *It's Just Different:* These examples seek to consolidate learning by contrasting U.S. culture with accepted behavior in other countries.

For the student, these text boxes provide additional information on the chapter concepts. Instructors may wish to assign these text boxes as the basis for in-class discussion. With the understanding that there are regional and industry-specific variations in practice, a useful approach is to ask students where and why they would disagree with the advice given in the text.

■ ONLINE AND IN PRINT

Business Protocol: A Contemporary American Practice, Third Edition, is available online as well as in print. The online version demonstrates how the interactive media components of the text enhance presentation and understanding. For example,

- Chapter quizzes test students' knowledge of various topics and provide immediate feedback.

- Clickable glossary terms provide immediate definitions of key concepts.

- References and footnotes "pop up" with a click.

- Highlighting capabilities allow students to emphasize main ideas. They can also add personal notes in the margin.

- The search function allows students to quickly locate discussions of specific topics throughout the text.

- An interactive study guide at the end of each chapter provides tools for learning, such as interactive key-term matching and the ability to review customized content in one place.

   Students may choose to use just the online version of the text or both the online and print versions together. This gives them the flexibility to choose which combination or resources works best for them. To assist those who use the online and print versions together, the primary heads and subheads in each chapter are numbered the same. For example, the first primary head in Chapter 1 is labeled 1-1, the second primary head in this chapter is labeled 1-2, and so on. The subheads build from the designation of their corresponding primary head: 1-1a, 1-1b, etc. This numbering system is designed to make moving between the online and print versions as seamless as possible.

■ ANCILLARY SUPPORT

Atomic Dog is pleased to offer a robust suite of supplemental materials for instructors using its textbooks. These ancillaries include sample syllabi and PowerPoint® slides.

Included on our Instructor's Resource CD are model syllabi to show how the book can be used in semester-length courses or in a sequence of quarter-length classes.

A full set of PowerPoint slides is also available for this text. These are designed to provide instructors with comprehensive visual aids for each chapter in the book. These slides include outlines of each chapter, highlighting important terms, concepts, and discussion points.

ABOUT ATOMIC DOG

Atomic Dog is faithfully dedicated to meeting the needs of today's faculty and students, offering a unique and clear alternative to the traditional textbook. Breaking down textbooks and study tools into their basic "atomic parts," we then recombine them and use rich digital media to create a "new breed" of textbook.

This blend of online content, interactive multimedia, and print creates unprecedented adaptability to meet different educational settings and individual learning styles. As part of *Cengage Learning,* we offer even greater flexibility and resources in creating a learning solution tailor-made for your course.

Atomic Dog is loyally dedicated to our customers and our environment, adhering to three key tenets:

Focus on essential and quality content: We are proud to work with our authors to deliver a high-quality textbook at a lower cost. We focus on the essential information and resources students need and present them in an efficient but student-friendly format.

Value and choice for students: Our products are a great value and provide students with more choices in "what and how" they buy—often at savings of 30 to 40 percent over traditional textbooks. Students who choose the online edition may see even greater savings compared with a print textbook. Faculty play an important and willing role, working with us to keep costs low for their students by evaluating texts and supplementary materials online.

Reducing our environmental "paw-print": Atomic Dog is working to reduce its impact on our environment in several ways. Our textbooks and marketing materials are all printed on recycled paper. We encourage faculty to review text materials online instead of requesting a print review copy. Students who buy the online edition do their part by going "paperless" and eliminating the need for additional packaging or shipping. Atomic Dog will continue to explore new ways that we can reduce our "paw-print" in the environment and hope you will join us in these efforts.

Atomic Dog is dedicated to faithfully serving the needs of faculty and students—providing a learning tool that helps make the connection. We hope that after you try our texts, Atomic Dog—like other great dogs—will become your faithful companion.

■ ACKNOWLEDGEMENTS

Two influences on my thinking deserve recognition. Edward P. Bailey, Jr., clearly articulated the application of "Plain English" in business communication education, and Judith Martin (who writes as "Miss Manners") has a practical approach to etiquette that modernized a dowdy field.

I bear a debt of gratitude to many colleagues who guided me through this process. Donny Chia first suggested the need for a book to bridge business communication and etiquette. Jill Steinbruegge and Victoria Whetstone have been generous in sharing examples of real-world business problems and have been tireless in debating solutions with me. Steve Scoble and Sarah Blasco have been supportive publishers and editors, particularly useful in distilling comments from adopters of the two previous editions. My students at the University of California, Berkeley, and my friends in China and Viet Nam have brought new issues to my attention and challenged my thinking.

David Robinson

ABOUT THE AUTHOR

David Robinson is a Senior Lecturer at the University of California, Berkeley, and has taught at Stanford University, the University of San Francisco, and Santa Clara University. He has taught short courses in places from Hungary to Viet Nam. He studied at the University of Durham in England and then at Oxford. His Ph.D. in Psychology is from Brown University in Rhode Island and his MBA is from the University of North Carolina, Chapel Hill.

Every year more than 1,000 students enroll in his Principles of Business class at Berkeley and he has led several study tours to Asia. Observing intercultural differences in behavior led him to write about American practices that people take for granted. His column "Business Protocol" appears each Sunday in the *San Francisco Chronicle* (sfgate.com).

Chapter 1

A Real Professional

Professionalism begins early.

Sitting down to enjoy a healthy lunch from the company cafeteria, which features low-fat, organic food, Taylor is a little embarrassed to be overhearing a conversation between two senior managers at the next table:

"That intern was just so unprofessional!" one of the managers declares.

"Nothing that was a firing offense, of course, but once this summer's over, that's it—out of here. No chance for permanent hire."

"Of course," concurs the colleague, sympathetically.

Taylor is left to wonder: "Good heavens! What did that poor intern do—or not do? I would never want my manager to describe me as 'unprofessional.'"

■ 1-1 YOUR AIM IS TO BE PROFESSIONAL

If you could have just one word used to describe you in business, you'd want to be known as **professional**. This adjective is hard to define. You know from everyday speech that people use the word to mean something much more than the dictionary definition, "A member of a learned profession such as a physician or attorney." You blush with pride when the word is applied to you, for it is the highest compliment. So what must you do to deserve it?

Professional people show *commitment*. They know what tasks have been assigned to them and what their duties are, and they take full responsibility for getting work done on time. They are single-minded in their tasks, and once they begin a project, they make sure it is completed and done well. If something goes wrong, professionals find extra resources to complete their tasks and don't waste time blaming other people. If you think about people you know who show good professionalism, you'll notice that part of demonstrating this commitment is the ability to know when not to accept a responsibility: "I'm sorry—I shouldn't commit to that. I'm on vacation next week, and I know that I couldn't get you the

Table 1-1 The Key Characteristics of Professional Businesspeople

Make commitments and keep to them.

Do not overcommit.

Act with integrity.

Demonstrate flexibility.

Show discretion for confidential information.

Maintain expertise by continuous learning.

Treat others with consideration.

Speak diplomatically.

Have a neat personal appearance.

figures you need in time to be useful. Can I have you talk with my colleague, who could do that for you?"

In contrast, unprofessional people are constantly tripping over themselves with seemingly unavoidable conflicts in their lives: "Oh, I know I promised you the figures, but I had to work on the quarterly report and I didn't get around to it." Or, worse yet, they hide behind the catch-all phrase "Something came up."

So, let's begin to develop a working definition of "professional" (see Table 1-1). It's already been noted that a high-functioning professional knows how to manage her or his own schedule. You'll also observe that highly professional workers are *self-directed*—they don't constantly need supervision.

Part of being a professional involves having *integrity*. Again, that's another word that we use every day that is hard to define. It means being consistent and being of one piece, or whole. For example, there's nothing worse than dealing with a service worker who is charming to customers and then turns and shouts at coworkers. This worker looks like two parts (charming and mean) in one fractured body. We show integrity by behaving consistently in all elements of our working lives. Integrity is fundamentally important in public life; inconsistency between personal behavior and public expectations can destroy a career (see *Business Protocol in Action: An Impression of Integrity Can Be Quickly Damaged*).

Now, to be truthful, being a professional often involves the denial of personal feelings. Suppose you have a bad fall from your bicycle and end

Business Protocol in Action: An Impression of Integrity Can Be Quickly Damaged

In early 2009, great excitement accompanied the swearing in of Barack Obama as the 44th President of the United States. However, the expected "honeymoon period" of goodwill between the new president and Congress was soon interrupted by the revelation that several of his nominees for cabinet positions had failed to pay part of their taxes in previous years. By the time they faced Senate Committees for approval of their nominations, all of the candidates had rushed to make restitution, paying the taxes owed with interest.

After using political persuasion to push through the confirmation of the first candidate with tax problems, President Obama agreed to let other candidates withdraw. He realized that although each incident of tax evasion was relatively minor, the cumulative effect was to give his new administration an aura of lack of integrity: Here were people who were being put forward to run government who didn't seem to be particularly careful about following the rules that apply to average citizens about paying taxes when due.

President Obama acknowledged the problem quickly and gave several TV interviews in which he said: "I've got to own up to my mistake. Ultimately, it's important for this administration to send a message that there aren't two sets of rules—you know, one for prominent people and one for ordinary folks who have to pay their taxes."

up in a hospital emergency room. You don't expect the nurse to come in and say, "Ugh! That's really disgusting—you've got blood coming out all over! I think I'm going to throw up." Even though a nurse may feel that way, he or she would not make such a comment. What you hope will happen is that the professional will set aside his feelings and treat you in a calm and efficient manner.

One aspect of denying personal feelings involves setting private matters aside while at the workplace. Sooner or later you'll have a colleague whose entire life seems to be one dramatic episode after another. The worker may come into the office late, be unkempt, and begin a long narrative of the drama in the latest episode of his or her life. No single aspect of behavior is less professional than chatting about personal issues while at work. So part of "integrity" involves separating out personal issues while in the workplace.

In our private lives, we can choose with whom to associate. If someone in our social circle is beginning to irritate us, we can choose not to spend time with him or her. Of course, this just isn't possible at work. Although the people from the Accounting Department may be unhelpful or even unpleasant, we don't have the option to say, "I just hate Accounting—I won't even go over there!" Again, professionalism requires that we set aside our own feelings while on the job.

If you think about any job you've had (even working with peers on school projects), you'll be able to identify people with whom you've enjoyed working in the past. Thinking about your favorite colleagues, one common feature is likely to be that, although they focus single-mindedly on the task at hand, they balance this with some flexibility. For example, a sales executive making an important presentation opens up her laptop and finds that it won't work. Checking the power cord and battery and attempting to restart it both end in failure. She turns to one of her custo-mers' managers and calmly says, "Well, clearly my laptop just died. I wonder…could I possibly borrow yours? I have my presentation here on a flash drive." Note that there is no drama, no cursing of the machine, and no losing track of the purpose of the meeting.

Professionals are absolutely *discreet,* that is, they can keep a confidence. Doctors know all kinds of things about their patients, but the last thing that you would want to know was that your doctor was telling stories about you. "He was such a whiner! It was just a simple shot and he was screaming like I was cutting his arm off." Of course, you wouldn't expect this behavior. In business, you might obtain information that is really "juicy," but if you want to be professional, you'll keep it to yourself. You may inadver-tently hear who is leaving the firm, who has just been promoted, or who is being disciplined, but it's important to keep this information to yourself.

A good way to practice discretion is to avoid indulging in office gossip. There's nothing more appealing than a coworker beginning a con-versation with a half-smile, a pause, and the words, "I really shouldn't be telling you this…" But spending time on gossip is wasting time that could be more productively employed, and spreading gossip is likely to destroy good working relationships. The best reply to people who begin: "I really shouldn't be telling you this" is, "Well, perhaps you shouldn't, then!" Professional people often have access to private information, and it is essential that they maintain that confidentiality (see *Doing the Right Thing: Don't Take Advantage*).

If you're in any doubt about what information to share with a col-league, a good standard is to apply a test of **need to know**. Does my

Doing the Right Thing: Don't Take Advantage

There will be many times in business when you hear something that is someone else's private business. Especially if you work in financial services, you'll have access to information that allows you to find out what people are buying, who has money to spend, and so on.

If you are ethical, you will treat this information as "privileged." That is, it is information given to you so you can do your job, but not information you should act on in your private life. Learning to keep confidential information confidential is an important part of being successful and respected.

colleague John need to know that his personal assistant is talking openly in the break room about quitting at the end of the month? Absolutely. Do I need to tell my personal assistant that I heard that one of the other PAs is having twins? Probably not.

Every rule has its exceptions, and, of course, there are times in business when you should not keep quiet. In the past few years, there has been a rash of corporate scandals in the United States. In their simplest form, most of these have involved people making false entries into a company's official records. If someone asks you to do something that you know is wrong (for example: "Let's just enter this contract as if it came in last year, okay?"), it's a time not to be discreet. Refuse to make the transaction and be prepared to let senior managers know what is happening.

Professionalism certainly includes the concept of specific expertise. For example, a dentist earns a degree to be able to do things with teeth that other people can't. But although the dictionary definition of "professional" refers to the "learned professions" (doctors and lawyers), plenty of people in other jobs can show true professionalism through their behavior. You can be a thoroughly professional janitor just as you can be a thoroughly *unprofessional* neurosurgeon, depending on your behavior in your role. Part of being an expert is committing to continuous learning. Think about the office machines you have to use every day. The fax sometimes works and sometimes doesn't. Instead of just accepting this inconsistency, you should read the manual to learn more and understand why the machine won't work. Your colleagues will respect you when you say, "Well, when it acts like this, you have to press the reset button. Then it'll work."

A real professional makes an effort to communicate to customers and coworkers that transactions will be handled efficiently and accurately. The professional signals this by always treating other people and the situation with *consideration*. For example, a stockbroker might ask a customer if he or she is familiar with the firm's business systems: "Okay, have you made a fund transfer before? Let me help you with the steps..."

Professionals speak with tact. There are plenty of times when customers ask for the impossible, or coworkers are unreasonable, but it rarely helps the situation to state this directly. "You know, you're always late with projects, and this makes it very difficult to deal with you!" may be true but is unlikely to make a colleague act in a more timely manner (see *It's Just Different: The Language of Diplomacy*).

The final way in which professionals communicate their commitment to their work (and to their customers or patients) is through their *personal appearance*. Have you ever wondered why people wear business suits to conduct commercial transactions? It is a symbol of a personal commitment to the task at hand. The suit says: "I prepared for this meeting.

It's Just Different: The Language of Diplomacy

If you watch the news on television, you may have wondered about the strange turns of phrase used to describe meetings between foreign ministers and ambassadors (diplomats). The language sounds prissy and quaint, almost antique. After days of negotiation, talks may break off with a comment that "both sides have made substantial progress" (code for: "'We are close to an agreement"). Or the comment might be: "We had a frank exchange of views" (the diplomatic way to say: "We are nowhere near agreement, and just got as far as telling the other country why we think they are wrong").

Although this almost antique, courtly style of language may strike you as odd, it has a purpose. Diplomatic language is deliberately tactful and is a way for participants to comment without escalating tense situations. For example, if a minister came out of a meeting and commented to the press: "We've been banging heads all morning! These people are idiots and we're wasting time here," there's little chance that a crisis could be peacefully resolved.

There's much to be said for learning to be diplomatic in business. "I wonder if I could get you to copy that for me at once? I'm leaving the office for a meeting" is likely to get you much better cooperation than saying: "I need it now!"

I am not merely fitting in this meeting while I am in the middle of working on some matter in my personal life."

Along with wearing the right clothing, professional people are perfectly groomed. Grooming means paying attention to personal hygiene and neatness. The waiter whose shirt is untucked and whose hair is flying wildly may take your order quickly. But his sloppy appearance will make you wonder whether he will correctly respond to your requests, and whether he isn't being sloppy in the kitchen, too.

A good self-presentation will communicate to customers, supervisors, and interviewers that you have the skills to succeed in the business world and that you understand the importance of communicating your professionalism through your personal appearance.

◼ 1-2 PROTOCOL MEANS MORE THAN REVIEWING HONOR GUARDS

When you think about the word **protocol**, you may have an image of foreign dignitaries arriving at the White House on a state visit. You might wonder about the correct protocol: Does the premier's husband stand behind her while the national anthem is played or beside her? Should they shake hands with the president, or is this the time for a hug? But protocol turns up in everyday situations, too. In every business situation in every country in the world, there are unspoken rules of conduct that determine how people expect one another to behave. Just as Woody Allen said that time is "nature's way of keeping everything from happening at once," you could say that protocol is the way we limit an infinite range of human activities to some reasonably predictable set of behaviors.

The term **business protocol** refers to a concept that includes some aspects of business communication and the parts of **etiquette** that relate to professional life. It's easy to scoff at etiquette as a silly set of rules that apply to society matrons (do I have to wear white gloves after Memorial Day?). However, Judith Martin (who writes wonderfully entertaining and insightful columns under the byline "Miss Manners") has cleverly said that etiquette is just a set of rules that enable us to live together without killing one another. All of us have experienced a brief moment of rage at a coworker and the passing thought, "Why, I'd like to kill that…"—but we don't.

Protocol can also serve a negative function in a society. Lapses in protocol often signal who is a stranger to a group. Such lapses served a useful function in prehistoric times, when it was helpful to know who really belonged to a tribe. But now that we don't operate in a tribal society, feeling out of place as a newcomer can interfere with establishing effective working relationships. Studying business protocol is frankly a good investment in your personal advancement. It will help you fit into a business environment in which you will experience professional success.

▪ 1-3 BUSINESS LIFE IN THE "DOMINANT CULTURE"

The United States, with less than 5 percent of the world's population, contributes almost a quarter of the world's economic output. That leads some people to feel that Americans have come to have overwhelming influence in how international affairs and commerce are conducted, so much so that the American way of doing things has now become the **dominant culture**. The concept of dominant culture implies that even if other countries have a different way of doing business, they will have to conform to American practices because the United States tends to control most international commerce. As cruel as this required conformity sounds, we should not be too coy: American firms are very good at what they do. People come from all over the world to study at American business schools, and perhaps more importantly, some of the brightest, best, most hardworking individuals in the world immigrate to the United States to work for American firms.

While we're being honest, there is no use in denying that English (and American English at that) is the universal language of business. Watch a Japanese tourist settle his bill in an Austrian hotel, and after a few minutes, both participants switch to English. Although this trend was well underway before the advent of the Internet, online communication has removed any doubt. Of course, there are many Web sites in Swedish, Thai, and Arabic, but it is obvious that the dominant language of the Web is English. As a consequence, young people throughout the world have a hunger to learn English and the American way of doing business.

Many aspects of American culture may seem ugly to people arriving from other countries: Public spaces are often dirty, advertising signs are garish, and there seem to be more beggars on the streets of U.S. cities than in the poorest countries in the world. When American businesspeople travel abroad, they are often seen as impatient and demanding, and they are often spectacularly ignorant of other countries' cultures and customs.

Despite foreigners' misgivings about life in the United States, there is almost universal admiration for the American approach to business. It's energetic, practical, and pragmatic. Decisions are made according to the profit motive, not family ties. Promotion is according to merit, not social class or longevity. U.S. corporations have a notoriously "flat" hierarchy with little bureaucracy and few layers of government, so new ideas are rapidly embraced. Although Americans traveling abroad are sometimes seen as pushy, they are more often highly regarded for their interpersonal warmth, enthusiasm, and openness. Although we can't say that corruption is nonexistent in U.S. business, whenever it's discovered, it becomes front-page news and it's very severely punished. As a result, people in the United States who've never met one another do business with full trust; when businesspeople interact with government agencies, they have the expectation that the rule of law will be followed and administrators' decisions will be fair, equitable, and just.

To an outsider coming from another county, U.S. business appears to have no structure, and it's hard to see how companies can function in an apparent state of anarchy. Chief executive officers (CEOs) of large corporations—some of the richest people in the world—routinely give interviews humbly dressed in a T-shirt and jeans. People don't seem to stand on ceremony, and it appears as if there is no code of behavior at all. The lowliest summer intern can greet the company president in the firm's cafeteria with a cheerful, "Hi, Larry!" and the president is likely to reply, "Let's go jogging together sometime!" For all the apparent casualness, however, U.S. business does indeed have its own protocol, its own unspoken rules.

▪ 1-4 CULTURES AND SUBCULTURES

When we talk about American business protocol, there is an implication that everyone in the United States does everything the same way. You may already have enough experience to know that there are subtle variations in customs, rituals, dress, and styles of communication. Some of these variants are regional subcultures. For example, a casual business get-together in the southeastern United States is likely to feature a "pig picking," in which a whole pig is roasted and the main dish at dinner is pork "picked" from the grill. In New York City, where many people have religious prohibitions against eating pork, roasted pig would never be considered as a menu item.

There are also variations in behavior among industries. In the entertainment industry based in Los Angeles, most professionals spend much of their day on the phone. It's not unusual for an executive to return 80 to 100 calls a day. In that industry, people expect to do a lot of business by phone. In contrast, a life insurance sales rep in the Midwest would expect to spend most of the day in face-to-face meetings with customers. Someone who joined an insurance agency in Des Moines, Iowa, hoping to do business largely by phone probably wouldn't be very successful. These industry-specific patterns of expected behavior are also a subculture.

Within the overall American culture, then, we can observe regional and industry-specific variations in patterns of behavior. However, there are many common themes that you will observe in any good professional behavior, and we will begin with a guiding principle, a new "Golden Rule."

■ 1-5 A NEW GOLDEN RULE

A good place to start your study of business protocol is with a new version of the Golden Rule. You'll probably remember people telling you when you were younger that the Golden Rule is: "Treat other people as you would wish to be treated yourself." In business, we can do better than that: We have to treat others people in such a way that they can do their jobs as easily as possible. The **New Golden Rule** is this:

> In business, you have but one job:
> to make it easy for other people to do their jobs.

To do this, you have to treat other people with more than just polite consideration. You have to stop and think: "How does this person do his job? What information does he need from me, and in what order? What will he need next?"

Let's look at an example. You arrive at a large hotel at the end of a long business day, tired from your flight and the struggle to get a taxi at the airport. Balancing your briefcase, overcoat, rolling luggage, and newspaper, you join one of several lines at the front desk. In the line to your right, you notice a harried businessman talking loudly on his cell phone. As the line advances and he reaches the front, you hear him say: "Well, tell them they're all IDIOTS!" and then mutter "Lea" to the bewildered desk clerk, who responds with, "Checking in or checking out, sir?" The businessman interrupts his cell phone tirade to spit out: "Checking in, of course! Lea! I told you."

After looking at the computer screen, consulting some paper files, and checking with a colleague, the desk clerk interrupts the cell phone rant to say: "I'm sorry, sir. I'm not finding that reservation. Do you have a reservation number?" The angry customer slams his cell phone down onto the desk, reaches into his briefcase and pulls out a sheaf of travel documents, saying: "Here, you find it," and returns to the phone conversation.

"Ah, that's Lea, L-E-A," says the desk clerk. "I've found your registration, Mr. Lea. Now here's your key," then adds, "And is there anything else we can do for you?" as the customer turns without a word of thanks and walks away.

In the silence left by the cell phone screamer, you notice that you are now near the head of your queue and you observe the following interaction as the customer in front of you gets to the desk: "Good evening. I'm Sharon Johnston, that's Johnston with a T. I have a reservation for two nights." You observe that Ms. Johnston already has out her credit card, turned so the clerk can read "Johnston" and understand the spelling of her last name.

"Ah, yes, Ms. Johnston…welcome back to the hotel. We have you close to the pool—is that alright? It might be a bit noisy?"

"No, that's fine, I'll be doing my laps myself in a few moments. One question, though: What time is breakfast open?"

The clerk replies: "From 6 to 9 A.M., in the coffee shop."

"Hmm, that'll be a problem on Wednesday. I have a 6 A.M. flight …"

"Well, room service operates all night—you could order an early breakfast or a box meal to take with you if you'd prefer."

Ms. Johnston understands that the spelling of her last name is a little unusual; she anticipates that it will be easier for the clerk to find the reservation if he can both hear and see her name (holding up her credit card was a good way to do that). Ms. Johnston's chief concern is about her early checkout, but she waits until the right time before asking the clerk. Note that she asks about the restaurant and doesn't begin with: "I have an early flight." (So what?)

The old-fashioned Golden Rule would have Ms. Johnston greeting the clerk with: "Well, I imagine you're exhausted. Is this the end of your workday? Have you been on your feet since eight o'clock this morning?" Pleasant, for sure. Empathic, yes. But it does nothing to get the business transaction started.

Like all rules, the New Golden Rule has a corollary, something that naturally follows from the original premise. In this case, the Rule tells us what to do when someone else shows a lapse of etiquette; our duty is to correct the situation as quickly as possible by establishing good business protocol. Again, our goal is to help them do their job as best as possible. For example, you come to a hotel front desk and you are the only customer. The two clerks are chatting about last night's social encounters. No matter how much you are tempted to bang the desk and say, "Hey! You have a customer here! How about a bit of service!", it is better to alert them (your briefcase bangs on the desk) and, then if there is no response, say, "I wonder, could one of you help me with check-in?"

The corollary of the New Golden Rule involves applying generous amounts of forgiveness. Suppose you're at a business meeting and you join a conversation involving one of your subordinates. If your colleague fails to introduce you to the other person, you can introduce yourself. Helping other people overcome their lapses involves two parts: First, you must take responsibility for making the situation work smoothly. Second, forgiveness implies forgetting. Don't brood on other people's lack of courtesy—show them by example how to do things better.

▶ > > PUT THIS CHAPTER INTO PRACTICE

1. For a complicated transaction, such as going into a branch of your bank and cashing a check made out to you by a friend, think through: What information will the clerk need and in what order?

2. Review Table 1-1 and note the attribute of professionalism at which you see yourself being weakest; then make a plan to practice

improving that skill. For example, can you identify any projects within your work group (or student club) in which there's been no progress because no one has committed to managing the project?

KEY TERMS

business protocol

dominant culture

etiquette

need to know

New Golden Rule

professional

protocol

Multiple Choice Practice Questions: To take the review quiz for this chapter, log on to your Online Edition at www.atomicdog.com.

Chapter 2

Introductions

Confident introductions demonstrate your maturity.

Two job candidates sit nervously in an outer office, waiting for an interview. A smartly dressed young woman enters the room, and the candidates aren't sure whether the new person is a secretary, another candidate, or the executive who will be the decision maker for the job. One candidate stands up, makes eye contact with the newcomer, and extends his right hand.

"Hi. I'm Subata Anaya, and I'm here for a 3 o'clock with Leslie Stein."

"Good! I'm Leslie. I'll be interviewing you. Nice to meet you."

Trivially simple, right? But the other candidate has just lost the critical opportunity to make a positive first impression.

So why do so many people overlook the chance to introduce themselves? We would all agree that there's a sense of awkwardness when we're in a business situation and we don't know exactly who's who. And yet we often hold back.

Perhaps this reserve comes from a very formal (and outdated) type of English etiquette in which it was considered brash and impolite to ever introduce oneself.

2-1 A GOOD INTRODUCTION GIVES YOU A GOOD START

Nothing starts off a business encounter better than a clear, confident introduction. While Europeans may laugh at: "Hello, my name is Tom and I'll be your server today" (why do you need to know the waiter's first name?), it is the type of friendly interaction that Americans expect.

In professional selling, instructors teach young salespeople the ABCs of selling: *Always Be Closing* ("closing" means asking the customer to close the deal or place an order). We can say the same about introductions: Always Be Introducing Yourself (that is, you can never introduce yourself too often).

Some people are reluctant to introduce themselves because they feel shy. But just as often, people hold back from beginning the process of introductions because they don't want to seem pushy. A great example worth watching is actor Tim Robbins playing the character Griffin Mill in the movie *The Player*. Robbins plays the part of a Hollywood movie studio executive, and in each scene he always introduces himself (using first and last name) to all the famous actors who come across his path.

When you've met someone before, there's sometimes a moment of tenseness while each person wonders if the other has remembered her or his name. An immediate, simple restatement of your name (accompanied by a slight tap of your right hand to your upper body)—"Hi, Tom Studebaker"—offers a polite reminder and could never cause offense. Once you miss that first-moment chance to re-introduce yourself, it becomes increasingly difficult to find the right time in a conversation to say: "Oh, and I should've told you my name."

If you get stuck in a conversation in which you missed that first opportunity, and it's clear that the other person is searching for your name, it's polite to help him or her out. Saying

> "I should've told you: I'm Libby Daffner."

puts the other person on the spot and implies that he or she made an error in not remembering you. The nice way out of this situation is to imply that the person probably does remember *part* of your name but—for good reason—doesn't remember the other part. For example,

> "Oh, I should've told you: My name's Libby *Daffner* since I got married this summer."

Or, using the context of a mutual colleague:

> "I'm not sure Harry gave you my first name when he said I'd be working on your account. I'm Elizabeth Daffner, but please, call me 'Libby.'"

Or perhaps an e-mail or phone identification will provide you with a gracious way to state your name:

> "My e-mail is the same: libbydaffner@sales.org—that's Libby Daffner, all one word, no period or underscore. Just ask for Libby Daffner in Technical Sales when you call."

2-2 CULTURAL NORMS

Americans are friendly, outgoing people. Although they respect hierarchies and give deference to superiors, they usually choose a decidedly casual level of formality in most business interactions. The chief executive officer (CEO) of a large corporation will most likely greet a lowly sales-person with, "Please, call me Steve."

Of course, this type of behavior isn't true all over the world. Every society has its own **cultural norms**. An exaggerated stereotype of the rule for introductions in English upper-class society is that one should never introduce oneself. That is why characters in Victorian novels are always begging their hostess at a social function to make an introduction. There is an old joke that in England, it is very rarely permissible to introduce yourself, say if you're stuck in an elevator for more than 24 hours. At the beginning of the second day, you stiffly extend your hand, with these words: "I wonder if you would permit me to introduce myself? My name is Johnson." (Note, not "Tom" or even "Tom Johnson.")

But Americans like action and are very egalitarian. Successful busi-nesspeople are comfortable introducing themselves. The following rules show how to make introductions correctly:

- If you're expected for an appointment, always announce yourself by your first and last name: "My name is Ronnie Mora, and I'm here to meet Ms. Lee in purchasing." (It's impolite to ask for the other party—Ms. Lee—without giving your own name, too, so the simple "I'm here to see Ms. Lee" is wrong.)

- Never refer to yourself by a title ("Mr.," "Mrs.," or "Ms."). Because "Mr." is an **honorific** (in full, "honorific title," meaning a formal style of address, such as "mister" or "doctor"). Other people can use it about you, but you shouldn't say, "I'm Mr. Mora." "I'm Ronnie Mora" and "My name is Mora" (for example, on arriving at a rental car counter) are acceptable forms.

- Whenever possible, repeat your name in a way that helps people with unusual pronunciations or spellings:

  "I'm Tony Lam—that's just L-A-M, no B."

  "I'm Tom 'Shevorsky'—that's spelled 'Przeworsky.'"

- When you are introducing yourself, speak almost artificially slowly and distinctly. Your name is very familiar to *you* but may be hard for someone from a different ethnic or cultural background to understand at first hearing. Most people rush and mumble the pro-nunciation of their own name, and this doesn't help good business communication.

■ 2-3 NONVERBAL COMMUNICATION

Although we think about spoken and written words when we use the term "communication," we form a lot of impressions of other people in social contexts from **nonverbal communication**. This means how people stand and sit, how they use gestures, and whether they touch one another. In U.S. business situations, most people begin and end a meeting by extending their right hands for a handshake. The handshake is immediate, firm, and brief. It's never wrong to extend your hand first (see Figure 2-1).

Figure 2-1   New Zealand Ambassador with Chinese World Trade Organization Negotiator

Most American businesspeople are accustomed to being greeted by a handshake rather than a kiss. Americans expect an easy smile and good eye contact upon meeting someone.

SOURCE: © AP Images/Donald Stampfli.

There's a range of style in handshakes, and this is, in part, culturally determined (see *It's Just Different: Greetings Around the World*). For example, while shaking your right hand, some people may routinely use the left hand to also grab your right shoulder or upper arm. Although this style of handshake may be uncomfortable for you, not much is meant by it; the other person is just attempting to be friendly.

It's Just Different: Greetings Around the World

In general, Europeans (especially Swiss and Germans) are more likely to shake hands, and to do this more often, than Americans. German handshakes are firm and hearty. European women often shake hands (for example, two lady friends ending lunch in Geneva might well expect to shake hands). Some American women don't expect to shake hands, but this is generational—younger women in business expect to be taken seriously and routinely offer to shake the hands of either women or men with whom they are about to do business. In Korea, handshakes are gentle (they'd strike most Americans as "weak"), and a Korean businesswoman might be surprised if a stranger reached to grab her hand.

The Japanese bow to one another, slowly and quite deeply, but Americans almost never bow to one another.[1] This brings up the question: "What do I do if I'm an American businessperson welcoming important customers from Japan who are visiting my company?" You can show your cultural sensitivity by beginning your greeting with a short bow, and then adding a handshake. Remember, most visiting businesspeople have read extensively about U.S. business practices, even if this is their first trip to the States. If you find yourself in an awkward situation (you shake hands with a woman who clearly wasn't expecting it or you have just been given a bear hug by a Mexican colleague), you can cheerfully comment on the cultural differences and get conversation going.

Although handshakes are the norm in the United States, hugs and "air kisses" are the norm in some industries, such as entertainment and fashion. An air kiss means placing right cheeks close but not actually touching, and miming a kiss. (In Hollywood, this degenerated into the verbal expression "Kiss-kiss, darling" without the pantomime.) Men almost never hug or kiss other men (except at moments of extreme joy, such as when a soccer team scores a winning goal), and the French or Arabic style of fraternal kisses (right cheek, left cheek, right cheek) is extremely uncomfortable for most Americans —no matter how well intentioned the gesture. So it's best to stick with handshakes unless you are sure that you have correctly observed the behavior of other people in a particular business situation.

[1]An excellent book that details the differences in nonverbal communication is *Kiss, Bow or Shake Hands* by T. Morrison, W. Conaway, and G. Borden, Adams Media, 1995.

Americans never avoid making eye contact and, even when greeting a superior, look the other person straight in the eyes. A natural, unforced, easy smile (look on the Web at pictures of the late President Ronald Reagan for a good role model) is expected and does not signal a lack of serious purpose, as it might in other parts of the world. Elsewhere, avoiding eye contact is a way to show respect. Unfortunately, in the United States a lack of strong eye contact is interpreted as signaling that something is wrong and that the transaction at hand won't be honest and forthright.

■ 2-4 YOU'LL HAVE AT LEAST TWO FORMS OF YOUR NAME

Most people have a number of different forms of their name, which range in use from the most formal to the most casual. For example, General Motors chairman George Richard Wagoner, Jr., is universally addressed as "Rick Wagoner." The formal version of your name is technically the words that are on your birth certificate and passport, and for students, the name you use when you register at the university.

U.S. government officials and businesspeople will expect your family name to come at the end. If the family name is Louie, you introduce yourself as follows:

Zeming Louie

not Louie Zeming (although that's how the name would be spoken in China).

An exception to this is printed lists of names (such as directories) that are alphabetized first by the last name and then the first name:

Louie, Freddy
Louie, Zeming
Louis, Sean

In this example, the last person would introduce himself, "I'm Sean Louis."

If you do business in other countries, be alert to the possibility that the name order will be different. In America, the order is forename, middle name, family name, but in China, it is family name, forename, middle name, and in Viet Nam it is family name, middle name, personal name. So former Singaporean prime minister Lee Kuan Yew has the family name "Lee" (not Yew), and Vietnamese prime minister Nguyen Van Dung, has "Dung" as a personal name.

In addition to their full, legal name, most people have two or more familiar forms of their name by which they prefer to be called (for example, "Bill Clinton"). Although some people have a childhood name ("Bobby" or "Buddy," for example) that is used only within their family, many Americans use familiar, diminutive forms of their names at work (for example, former U.S. president James Earl Carter is known worldwide as "Jimmy Carter"). Using such names is consistent with American friendliness and informality, and it is almost never wrong to use the familiar form of the name after you notice other people in your work group using it. Finally, many Americans have a nickname, a name that is based on a personal characteristic and that has no relation to the formal name —for example, former vice president Richard Cheney's chief adviser, I. Lewis Libby, was known as "Scooter Libby" in business and government.

■ 2-5 BE THOUGHTFUL ABOUT YOUR OWN NAME

In business, you can choose how you are addressed. If there's a short form of your name that you prefer, you can use it all the time. On the other hand, if you want to keep a personal name just for family and go by a different name in business, that's perfectly acceptable. If your name is Robert, your family has always called you "Bobby" (and you hate it), and you prefer to be called "Bob," you can gently correct people:

> "Good to see you, Robert."
> "Please, call me Bob."

If you have to repeat the correction, you can be firmer:

> "Well, Dick…"
> "Actually, as I've told you, I prefer to go by 'Rick.'"

Think about the consistency of your name, however, and don't set people up to make a mistake. If you really prefer to be called "Kristy," rather than "Kristen," consider having "Kristy Wells" printed on your business card so that you don't have to constantly correct people. Some people have a nickname in quotation marks on their card and on their signature line for letters:

> B. J. "Bugsy" Littlejohn

However, increasingly in business, people will drop the formal part of their name, and the business card will just show how they wish to be addressed (without the quotation marks):

Bugsy Littlejohn.

Occasionally, you'll find people who wish to be addressed by their initials, as in "BJ"; you can guess that they have two forenames, neither of which pleases them. Just follow their lead: If someone says, "Please, call me 'Bee-Jay,'" then that's how you should address him or her.

In some parts of the United States (particularly in the Southern states), naming firstborn sons after their fathers and grandfathers is a family tradition. These people then need a **suffix** (such as "Senior") on their legal name so that property and legal communications go to the right person. The form is

Rhett Butler, Sr. (the grandfather)
Rhett Butler, Jr. (the son)
Rhett Butler III ("Rhett Butler, the third" for the grandson)

The form "II," as in "Rhett Butler II," is used when a son is named not for his father, but for another relative such as an uncle.

In business, most suffixes aren't needed. Indeed, someone who has

Alex Proudfoot IV

on his business card probably won't make a good impression; Americans rejected royalty when they overthrew King George III. Some exceptions are when two people with the same name work in the same firm or when customers want to know whether they should be asking for Albert Gore, Jr., or Albert Gore, Sr., when they call. Table 2-1 provides a summary of some things to think about to make a good introduction.

Table 2-1 Tips for Making a Good Introduction	
Did you remember to…	announce yourself by name?
	never refer to yourself by a title?
	repeat your name in a way that helps people with unusual pronunciations or spellings?
	speak almost artificially slowly and distinctly?

■ 2-6 WHEN YOU'VE FORGOTTEN SOMEONE'S NAME

A situation that everyone dreads in both business and social contexts occurs when you run into someone you know—perhaps quite well—and you just can't remember his or her name. If the other person doesn't make a quick self-introduction, you can easily become stuck in a conversation, desperately trying to search for the name. As hard as you try, you can remember all kinds of details about this person, except his or her name.

Meeting this challenge straight on is best:

> "I'm terribly sorry [shaking head, with eyes scrunched]. I just blanked out here. Please, would you remind me of your name?"

> "I remember we met at the convention last year…and I'm remembering everything about you, but—forgive me—I just can't come up with your name."

In many business situations, you can work around this situation by saying

> "I wonder, do you have a copy of your (business) card?"

Of course, this can backfire if the person replies: "No, I'm afraid I don't have one with me."

■ 2-7 INTRODUCING OTHER PEOPLE

Learning how to make gracious introductions between business acquaintances will get you ahead in U.S. business. Because people are often not very good about introducing themselves, your efforts will be gratefully received. Introductions put everyone at ease and facilitate business. Learning how to make courteous and confident introductions will make you look good.

The rule for introducing people is simple. You always introduce the lowest-ranked person to the highest-ranked person:

> "Mr. Jobs [chairman and Chief Executive Officer (CEO) of the firm], may I introduce Jacqui Williams? Jacqui is a summer intern from Stanford University, working in our marketing department."

Note that part of the introduction is to give a context and to make a reason to repeat the name. As with your own name, if it's a little unusual, link the name to something familiar:

> "This is Orly Katzoff. Orly—that's just like the airport in Paris—is working with us in testing this summer."

The form "May I introduce…" is quite formal and appropriate when you're talking to a superior, but in many contexts, the form "This is Sheila Wong…" is perfectly appropriate.

After introducing the junior person to the senior person, you then reverse the process, but without stating the obvious (in this case, "Mr. Jobs is head of the firm"). Again, you should give some context (as illustrated in Figure 2-2):

> "Jacqui, as you know, this is Steve Jobs. He was just on campus last week, speaking to the Board of Trustees."

Unless the context is a reception line for very senior executives, you can dismiss yourself once you have made the introduction:

> "And, if you'll excuse me, I have to talk with some people in Production."

Figure 2-2 Introductions
When you're introducing a lower-level worker to an upper-level one, always introduce the lower-ranked person to the higher-ranked person.
SOURCE: © 2009 Jupiterimages Corporation.

Doing the Right Thing: Choose Neutral Descriptions When Pointing People Out

When you are trying to point out someone in a crowd, it is often tempting to identify them by a physical characteristic that really stands out. For example, you ask a colleague at a cocktail party: "Who's the really fat guy over there, stuffing himself on the hors d'ouevres?" To your horror, your coworker turns and says: "Hey, Tommy! Come over here—my friend here thinks you're a fatso!" Little did you know that Tommy was a golfing buddy of your colleague.

So it's a good idea to stay away from any personal description that could have negative connotations. No matter how obvious the negative feature is, choose something neutral: "Yes, the gentleman in the blue suit, next to the staircase."

If you'd like to be introduced to someone else at a social function, it's perfectly appropriate to ask: "And would you introduce me to the head of Marketing?" to someone you reasonably believe knows you both. But choose your wording with care (see *Doing the Right Thing: Choose Neutral Descriptions When Pointing People Out*).

Most Americans refer to one another simply by first name, last name (for example, "Steve Jobs"), even if someone is quite senior. The form "Chairman Jobs," which is common in Asian countries, is never used, but the form "Mr. Jobs" would not be wrong under circumstances of considerable formality (for example, a job interview as opposed to a party). When you're addressing and referring to women, you'll have to make a decision as to whether to use "Ms.," "Mrs.," or "Miss." "Ms." is never wrong and is increasingly used in business to the exclusion of the two forms that indicate whether someone is married. (The pronunciation of Ms. is "muz" where the /u/ sound is like the unstressed 'e' in "the.") As a matter of personal choice, some women may change their last name after marriage, but it's not necessary to do so for business (see *Business Protocol in Action: How to Handle a Name Change*).

In business, few married women prefer to be addressed as "Mrs. Lastname," but you should be sensitive to those who do (follow the lead of people in her immediate work group). In general, even people with Ph.Ds aren't referred to as "doctor"—former CEO of General Electric Jack Welch was almost never referred to as "Dr. Welch." Former U.S. secretary of state

Business Protocol in Action: How to Handle a Name Change

In most Western countries, when women marry, they have traditionally changed their last name to that of their husbands. There's no law that requires this, and some women keep their own name, while some use the husband's name for social functions but retain their own last name at work. For example, if Jasmine Wong marries Michael Tse, for business purposes she can choose to still be known as Jasmine Wong, or she can switch to Jasmine Tse.

This differentiation brings up the question of how to handle the transition. Clients might be confused that their business is now being handled by a different person. To show the continuity, many married women append the husband's family name, rather than replacing it. In this example, Jasmine's letters would end with:

Jasmine Wong Tse
Account Representative

and her business card would show all three names. In introductions, Jasmine would likely just use two names: "Hi, I'm Jasmine Tse."

A similar problem occurs when the name change is the result of a divorce. After years of being known simply as Michelle Gerber, Michelle's marriage ends and she returns to her original last name, Woods. She might then include her old name in parentheses to show the continuity:

Michelle Woods (Gerber)

and introduce herself as follows: "I'm Michelle Woods—I think we've met. It used to be Michelle Gerber, but I've had a name change, now its Woods." Note that Michelle doesn't have to give details about why she is reverting to her unmarried name.

Madeleine Albright made it clear that despite her Ph.D., she wanted to be addressed as "Mrs. Albright" (a curious choice because she had been divorced decades before), while her later successor, Condoleezza Rice, was pointedly referred to as "Dr. Rice" in briefings by her colleagues.

No matter how uncomfortable you may feel or how much you "hate" introductions, learning the correct protocol and practicing at every possible opportunity will increase your self-confidence and your professional image. And, of course, once you've gained confidence, you won't hate introductions. When it comes to addressing other people, be aware of the possibilities and address people the way they choose to be called.

▶ ❯ ❯ PUT THIS CHAPTER INTO PRACTICE

1. Thinking of someone you know well, such as a family member or roommate, see how many names they have according to different contexts, such as close family, neighbors, work situations, and so on.

2. Take the lead in club functions to practice making semiformal introductions of people to one another.

3. With some friends or classmates, role-play greeting some people from different countries.

▮ KEY TERMS

cultural norms   nonverbal communication

honorific   suffix

Multiple Choice Practice Questions: To take the review quiz for this chapter, log on to your Online Edition at www.atomicdog.com.

Chapter 3
Effective Communication

Why is no one here?

At a fast growing hi-tech company, the two founders survey the conference room. "It's two o'clock—where is everyone?" asks the CEO (chief executive officer). "This is supposed to be an 'all hands' meeting for everyone in the firm and there's just the two of us and a couple of interns. Didn't you tell people about the meeting like I asked you?"

"Sure," replies the COO (chief operating officer). "I sent out an e-mail last Monday telling everyone to be here."

Although e-mail is undoubtedly the preferred mechanism of communication in most American companies, the two company founders discover that simply sending an e-mail doesn't necessarily accomplish their communications objective.

■ 3-1 CHOOSING THE RIGHT CHANNEL OF COMMUNICATION

Whenever you have a business message to deliver, you have a choice of several different channels of communication. The **channel of communication** is the **medium** (plural: **media**) through which a message is sent. Suppose, for example, you are in charge of arranging a routine lunch where your firm will be hosting some executives from an existing customer of your firm. You are in the Marketing Department, and your team has agreed that it would probably be a good idea to invite some people from the Product Engineering group. There's no specific agenda, but you want to show the client the range of professional expertise at your firm, and during informal conversation you hope to get some good ideas for new product development. Your team has decided that the best engineer to invite would be a colleague, Heidi Lin, who has roughly the same standing in the firm as yourself. In business, we'd say that Heidi is your **peer** (a coworker of the same rank and status—not a supervisor or someone who reports to you).

To invite the colleague, you are faced with many choices for how to enlist her help with the meeting. You might pick up the phone and call her. This will get you an immediate answer, and you could do some negotiation because the telephone is a **two-way communication,** one that includes the recipient in the final form of the message. You propose the lunch and Heidi says: "Next Tuesday? Well, I could do that ...but only if it's early and I'm absolutely out of there by one o'clock."

But Heidi might be a little grumpy and terse with you. What does this mean? Have you imposed by asking her to attend? Does she dislike working with your group, or has she had a bad experience with this customer? The answer may be simple: Heidi was working on a complicated calculation, and your phone call interrupted her. Although the business lunch is important to you, important to the firm, and even important to Heidi's team, making the arrangements are not time sensitive from Heidi's point of view. There was no reason to interrupt. The problem with a phone call is that although it provides **place shifting** (you don't have to be in the same place as Heidi for the message to go through), there is no **time shifting** (Heidi has to interrupt her work to talk with you).

If instead of the phone call you choose to send an e-mail, Heidi can reply to you when she's taking a break from calculations. And because an e-mail creates a **permanent record,** unlike the phone call, on the day of the meeting she can readily check the copy of the e-mail to confirm the time and location. If she can't oblige you, she can write back: "Sorry, I have to be in Houston that week. See if Albert can go instead." Although the message is brief, you probably wouldn't experience the answer as curt if you and Heidi already had a good working relationship.

Making a permanent record is important for many business transactions, from ordering supplies and materials to writing down what has happened in a workplace incident. When a supervisor has to discipline an employee for substandard performance or for failing to follow company rules, there will usually be a sequence of steps. The first instance will cause the supervisor to give an oral warning (simply speak to the employee about the matter). A subsequent repeat of the same problem will lead the manager to issue a formal written warning. Although this might be a typed letter sent to the employee with a copy placed in the worker's personal file, it would not be exceptional to have this communicated by e-mail:

Amelia,

This is a note to document our discussion today about your repeated late arrival for your shift. Your supervisor has mentioned this to you several times in the past and we have not seen any improvement. As you know, the firm needs the front desk staffed before the doors open to customers at 9 o'clock.

> While we understand that you take public transportation to work, and that buses occasionally run late, this must be an exceptional event. You may need to set out to work sooner and take an earlier bus.

Note that in this e-mail, the manager uses the verb *to* **document.** Literally speaking, *document* means to make a written record on paper. However, it's important to know that the meaning has evolved to mean: "to make a written record," which may include an e-mail. If you are asked to document an incident or someone else's behavior, it would be prudent to ask: "Do you need a memo from me, or will an e-mail be sufficient?"

Would you ever issue an invitation to a colleague in person? Well, let's assume that Heidi works at the same general location as you, but in an adjacent building. Walking over to her work area and inviting her in person would take some time out of your workday. But on some occasions, you would make the extra effort. Suppose you knew that Heidi had had a bad work experience with this customer in the past—the client had insisted on many last-minute design changes. You might want to influence and encourage Heidi to set the previous experience aside and try to develop a better working relationship with the client. At the least, you would want to let her know that you understand that the meeting might be difficult for her. The **emotional impact** (how the message recipient will likely feel about receiving the message) is quite different when a colleague sees that you have taken the time to make a visit in person. It signals consideration and understanding.

If you knew that it might take some persuasion to encourage Heidi to join the meeting, you probably wouldn't use e-mail. It would be wrong to make negative comments about a customer in writing: "Heidi, I know the people from Acme Co. are a pain, but could you see your way..." (see Chapter 5). And when persuasion is necessary, Heidi might never read your comments that indicate your anticipation of her reluctance if she read your message on a handheld PDA (personal digital assistant). After reading the first few words: "Are you available to meet with the people from Acme...," Heidi responds: "Sorry. Buried over here with new projects. Can't make it."

What about sending a *letter* of invitation to Heidi? Common sense suggests that you wouldn't send Heidi a written invitation to a business lunch. A letter to a colleague at the same firm would be a strangely **formal** medium of communication and would signal that the lunch has a greater significance than is true (formality indicates seriousness and importance). A memorandum ("memo")—like a letter—suffers from being a **one-way communication.** One-way communication means sending a message

Table 3-1 How Channels of Communication Differ from One Another

1. One-way or two-way communication—does the recipient contribute to the content?

2. Permanence—the communication generates its own written record.

3. Time and place shifting—must the sender and recipient be in the same place, or deal with the message at the same time?

4. Emotional impact—would the message be considered upsetting if delivered on one channel rather than another?

5. Level of formality—communications sent by postal mail and one-to-one conversations scheduled in advance are examples of channels that are inherently formal.

but not having a discussion. In the phone call, Heidi was able to agree to the date but negotiate the time. Sending a memo would be as if you were almost ordering her to attend—clearly inappropriate for someone who is a peer in your own firm. Although a casual in-person visit to Heidi's cubicle wouldn't necessarily signal formality, imagine if you wrote an e-mail saying: "Heidi, could you let me know when you have a half-hour to discuss something in person?" You would signal that the meeting is highly formal (and quite inappropriate for the task at hand here).

The use of **postal mail** (communications written on paper and delivered by internal mail within the firm, by the U.S. Postal Service, or by a courier like Federal Express or United Parcel Service outside the firm) is becoming increasingly rare in American business. It is slow compared with e-mail, and for this reason technology workers sometimes call postal mail "snail mail." Postal mail has been largely replaced by e-mail—not just for communications within a firm, but also for messages to other firms and customers—and is used quite rarely in many U.S. companies. Table 3-1 summarizes the factors that make various channels of communication different from one another.

■ 3-2 ADVANTAGES AND DISADVANTAGES OF DIFFERENT CHANNELS

Although it may seem that all of American business communication has been reduced to just one or two channels—e-mail and cell phones—there is actually a wide variety of different media available to most executives.

Table 3-2 Advantages and Disadvantages of Using Media

Medium	Advantages	Disadvantages	Best Used for
Face-to-face one-on-one meeting	Promotes trust. Easy to adjust content and level of formality while the meeting is in progress. Disagreements can be negotiated.	Expensive use of staff time—no place shifting. No leverage—communicates with just one person. No written record.	Recruiting. Confidential and sensitive personnel issues. Complex sales negotiations.
Face-to-face group or team meetings	Social benefits of meeting other people. Likely to generate new ideas.	Hard to schedule everyone at one time and place. Travel may be expensive.	Brainstorming, developing new ideas. Communicating a change in strategy. Generating new business.
Phone	Immediacy—no waiting for an answer. Opportunity to restate or clarify if the recipient doesn't understand.	No time shifting—interrupts work flow. Tend to go on too long. Hard to judge emotional component. No permanent record.	Quick "fact checking" and scheduling. Social interaction.
Web meeting	Much cheaper than arranging a face-to-face meeting. Easy to see computer files of presentations or spreadsheets.	Can be hard to sustain attention during a long meeting. Unlikely to promote creativity or breakthrough ideas.	Used extensively for training. Very effective for collaborative projects that are computer-based.

(Continued)

Medium	Advantages	Disadvantages	Best Used for
Videoconference	Can be a "milestone" event—the day and time by which work groups report progress. Relatively inexpensive compared with in-person meetings.	Interactions are likely to be stilted. Takes substantial organization to get all participants available at the same time (especially across time zones). Limited possibility for "breakthrough" success if participants haven't previously met face-to-face.	Routinely scheduled team meetings where team members are in different geographical locations. Client presentations where travel costs are prohibitive.
E-mail	Easy to copy several people at once. Can be saved or printed. Time-shifting does not interrupt recipient.	Lacks emotional cues, so may lead to misinterpretation. Recipient may not read the whole message if reading on a "smart phone" or personal digital assistant (PDA).	Normal communication between coworkers. Routine business correspondence with partner firms.
Text messaging	Instant communication. Contents can't be overheard.	Responding to each message leads to a poor attention span. Temptation to reply too quickly without proper consideration. Records may be difficult to retrieve.	Routine transactions (appointments and inquiries) within established work groups.
Memo	Permanent record for policy decisions. Can be referred to in the future.	Communicates decisions without promoting cooperation or "buy-in." Difficult to trace precise authorship.	Almost never used in business—replaced by e-mail. More common in law firms and legal departments.

(Continued)

Medium	Advantages	Disadvantages	Best Used for
Letter (postal mail)	High formality indicates seriousness. Can be the basis of a formal contract. Permits sober reflection and analysis of proposals.	One-sided communication—does not permit adaptation or negotiation. Time-consuming to prepare well. Response is likely to be delayed.	Documenting items agreed on at a face-to-face meeting. Statement of terms and conditions of a business deal. Formal introductions (of yourself or your firm). Formal warnings (to suppliers, people who owe the firm money, and employees).

Later chapters will treat these communications options in detail. Each one has its own advantages and disadvantages. These are shown in Table 3-2 relating to the five factors introduced in Section 3-1.

■ 3-3 FIRMS (AND PEOPLE) HAVE THEIR PREFERRED METHOD OF COMMUNICATION

When you join a new firm, you'll soon find that the company as a whole, or perhaps just your work group, has a definite preference for the medium of communication. For example, in the large international strategy consulting firms, consultants are often working at the client site, away from their own offices. Many prefer not to rely on PDAs, as they can be distracting in client meetings. They carry laptop computers, but powering up the laptop and "replicating" (downloading e-mails from the firm's server) take quite a long time, so consultants may check their e-mail only once or twice a day—perhaps less often if they are out of the country. However, they can check voice mail relatively easily, from airports while waiting for flights or even from a client's office between meetings. So consultants often have a strong preference for voice mail (phone messages).

In some firms, frequent phone calls are a primary method of communication, but in other firms, they are considered a nuisance that invariably interrupts the work at hand. For example, in financial services firms in which securities are traded from moment to moment, a failure to answer a telephone on the first ring would be considered poor job performance. In contrast, in medical fields, almost no professional would be expected to pick up her or his phone when examining a patient or consulting with a colleague.

Within each firm, individual managers always have their own preferences for how they want to receive information. For example, a few older executives readily admit to being "not very good" with e-mail. They rely on their assistants to handle it, and some even have each message printed out. If you know this is true about someone you have to work with, you can adapt to the manager's style and use the phone or in-person visits, even if you typically use e-mail for everyone else in the firm. One famous executive, however, is insistent on using his BlackBerry® "smart phone" (see *Business Protocol in Action: Our First BlackBerry® President*).

Similarly, some individuals strongly prefer face-to-face conversations to receiving phone calls from colleagues within their own firm. They deflect phone inquiries with: "Why don't you wait until we can chat about that in person?" Again, once you understand a colleague's personal style, you can probably make a good adaptation. You may also have to adjust your own preferred style to take into account the cultural differences of communication styles that you will encounter in international business (see *It's Just Different: Please Don't Call for an Appointment*).

■ 3-4 WHY FACE-TO-FACE MEETINGS STILL MATTER

Business trips are very expensive. When you add the cost of airfare, hotel, taxi, and meals, the total comes to several thousand dollars before you add in the lost productivity caused when one member of a firm is away from the office. But despite the advent of the telephone, e-mail, Web meetings, and videoconferencing, most businesspeople still rely heavily on face-to-face meetings (as illustrated in Figure 3-2).

Business Protocol in Action: Our First BlackBerry® President

Figure 3-1   President Obama and His BlackBerry®
President Barack Obama was reluctant to give up text messaging, despite the security concerns.
SOURCE: © AP Images/Jae. C. Hong

When George W. Bush took office as President of the United States, he reluctantly signed off from his e-mail account. As a businessman and candidate, he'd come to rely on the instant communication and the ability to send a single message to many people at once.

But presidents face a number of problems in using electronic communication. The first is the possibility that confidential messages with national security implications could be intercepted and sent to unintended users. In addition, occupants of the White House are subject to strict laws that require all communications to be preserved and turned over to Congress or the courts under certain circumstances. Although a private conversation can remain "privileged" (both people in the conversation might refuse to disclose what was said), it may be harder to keep an e-mail message confidential.

President Barack Obama was well known as a candidate for being a "BlackBerry addict"—he was often photographed with his text-enabled "smart phone" in his hands and he relied on sending and receiving dozens of short e-mail messages each day (see Figure 3-1). Indeed, e-mail communication with supporters was an important part of his campaign strategy.

On taking office, he vowed to never give up his BlackBerry, and government technology experts began scrambling to find truly secure methods of communication. Only time will tell whether, like his predecessor, he'll have to send a "signing off" message.

It's Just Different: Please Don't Call for an Appointment

American salespeople are used to phoning or e-mailing any firm to ask for an appointment—and they expect to get it. In many other countries, commerce does not move as quickly and people are suspicious of beginning new business relationships. Very often the first contact must be made by letter, and a salesperson needs to present a great deal of background information on her or his company before even making a presentation about a specific product or service.

The officers of the firm that has been contacted will not reply at once. They are not ignoring the request to visit—they are checking with colleagues to see if they've ever heard of the salesperson's firm to determine whether they will even grant an appointment. Statements in the background briefing, such as "We are the second largest operator of budget hotels in Asia," will be carefully researched.

In much of Latin America, even a written approach from a stranger may not get an appointment. Often business relies on intermediaries such as attorneys and local politicians, who have an important social function in making appropriate introductions. The salesperson who lacks these introductions won't get very far.

Executives are paid to make decisions, and as we like to say in business school, to make decisions in the face of uncertainty. Managers have to make plans for the firm even when they don't know whether the economy will boom or be depressed next year, whether the firm's chief competitor will launch a rival product or abandon the field entirely, and so on. Making decisions involves two parts. First, an executive has to gather enough information. Note that the word is "enough"—usually there won't be sufficient time or resources to gather all possible information. Then the executive has to make a choice between various possible courses of action, such as whether to substantially increase advertising expenditures or wait until market opportunities seem more profitable.

Businesspeople expend money on face-to-face meetings because the quantity of information is greater and the quality of information is richer. For example, potential suppliers may describe themselves as "very sophisticated," but site visits to their factories may reveal broken-down equipment and little evidence of research and development activity. A retailer with 25 stores can see from sales reports that some outlets are doing better than

Figure 3-2   Face-to-Face Meetings
Sometimes a face-to-face meeting is better than sending an e-mail or calling, even within an office.
SOURCE: © 2009 Jupiterimages Corporation.

others. But only an in-person visit will help to diagnose *why* the low-performing locations are not doing as well as the best stores. Perhaps the problem is that the staff members are undertrained and unhelpful to customers; or the staff could be wonderful, but the problem is that road work has cut off access to the store. An in-person visit resolves the uncertainty.

A great deal of business depends on trust, and this is where business-people make a qualitative assessment. If customers keep you waiting despite a scheduled meeting, you begin to wonder how prompt they'll be about paying their bills. If a supplier goes out of his or her way to drop you off at the airport so you can take an earlier flight home, you have a good sense that he or she will work hard to deliver the right goods on time.

So, although success in business depends on careful calculation and rational decision making, an emotional element always comes into play. Consciously or not, executives make a judgment about how they feel about their business partners, and to date, no one has come up with technology that can supplant the experience of a face-to-face meeting.

A great deal of business is still conducted face-to-face, and managers look forward to trade meetings and conventions. But these events come with special rules (see *Doing the Right Thing: Meeting with Competitors Is Risky*).

Once you've decided that a situation calls for an in-person meeting, you then have to decide whether to meet with each person one-on-one or with a group. In general, whenever there is a problem with a specific individual, it is always best to meet privately—for instance, to understand low performance and to coach a worker to better results. However, as we learned in the example of asking Heidi to a half-hour meeting, scheduling one-on-one meetings may have the unintended effect of overstating the importance of the issue at hand.

Doing the Right Thing:
Meeting with Competitors Is Risky

Most industries have conventions and conferences in which all the competitors in a particular line of commerce come together to identify new trends and to address common problems. Competitors show off their latest products and try to win new customers.

If your firm encourages you to attend one of these events, you'll be excited that it provides you with a way to learn about your competition. You may even be introduced to people at competing firms. You may be surprised to find that your firm gives you specific instructions to avoid executives from other firms, even from having a casual drink with them in a bar. It's not that your firm worries that you will gossip and give away trade secrets. The concern is the enforcement of antitrust laws that prohibit firms from colluding (making private agreements) on price. In some cases, antitrust violations have been found where one participant in a casual, off-the-record conversation stated, "It's time that we all raised our prices in this industry," and the other participants neither particularly agreed nor disagreed. When many firms in the industry later raised their prices at the same time, they came under suspicion.

So you may find yourself under restrictions not to meet with competitors, to meet with them only under certain circumstances (such as when your boss is present to observe what is said), or to specifically avoid certain topics such as prices or how much profit your firm is making on a particular product line. You don't want to be accused of doing something you weren't doing, so it is good to be sensitive to these issues and avoid a trap.

Group meetings are efficient if something needs to be conveyed to every member of a team, such as a new initiative or a change in an existing business strategy. Group meetings are appropriate for problem resolution and for coming up with new ideas—there are synergies from the social interaction that provide better results than endless one-on-one conversations. If the conversation in a group meeting seems to be going nowhere and one person is offering endless objections to a reasonable plan, an appropriate response is go back to an individual meeting: "Perhaps it would be helpful if we talked about this privately?"

■ 3-5 DEVELOPING AN INTEGRATED COMMUNICATIONS CAMPAIGN

Let's return to our opening scenario where two entrepreneurs have asked all their staff members to turn up to a meeting, but no one except the interns shows up. What can be going on? It could be an act of rebellion. Perhaps the staff members are so angry about a change in benefits that they have decided to communicate their disapproval by boycotting the meeting. It is possible. But it's most likely that the single e-mail message was insufficient to convey the importance of having a meeting with everyone present. It's quite possible that staff members were working hard to complete a project by a deadline and they assumed that someone or other would fill them in later on the content of the meeting.

The COO's mistake here was assuming that a single e-mail message would accomplish the objective. Although logically his message was sufficient, human behavior isn't always strictly logical. Advertisers know that customers are unlikely to understand a promotional message the first time they hear it, so they plan for repetitions. However, there's more to convincing customers than just sending out the same message several times. In advertising, it's generally agreed that good communication involves a sequence of events referred to as: **inform, persuade, or remind.** Many advertising professionals feel that you can do only one of these tasks effectively at a time. That is, an ad that is good at *reminding* existing customers about a brand is unlikely to work to *persuade* nonusers to try the company's products for the first time. The same rule applies to all business communications. Even a simple task like convincing everyone in a work group to turn up to a meeting may involve a campaign with the three elements of informing, persuading, and reminding.

In the case of the two founders trying to meet with all of their company's workers at one time, the COO should have planned a sequence of messages to inform, persuade, and remind. The idea here is that it's difficult to *persuade* people until they first have an idea of what you are proposing. So, assuming for the moment that the COO thought it was appropriate to rely solely on e-mail to set up the meeting, he would have planned for three messages and would begin with a simple announcement designed to *inform:*

Subject: All hands meeting, Wednesday 2 P.M.

Folks,

There will be an "all hands" meeting next Wednesday, 3 March at 2 o'clock in the dining commons. Jeff and I will be outlining new strategic directions for the firm, so we need everyone to attend.

The second message will develop the idea of the importance of the meeting and will have a specific goal of *persuading* people who are thinking of skipping the meeting. Within the context of a small firm, the COO's second message might read as follows:

Subject: Yes, you have to be there: All hands meeting, Wed 2 P.M.

Several people have asked me if they really have to turn up to the meeting next Wednesday afternoon.

The answer is: Yes! We want everyone together in one place and one time.

As you know, we've just completed our second round of financing, and this gives us the opportunity to pursue some exciting new projects. We want everyone to be on the same page [*colloquial:* to understand the same facts and come to agreement] and not hear the message second-hand from others.

So, please arrange your work week—including rescheduling client meetings if necessary—so that you can plan to attend.

In the second message, the COO is using persuasive language to show the importance of the event (even inconveniencing the firm's customers). He explains why the meeting is important and why staff members can't skip the meeting.

Lastly, he'll plan for a *reminder* message. In business, few workers willfully disobey their superiors, but most people are very busy and sometimes even important matters can be overlooked. Compliance is much greater when a reminder message comes out one day before the event:

> Subject: Reminder: All hands meeting 2 o'clock tomorrow dining commons

> Just a reminder that Jeff and I are looking forward to meeting with everyone on staff tomorrow, Wednesday at 2 o'clock in the dining commons.

> We plan to present our new strategy for about 20 minutes and then take your questions. The meeting should end by 3:15 P.M.

Note that the Subject line alone conveys all the necessary information for someone who might be reading this message on a cell phone or PDA. The message conveys one more piece of information—an estimate of how long the meeting will last.

Although three e-mail messages might be successful within a high-technology firm (where almost all the communication is conducted by e-mail), many managers would choose to use several different media to get the message across. For example, they might choose to send the first, "inform" message by making an announcement at a routine team leaders meeting, adding: "Please tell everyone on your team and let them know it's important."

Effective communication involves the careful selection of the appropriate medium or media to deliver the message. Getting important messages across often involves developing a communications campaign with a carefully designed sequence of messages.

▷ ▷ ▷ PUT THIS CHAPTER INTO PRACTICE

1. Take any routine communication you've recently received (such as a phone message to come in for an interview) and consider how the same message would be structured using a different medium (such as an e-mail or letter).

2. Identify a project that involves communicating a new strategy to people who will actually do the implementation. How would you use various media to accomplish the overall communication goal?

3. Ask professional businesspeople what medium of communication they prefer and why; and as a follow-up, ask them why they do not prefer another medium. For example, if your interviewee says: "I'm an all e-mail person," ask her what she doesn't like about using the phone.

KEY TERMS

channel of communication

document

emotional impact

formal, formality

inform, persuade, or remind

medium, media

one-way communication

peer

permanent record

place shifting

postal mail

time shifting

two-way communication

Multiple Choice Practice Questions: To take the review quiz for this chapter, log on to your Online Edition at www.atomicdog.com.

Chapter 4
Creating Compelling Messages

Bureaucratic language obscures meaning.

"Per Margo Smith, I have ascertained that you are ineligible for benefits due to the temporary nature of your appointment."

What does this sentence mean? Dung Nguyen has just written to a recruiter with the simplest of employment questions: "Will I be covered on the company's health insurance this summer?" The recruiter, Sandy, had to check with the firm's Human Resources Department but writes back quickly. If Sandy had phoned Dung, she might have left this message: "Dung, I checked with Margo Smith in HR, and unfortunately we don't cover health insurance for summer interns, as you'll just be a temporary hire." So why does she switch to a strange archaic form of language when the message is written? It's a false attempt to appear erudite and sophisticated. Instead of conveying her meaning clearly, Sandy spent a great deal of time crafting a message that Dung has difficulty understanding.

■ 4-1 BEGIN WITH THE END IN MIND

Perhaps the most important habit described by Stephen Covey in his best-selling book, *The Seven Habits of Highly Effective People,* is: "Begin with the end in mind." That is, if you take a pause before you start a business activity and ask yourself, "What do I want to accomplish here?", you are likely to be much more successful. Use this rule for every e-mail, text message, and letter you write, for every phone call you make, for every meeting you set up, and for every speech and presentation you deliver. Even when the task is complex and involves millions of people in several countries, single-minded attention to the end goal can lead to success (see *Business Protocol in Action: Switching to a Single Currency*).

Suppose your boss concludes a conversation by saying: "I guess you better write to their legal people." The letter to the attorneys in another firm is not an end in itself. You should stop and think: "If this letter is successful, what result do I want to see for the firm? Do I want them to agree with our interpretation of words in a contract, or do I want them to rewrite

Business Protocol in Action: Switching to a Single Currency

Imagine reading a news story that the money in your pocket was about to become worthless. You'd likely be surprised and angry. But that was the situation that faced millions of residents of the European Union (EU) at the beginning of 2002 as national currencies such as the French franc and the German deutsche mark were replaced by a common currency, the euro.

Of course, people didn't read about the switch one day in the newspaper. The message had been conveyed in every possible medium over a period of several years. The initial agreement for the common currency had been announced ten years before, in 1992. Although many people objected to the loss of their national currency, the long lead time was sufficient for their concerns to be heard and addressed. Politicians in each country engaged in every kind of debate to convince citizens of the merits of the common currency.

A key component of the message was a theme of inevitability: This change was coming on a certain date, New Year's Day, 2002. Repeated unwavering statements from government leaders made it clear that the changeover would occur on schedule. The "big bang" single date for all consumers to begin using the euro was coupled with some careful gradualism that fit with the theme of inevitability: From 1996 to 1998, central banks maintained interest in the story by periodically releasing pictures of the designs for the new notes and coins. In 1999, government bonds began to be issued in the new currency, and interbank transfers were recorded in euros. During 2001, a massive poster campaign reminded people of the changeover date, and souvenir starter packs of the actual coins (not yet legal tender) were sold by banks throughout the EU. These tactics convinced ordinary consumers that the euro really was going to launch on time.

The old legacy currencies were legal tender for two short months in January and February of 2002, but they were soon swept up by the banking system: As people deposited legacy currencies, banks issued only euros. Despite fears of chaos and rampant inflation as prices were changed to euros, the launch of the new currency went just as planned. The success was due to conveying the message consistently through a number of different media so that everyone received the message.

the contract and send it to us again?" You can see that being clear about your objective from the beginning will help you to structure your communication effectively.

There's an important corollary to thinking about the "end in mind." When you plan a communication, you should also ask: "What is it that

I do NOT want to have happen here?" In the example of "write to their legal people," what the firm does not want to have happen might be that the contract is canceled or the customer refuses to enter into further negotiations.

■ 4-2 TYPES OF BUSINESS COMMUNICATION

If you were to ask a businessperson: "What sort of messages do you send out each day?", a reasonable reply might be: "Oh, good heavens! There are all sorts of messages for a number of different purposes." However, it's not too difficult to define some general categories of messages that apply across various media such as e-mail, letters, and phone calls. Before turning to each one in detail, Table 4-1 provides a summary.

Table 4-1 Types of Business Communication

Communication Type	Purpose and Description
Inquiry	Asking for information; asking about availability or requesting a favor
Response	Replying to an inquiry giving the requested information or agreeing to perform some task
Transmittal	A brief note to describe something that is being sent, such as a longer document or object
Request for action	Asking a coworker or service provider to do a specific task; sometimes done informally; often done by e-mail to provide a record
Follow-up	To repeat an inquiry or request for action when there has been no timely response
Documenting and warning	Often done as an "on paper" letter; to warn an employee or vendor that unsatisfactory service will have consequences if not improved
Negotiations and proposals	Usually begins with face-to-face discussions but may be reduced to a written proposal for further study

Inquiry.   Simply, you contact someone to request a specific piece of data. By letter, the request would be:

> Dear Ms. Hui:
>
> I am writing to ask if you can send us a copy of your report: "Marketing Opportunities for Baked Goods, December 2009." Please let me know if there is a fee for this or if you are able to send it free of charge.

Many e-mails also seek specific information:

> Julian,
>
> Can you send me the Travel Expense limit for my team for this quarter? I know we've cut back, but I don't remember the specific figure.
>
> With thanks, Anselmo

Response.   The person who receives the inquiry then makes a reply:

> We are happy to send you a copy of our December 2009 report on "Marketing Opportunities for Baked Goods" at no charge. It's one of a series of reports we offer on different industries.
>
> If you'd like to regularly receive our reports, please register with our Web site.

Of course, sometimes the response might be in the negative:

> I'm afraid we no longer have copies of the December 2009 report on "Marketing Opportunities for Baked Goods." It was a customized project and we feel the conclusions are no longer up-to-date, so we've withdrawn it.
>
> I've kept a note of your interest and will contact you if we offer a similar report in the future. I'm sorry I could not be more helpful on this occasion.

By e-mail, a response would take this form:

> Anselmo,
>
> Your travel budget limit is $12,000 (down from $15,000 last year). You can spend it as you wish—there are no restrictions on how it is used.
>
> Let me know if you need any other budget figures.
>
> Julian

An important part of good business protocol is to understand that almost all inquiries (all, that is, except e-mails to participate in scams and frauds) need a response. When the request can't be met immediately, the message should at least be acknowledged:

> Anselmo,
>
> You are right that travel budgets are likely to be cut substantially for this fiscal year.

Unfortunately, the negotiations haven't been completed. I hope to have the exact figures early next week and will write back with your allocation.

Sorry for the delay.

Julian

Transmittal.   When businesspeople are sending something as an e-mail attachment or postal-mail enclosure, the response becomes a "letter (or e-mail) of transmittal," a term that could also apply to a communication that is initiated by the writer, as in this example:

Dear Ms. Wang:

I am enclosing your employment contract for the coming year. Please look it over carefully and make sure that it fairly reflects the salary and bonus you negotiated with your manager, Jay Nagler. As you know, benefits are uniform for everyone at your career level within the company and are not part of individual negotiations. The current benefit schedule is shown on our intranet (click on the "HR Service for You" tab).

If you have any questions about the contract language, please contact your manager directly. If the contract is acceptable to you, please sign one copy and return it to me in the envelope included and keep the other copy for your records.

Sincerely,
Scott Craig
VP Human Resources
Enclosure: 2009-10 contract

In some circumstances, a voice mail message could be considered a letter of transmittal:

"Hi, Fernando, this is Celia in Publication. Just to let you know, I got your request for additional copies of the staff manual and I've sent them to Building 31 by the courier. Just let me know when you need more. Bye for now."

Transmittals by e-mails invariably involve an attached file. Because most e-mail users have been trained to be cautious about opening attached files (they may contain computer viruses), the content of the e-mail is particularly important. Because viruses can sometimes send messages that appear to come from a legitimate sender, a message such as:

Here you go! I think you'll enjoy this!

with an attached file should really make the recipient suspicious. So it's a good idea to indicate the specific materials that are being sent and indicate in the subject line that the message includes an attached file:

> Subject: Fiscal Year Budget Allocations (attached)
>
> Henry,
>
> The attached Excel file has the budget allocations by work group and expenditure category. These were approved by the Executive Committee last week, so should be considered final. Pritika Lahore

Request for action.   Many business messages are requests for someone to do something. Many of these are internal e-mails within the firm, like this:

> Subject: Issue Spare Key to Building 31, Office 240A
>
> Helen,
>
> I'm sending over my summer intern, Tuan Lei, to see you to request a key to my office. He has his security badge issued OK. I'll take responsibility for making sure the key is turned back in when he leaves at the end of the summer.
>
> In advance, my thanks,
> Paul Cua, *Finance*

A request for action by a customer (or from one firm to another) might be in the form of a letter, especially where it is necessary to document a problem:

> Dear Mr. Preis:
>
> I'm writing once again to ask that our account for trash service at 12 Benjamin Lakes Lane be re-opened in my name. As we've discussed several times with Customer Service, this is a holiday cabin which we only use for some months of the year.
>
> While there may be no trash to haul on some weeks, we're happy to pay your fee and consider this much easier than dealing with the inevitable delay to get service restarted each time we get cut off.
>
> Please would you let your operating staff know that we wish the account to continue?
>
> Sincerely,
> Irene Ellis

Note that the content here begins with a short statement of the problem, goes on to an explanation, and ends with the action step: What to do? Let Operations know to keep the account open.

Follow-up. In a perfect world, every problem would be instantly resolved and every request would be immediately granted. However, in the real world, in which front-line workers are busy and may be distracted by other demands, requests for information and for action sometimes fall between the cracks. When this happens, it can be helpful to remember the phrase: "People aren't evil—just busy." With that in mind, a follow-up should be courteous:

> Subject: Follow-up: Projector tube needs replaced, East Conference Room
>
> Emilio,
>
> Just a note that the tube in the projector in the East Conference Room clearly still needs to be replaced. When I checked this morning, the image was still very dim. We have client presentations all next week and need to look our best.
>
> Please could you have a technician work on this before the end of the week?
>
> With thanks,
> Emily Lindblad
> *Marketing Group*

Documenting and warning letters. As we saw in Chapter 3, although workplace problems are invariably first addressed face-to-face with a "friendly warning," it may be necessary to send a letter or e-mail to demand action when a problem has been identified and not corrected and to document that previous efforts at resolution have failed:

> Tom,
>
> My colleagues and I have called the building management repeatedly to complain that customers of the neighboring shopping center are using our parking spaces. As you know, we pay a considerable amount of money each month for exclusive, reserved parking spaces.
>
> I must warn you that unless the building security guards do a better job of policing the parking, I will instruct our accountants to begin withholding the substantial sum we pay for parking each month.
>
> Please attend to this at once.
>
> Yours truly,
> Zach Bellomy, CEO
> Indentured Solutions, Inc

This letter both documents the problem (creates a written record of something that has been only the subject of phone calls in the past) and raises a threat: Fix the problem, or we stop paying for parking. In personal correspondence between customers and companies, such letters are usually referred to as *complaint letters* and they are most often sent on paper, through postal mail. A good complaint letter is one that succinctly describes the problem and previous attempts to resolve it, clearly labels a proposed action that would resolve the problem, and backs up the seriousness of the complaint by explicitly stating what will happen next if the problem continues to be ignored. Vague threats such as "I'll report you to management" or "I shall refer the matter to my lawyers" have little effect—they are seen as posturing or bluster. Stating an explicit but reasonable *quid pro quo* (you do something for me, and I'll do something for you) is likely to be more effective. For example: "If your performance does not improve, we will withhold part of your annual bonus," or "If you can't keep your promise of a one-hour response time, we'll switch to a different service provider."

Many companies require formal warning letters as part of their procedures for dealing with employees who are failing in their duties. Such warning letters have some advantages, as they require a relatively cool tone (see *Doing the Right Thing: You Never Do What I Ask!*).

Negotiations, proposals.   In the last chapter, we explained why face-to-face meetings are still important in business. Complex collaborations depend on discussions that can sometimes stretch over several days and many meetings. Because letters and e-mails are one-way communications, they are unlikely to be the sole channel in negotiations. However, they do have a place. In a long series of discussions, a written proposal may be helpful to clarify an offer. For example, suppose a firm is trying to sell a very expensive piece of capital equipment to a customer. As the negotiations go along, it becomes apparent that the customer really needs the machinery but may have some difficulty in paying for it. The salesperson says: "Of course, you could lease the equipment from us, with the option to buy it at the end of the lease term." The customer's lead negotiator replies: "Well, that may help. But I'll have to run it by our Finance Department. Can you write me up a proposal and send it over?" It is then the salesperson's job to write a carefully crafted formal letter that describes the arrangement that might be made in a lease contract.

4-3 DEVELOPING THE CONTENT OF A MESSAGE

Most college-educated people are familiar with the concept of outlining: Before beginning to write a paper, you make a list of the topics that

Doing the Right Thing: You Never Do What I Ask!

Almost all well-run companies have a system of "progressive discipline" to handle substandard performance. The progression begins with orally noting the problem, then may move to a semiformal "counseling" session in which the manager spells out remediation—what the employee must do to improve. If the performance is still substandard, managers are required to write up the problem.

Most managers hate to spend time documenting poor work. When it comes to writing up a specific incident, it may sound trivial: "I asked you to run copies and distribute them before the three o'clock meeting. You didn't do this and when I went looking for you, I found you in the break room engaged in social conversation."

However, the positive side of formal documentation is that it is an opportunity to state the objective facts without coloring the message with emotion. Combative conversations that begin: "You never do what I ask!" are likely to get a defensive response and position the manager as an angry hothead.

In a well-run organization, poorly performing employees learn to read the seriousness of their situation without a lot of shouting and hollering.

you want to cover in the paper and organize them into major and subsidiary themes before beginning the actual process of typing the text. Although many business communications are short and are composed without taking time to write notes, there are other messages—long ones that handle complex topics and even shorter ones in which the message is of particular importance or sensitivity—that require some planning.

Developing the content of each message depends on balancing the need to provide sufficient **context** (the circumstances that led to the generation of the message) with the temptation to provide **too much information** (the endless recitation of details that, although true, obscure the heart of the matter). Look at this *response* e-mail:

Subject: Updated figures

Sorry, don't have them. Out next week.

Don't have what? In business, one worker, department, or firm may have sent out several inquiries in a short period of time. In this example, there is no context provided to remind the recipient what the topic of the e-mail is.

When responding to a complex inquiry, a good communication is one that breaks the situation down into component parts. Some brief history (that is, a summary of the *story* of the events as they happened) is often a good structure for a brief introduction that provides the context:

> Dear Ms. Xu:
>
> Thank you for writing to our head office about the difficulties you've encoun-tered in transferring your late grandmother's accounts to your name as Trustee of her estate. Apparently the local branch staff members failed to act on your first request, then made matters worse when you went in to follow up.

This succinctly sets the stage, without going through the whole "he said, she said" that was probably contained in the original letter.

If a situation seems unfathomably complicated, it may help to attempt to answer the familiar *six questions* that caring parents direct to teenagers who say: "I'm going out." Mom and Dad ask:

> "Who, what, when, where, why, and how?"

A full and complete answer to the six questions will invariably pro-duce too much information for a business communication, but it should be fairly easy to edit out what would be *too much information*. For example, *why* someone is requesting new toner for their printer is self-evident and doesn't need to be stated.

4-4 CHOOSING THE LEVEL OF FORMALITY

The next task in making a good business communication—whether it is written or oral—is to decide on the appropriate level of formality. People who teach English grammar like to define absolute rules, such as: "You should never begin a sentence with a conjunction." But in practice, even sophisticated English speakers often find good reasons to break the "rules." (The last sentence began with the conjunction "but," and you handled it well!) Here's another example of the very strict application of a rule: Most well-educated speakers of English know that "who" becomes "whom" when it is the object of a verb, as in "the man whom you saw yesterday," but in practice, most English speakers would say "the man who you saw yesterday."

If the rules can be defined but well-spoken people violate those rules, does this mean that the language is being corrupted and that even well-educated people are becoming careless users of it? Absolutely not! Expert speakers of English naturally adjust the **level of formality** to the context in which they are speaking or writing. For example, the sentence "Yeah, we'd better check with their rep" is appropriate for office conversation, although it has a low level of formality. "Please contact their sales representative and confirm their production schedule" means the same and would be appropriate in a letter—a context in which most businesspeople would naturally expect a higher level of formality.

Informal speech uses personal pronouns such as "I" and "you," abbreviations, **contractions** such as "don't" for "do not," and **colloquialisms.** A colloquialism is a use of speech that is understood by some speakers of a language but not others. For example, in Australia, "I'm going to stop in for a quick one" means "I am going to make a short visit to this bar for a drink."

There is a continuum of formality, and at the highly formal end of the scale, language has no contractions and writers avoid the use of personal pronouns. Certain vocabulary words also signal the level of formality: "Hope" is more informal than "expectation," for example. Words that would be perfectly acceptable in a social context (such as when standing in line waiting for a movie, chatting with a friend) might not be acceptable if you were making a presentation to the board of directors of your firm.

4-5 MATCHING LEVEL OF FORMALITY TO THE BUSINESS CONTEXT

Most well-educated native speakers of English—or indeed any other language—naturally determine the appropriate level of formality from the social context in which they're communicating. In business, the particular situation that you are dealing with will determine the appropriate level of formality. There is not a single level of language formality that is appropriate in every situation. Some business situations, such as a company party or celebration, are almost entirely social and demand a low level of formality. Greeting a coworker with "To whom were you speaking at the beverage table?" is grammatically correct but would seem strange because it's too formal; more likely you'd say: "Who were you talking to at the bar?" At the other end of the business context continuum, many business documents either are contracts or serve a contractual purpose— job-offer letters are an example. No matter how relaxed and casual a work environment the firm aims for, no one should write a letter that uses imprecision and colloquialisms of social speech: "We have great perks" doesn't mean the same as "You will be covered by health insurance after your first 90 days on the job."

The social context determines the level of formality in a manner best expressed by a diagonal region between the two scales, as shown in Figure 4-1. Note that at the lower and upper end of the scale in the figure, the context determines a very narrow range of acceptable choices: Contracts are always written in formal language, and office chitchat always uses very casual language structure. But in the middle of the range, the oval is broad, and this matches a range of acceptable levels of formality.

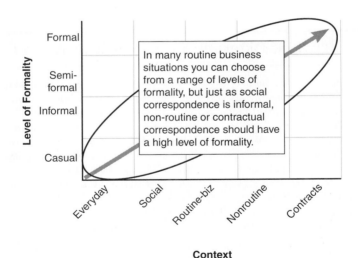

Context

Figure 4-1   Commonsense Rule About Formality
The middle of the chart indicates a range of acceptable levels of formality.

Routine business transactions include letters ordering materials and thanking customers. Nonroutine contexts include being unable to fulfill a previous agreement and sending warning letters and demand letters for nonpayment. So in many business situations, you have some flexibility between the informal side of semiformal and the quite formal side of semiformal. You are constrained, however: You can't use informal language and refer to customers as "you guys," nor should you use highly stilted formal language, such as "Under the terms of an agreement entered into on..."

Choosing the right level of formality is not difficult if you think about the communication objective. For example, an e-mail to a small group of coworkers would normally be considered routine and would demand a low level of formality. But if the purpose of the e-mail is to convince your colleagues that you are very concerned that no one is following an agreed-on plan to shut off office equipment at the end of the day to save energy, then a slightly higher level of formality would show that you are serious.

Also remember that the relative importance given to the written and spoken word differs considerably among countries (see *It's Just Different: Don't Put It in Writing*).

It's Just Different: Don't Put It in Writing

In Arab countries, nothing is more important to an individual's reputation and standing in the community than his or her word. Although it's not unusual for a business deal in the United States or Europe to conclude with the comment: "Well, put that in writing, and you have a deal!", in Arab countries, there might be surprise. "Why would I need to write it? I just gave you my word."

In Western countries, if a dispute arises in a commercial transaction, a businessperson will likely say: "Well, let's look at the contract—let's see what it says." This sometimes leads to a result that the businessperson did not intend: "Well, I thought we agreed that you'd pay for shipping, but I see we didn't put that in the contract, so I guess we'll have to pay." In other cultures, the dispute would be resolved not by looking at the written contract, but by face-to-face conversation—often at great length—until agreement could be reached. The discussion would likely be broad-ranging and include reference to previous favors and accommodations, which party is best able to bear the cost, and so on. Relying solely on a document would seem strange in those cultures.

■ 4-6 CHOOSING THE RIGHT TONE

In addition to level of formality, both spoken and written messages differ in their **tone**. Tone is a measure of friendliness or warmth in speech or writing. For example, given the business task of writing to a customer about an unpaid bill, it's possible to adopt a tone that is anything from a friendly reminder to a hostile demand. You can think of "tone" as the third dimension in a cube in which the other two dimensions are context and level of formality:

Hostile   Officious   Cool   Businesslike   Pleasant   Warm   Friendly

In social interactions, there are even tones beyond the ends of the continuum that has "Attacking" on the left and "Seductive" on the right. But you won't have much use for such tones in business.

You choose the appropriate tone by thinking through the "end in mind." If you want the customer to pay up and never do business with you again (in the example of writing to a customer about an unpaid bill), a frostily cool tone may well be your choice. On the other hand, if you want to get paid but also see the strategic importance of keeping the customer, you might choose a tone that is downright friendly.

Whenever you receive a letter or e-mail that irritates you, it probably violates some of the commonsense rules about matching formality and context and about choosing an appropriate tone.

■ 4-7 USING A PLAIN ENGLISH APPROACH

Plain English (www.plainenglish.co.uk) is an international movement to eliminate bureaucratic language that is unnecessarily complex and misleading.[1] The aim of the Plain English movement is to encourage people to write sentences that can be readily understood at their first reading. People who subscribe to the Plain English philosophy believe that even important legal documents can be written so that you do not need a lawyer to tell you what it means.

[1]Tom McArthur, ed., *The Oxford Companion to the English Language.* New York: Oxford, 1992, p. 785.

Once you've made a commitment to this approach, it's not particularly difficult to write in Plain English. There are just four main rules: Use simple, direct sentences; avoid the passive voice (defined in the following); use commonly occurring words in preference to obscure words; and use gender-neutral language. Let's look at these rules in detail.

■ 4-8 USE SIMPLE, DIRECT SENTENCES

Many concepts in business are quite complex (for example, selling a "put" option on a stock cannot be readily explained in one sentence), and most business transactions have important consequences. For example, your firm agrees to sell parts to a manufacturer who depends on them arriving on time. What penalty will you face for late delivery? But that's no reason to use convoluted, complicated sentences.

With the reasonable goal of being completely clear about the terms of transactions, many business documents have grown extremely long. Look at the next car rental contract you sign: On the back of the form you'll be agreeing to "terms and conditions"' that are printed in microscopic type and that few people who are not trained lawyers can actually understand.

There is no reason why even the most complex ideas cannot be expressed in simple sentences:

> If you don't bring back the car when you agree, we will begin charging you a late fee.

The Plain English movement has demonstrated that even complex legal documents, such as life insurance policies, can be rewritten in terms that are legally binding but are perfectly clear for a nonexpert to read.

There are many stylistic devices that authors use in great literature that should be avoided in Plain English. The most frequent violation of "use simple, direct sentences" is the **dangling participle.** In this construction, the subordinate clause comes before the main clause of a sentence and begins with the present participle:

> Having been founded in 1898, the company is one of the oldest in its industry.

What is bad about this form is that the reader doesn't know what was founded in 1898 until later in the sentence. A simple form may lack literary elegance, but it is easier to understand:

> The company is one of the oldest in the industry and was founded in 1898.

4-9 AVOID THE PASSIVE VOICE

The **passive voice** is a construction of language in which the object becomes the subject of the sentence:

> The ball was hit by Tom.

This sentence is written in the passive voice. In the **active voice**, the same idea is expressed as:

> Tom hit the ball.

From a literary standpoint, the first sentence focuses attention on the ball, and what happens to it, rather than on Tom. In contemporary American English, the passive voice is arcane, and in a country in which many people speak English as their second (or third or fourth) language, it's a sentence structure that can be very hard to follow.

With some effort, you can rewrite almost all passive sentences into the active voice. For example:

> Travel vouchers are to be submitted within seven days of your return to your regular place of employment.

You can restate this sentence in Plain English as follows:

> When you return to your office, submit your travel voucher within seven days.

Notice that as you edit out the passive voice, you'll have other opportunities to improve the wording to make a sentence into better Plain English form, in this case replacing "regular place of employment" with "your office."

4-10 AVOID OBSCURE VOCABULARY

The first step in avoiding obscure, bureaucratic language is to stop and ask why people would want to use such words and phrases as "pertaining to," "herewith," and "please find enclosed." Writers who use these terms are probably aiming to appear formal and serious—they are signaling that this is not a chatty note from a friend, and perhaps that's a reasonable purpose. But more often, the hidden text is that the writer wants to appear well educated and erudite. Indeed, the worst bureaucratic language comes from low-level government officials who have not had a good education, and some of the best Plain English comes from some Nobel laureates (look at the editorials and opinion pieces in *The Wall Street Journal* and *The New York Times,* for example).

The test for bureaucratic vocabulary is simple: If you cannot imagine yourself walking into a colleague's office and beginning a conversation with "Pertaining to…," then don't use it! (In this example, the conversation would begin with "I need to talk with you about…")

Now that's not to say that we write as we speak. In daily conversation we often use sentence fragments, and most speakers interrupt themselves to revise or amplify a point they are making. In written language, we avoid slang and most colloquial expressions that may be acceptable in spoken dialogue.

Of course, if you're writing a technical document such as the instruction manual for a heart defibrillator, you will use some terms that you wouldn't use in everyday speech. Edward Bailey[2] has defined these two simple rules for word choice:

* Use technical terms only when you need them (and make sure they are well defined).
* Use rare words rarely.

■ 4-11 USE GENDER-NEUTRAL AND NONSEXIST LANGUAGE

An important part of contemporary Plain English usage is to avoid referring to anyone in business documents by nouns or pronouns that indicate only one gender. The reason for this is that it is considered "sexist" (that is, diminishing the rights of women, in most instances) to refer to employees as "workmen" when some of them are likely to be women.

[2]Edward P. Bailey, Jr., *The Plain English Approach to Business Writing.* New York: Oxford, 1990.

The right approach is to choose a **gender-neutral** noun, such as "worker," "customer," or "employee." In some cases, new words have been created to provide a gender-neutral alternative: "congressperson" and "chairperson" are examples. Although these words were criticized by conservative individuals when they first came out, they've reached broad acceptance, and you'll demonstrate sophistication by learning to use them naturally.

When it comes to pronouns, we don't have a good gender-neutral form. If you write: "Each worker will report to his manager," this statement implies that all workers are male. Some writers add footnotes saying, "Whenever this document says 'he,' 'she' will also be included," but that seems awkward and continues to give the female gender a subordinate place. Similarly, going through an entire document and writing "he or she" and "his or her" will make your prose difficult to read.

Many businesspeople use the words "they" and "their" as if they were gender-neutral singular forms (although from a grammatical point of view, they are plurals). You'll find increasing use of the form "Each worker will report to their manager" as the preferred gender-neutral pronoun. You may encounter some people who think this use is ungrammatical because "their" is, strictly speaking, a plural pronoun, but you might ask them what gender-neutral term they prefer. The answer is that there is no convenient alternative. You can accept the "they, their, them" use in the singular as an almost mainstream practice and one that is likely to become more common in the next few years.

In informal speech, you'll often hear people referring to a group of themselves and coworkers as "guys." Technically, this word implies male gender, but in the form "The guys are going to work late and then go out together," it's inoffensive, even if some members of the group are women. A problem occurs when you look for the parallel form to refer to a group of women. The feminine of "guys" is "girls" (or "gals" in slang). But "girls" is also the parallel form of the diminutive "boys." So if you refer to a group of female colleagues as "girls"—even in a compliment such as "The girls have been working very hard on this project"—you may find some colleagues who will take offense. It's best to avoid using "girls" entirely in business contexts (unless you are running a daycare center!). You can say "the women" or "the ladies" (although "ladies" might be considered a little pretentious).

Finally, although you may often hear adult men half-jokingly refer to a group as "the boys," as in "The boys will all be going skiing next weekend to celebrate the end-of-quarter," it's not a good form of speech to follow. "Boys" like "girls" is a diminutive that you should almost always avoid in the singular. The term "boy" was common in a master-servant relationship and has unpleasant connotations of slave owning, and it should never be used. For example, even if you are being served by a waiter in an informal setting at the side of a pool at a country club, getting attention by calling out "Boy!" would be a big mistake in American culture.

■ 4-12 SOME LIMITATIONS OF PLAIN ENGLISH

No one would claim that careful adherence to the rules of Plain English leads to great literature. Indeed, Plain English documents are probably fairly boring to read if they are long. The Victorian English novelist Charles Dickens famously opened his story *A Tale of Two Cities* with the sentence: "It was the best of times, it was the worst of times." A joke in Plain English circles is that this should be rewritten: "There was a great deal of political and social uncertainty in Paris at the end of the eighteenth century." Although true, it's not nearly as eloquent as the phrase Dickens chose. Plain English has its place in business, but it is not a campaign to constrain the richness of the English language in other contexts.

To sum up, clear business communication depends on beginning with a clear objective, matching the level of formality to the business context, and selecting the tone that is most likely to achieve the objective. Messages delivered in any medium are more effective when they are crafted in Plain English.

▷ ▷ ▷ PUT THIS CHAPTER INTO PRACTICE

1. Find an example of bureaucratic language (the rules posted by tennis courts and swimming pools are often good examples) and rewrite them in good Plain English.

2. Identify a business conflict from a newspaper article and, taking the role of one side of the disagreement, outline how you would begin the next message to the other side.

3. Look through a Web site that defines policies and procedures (for example, the "claims procedure" at an insurance company, or the "refund" page of an online retailer) and see if the firm is using gender-neutral language throughout.

KEY TERMS

active voice

colloquialisms, colloquial

context, business context

contraction

dangling participle

gender-neutral

level of formality

passive voice

Plain English

tone

too much information

Multiple Choice Practice Questions: To take the review quiz for this chapter, log on to your Online Edition at www.atomicdog.com.

Chapter 5
Electronic Messages: E-mail, Text, and Instant Messaging

Instant communication is wonderful—but you can have too much of a good thing.

Jan is pleasantly surprised to find the office quiet for once. Within a few minutes of arriving at his desk, he has two browser windows open on his computer. In one, he's charting the moment-by-moment change in valuation of his imaginary stock portfolio, and in the other, he's watching a video of a Miss Universe contestant tripping on her ball gown. He opens up his Instant Messenger account and is happy to see that a friend from high school whom he hasn't talked to in several months is online. He begins a conversation with:

> Janmeister: sup? [meaning "what's up" or "what is happening"]
> HSFriend: not much u? [Not much. What about you?]

and before long, Jan is engrossed in a discussion of long-lost loves and great games from the past whose excitement will never be equaled.

When the BlackBerry® smart phone clipped to his belt buzzes, he reaches down and realizes that he must have left his personal cell phone at home this morning. The BlackBerry is for work, and his company "pushes" all his e-mail messages to his device so he can see them and respond whether he is in or out of the office. There are six or more new e-mails, but the first three are routine announcements about leftover pizza in the break room, birthday celebrations, and reminders to turn off computers at the end of the day, so Jan returns to his IM conversation.

To his surprise, the phone on his desk rings. This is unusual, as most people in his firm rely on messaging back and forth on their BlackBerrys. Jan pulls out the earphones from his iPod and cradles the phone to his ear. "Jan Schmidt, Mergers...?" he begins tentatively.

"Jan!" He instantly recognizes the irate tone of his "Third Year"—the senior analyst who controls his days (and often nights when work stretches beyond midnight). "Where have you been? I left you a voice mail this morning, I texted your personal mobile, and I just sent you an e-mail. Are you on another planet? The meeting isn't at our offices this morning—we're meeting at the clients' lawyers across town. Everyone else is here. What are you doing sitting at your desk?"

Poor Jan. He lives in a world in which he can connect to people on the far side of the Earth in seconds and he has a number *of different kinds of electronic communication devices. But you really can have too much of a good thing—and Jan is in trouble for being out of touch when his supervisor needed to reach him.*

5-1 E-MAIL IS THE NEW STANDARD

E-mail has every advantage as the predominant channel of communication in business: It's a medium that can communicate virtually immediately to any country in the world at almost no cost. It gives the recipient the advantages of *time* and *place shifting* (see Chapter 3) and automatically generates its own near-permanent record without imposing the environmental burdens associated with paper. It is easy to send a single e-mail to several people at once, and when a message is received, it can be stored, forwarded, or copied to someone else—again without measurable cost.

With all these benefits, it would seem that there's no reason not to use e-mail for every business communication. However, e-mail has its limitations: Although it's very good for short messages such as setting appointments and requesting data, it is much less satisfactory as a medium for communicating complex topics. E-mail lacks the emotional signals that are transmitted in face-to-face conversations and even lacks the nuances of tone that are communicated in a phone call. And the very ease of copying that makes e-mail an attractive channel of communication can also be damaging: It's just too easy for a disgruntled or malevolent employee to forward confidential information outside the organization.

It was just a few years ago that an executive would have asked a colleague who was visiting from another firm: "Are you on e-mail?" Of course, this inquiry would be unbelievable today when it is presumed that the visitor's firm would indeed have an e-mail system. Now that e-mail has become the new standard for communication (replacing the formal postal-mail *business letter*), the medium has achieved a new importance and an implicit new level of formality. In an earlier business environment in which employees might "chat" by e-mail but use postal mail for formal business correspondence, e-mail was treated lightly. However, now that it is the standard channel of communication, messages are ever more important and have taken on a slightly greater level of formality. E-mail's old role as the social chat channel has largely been overtaken by two other forms of electronic communication: **Instant Messaging (IM)** and *texting* (written messages sent over cell phones by the **Short Message Service [SMS]**).

5-2 ELECTRONIC COMMUNICATION OTHER THAN E-MAIL

Handheld devices.   There are several other systems for sending text-based messages. First, many professionals now carry a smart phone such as a BlackBerry. These devices allow people to read their e-mails (although with little formatting and on a small screen) when they are away from their desks. Miniature keyboards permit smart phone users to reply to e-mails at once. A big downside to this universal availability is that many meetings are inefficient if people who attend are reading e-mail messages rather than listening to the discussion (see *Business Protocol in Action: The Curse of the BlackBerry*®).

Business Protocol in Action: The Curse of the BlackBerry®

All young businesspeople want a BlackBerry. Better than driving a Mercedes, it's the unparalleled status symbol that shows that their input is so crucial that they must be capable of being reached anytime, anywhere.

However, once the initial novelty has worn off, many BlackBerry users begin to curse the day they took on the new device because of its immediacy. There's never an opportunity to say to the boss: "Oh, I'm sorry, I was traveling, I didn't see your message until I came back to the office," because you can be reached everywhere you go.

Worst of all, the instant communication means that, in the words of one BlackBerry addict, "Absolutely everything becomes urgent. You are in a meeting and you want to check your stock prices—maybe it's time to sell. You glance at your BlackBerry and you see a message: 'Pizza for lunch in the main conference room.' It's impossible not to dive in and reply, 'We've had pizza the last two times. Can't we have sandwiches for a change?'" Many presenters find themselves trying to catch the intermittent attention of audience members whose eyes—and minds—are elsewhere.

How should executives respond to the challenge of having a meeting with its participants being only half there? Some are insisting that the pagers and cell phones must all be turned off, and this prescription is likely to become more common for important meetings. On the other side, it's worth admitting that many meetings go on too long, and the "bit rate" is usually terrible (that is, the rate of flow of real information is usually very low). You can expect to see the American business culture adapt to the BlackBerry trend, and meetings will become shorter and more focused.

Most smart phones connect with corporate e-mail systems in a way that enables new messages to be "pushed" to the handheld device. That is, when a new message comes in to the corporate server, it is automatically sent out to the handheld. In addition to these devices, many cell phones and personal digital assistants (PDAs) can connect to the Internet wirelessly through Wi-Fi wireless so users can log on from time to time and download their e-mail messages.

If you know your recipient is likely to be receiving your message on a handheld device, you'll want to keep your message short and avoid adding comments to the *end* of a forwarded message—the recipient may never scroll all the way down to see what you wrote. Subject lines (discussed below) are even more important.

Text messages (SMS).   Even cell phones that are not fully Web enabled can usually use the Short Message Service (SMS) to deliver brief messages (typically about 160 characters long) from one cell phone to another. Because the messages are usually typed using the 12-key numeric keypad (rather than an alphabetic keyboard), a single character may require multiple keystrokes. The shortness of the messages results in a new cryptographic language (see *It's Just Different: Generation Text*).

In business it's important to remember two things about texting. First, only some people use text messaging. The distribution of users is largely generational (older people probably don't use texting at all). Second, although there are good reasons to use abbreviations when texting, the conventions of the SMS language should not spill over into semiformal office e-mails.

Instant Messaging.   Although IM began as a social communications medium, it is beginning to find a place in business for communication within small work groups. IM works by installing a specific program on the computer you are using. Then you can see which members of your group are online and can communicate back and forth with them in a type of electronic chatting. IM does not use subject lines and automatically generates the name of the sender:

> Monsterman: You in?
> Sherrystar: Just going to coffee. Wanna come?
> Monsterman: Nah, I'm buried here.

Some financial service firms are now using IM for communication between traders—but it could be dangerous. The medium is inherently

It's Just Different: Generation Text

It's not surprising that current college graduates are known as members of "Generation Text." They have grown up with cell phones always at hand, and many of their social interactions are made using their "mobiles." But they don't just phone one another—they spend much of each day writing and sending short text messages. For young people, the advantages of the SMS system are privacy (people can't overhear you talking) and the possibility to quietly send a message while in a meeting (or class!).

Texting has a language all its own: CUL stands for "see you later" and IDK communicates "I don't know." However, the "isms" of text messaging (or txt msg, if you will) may mean nothing to people not familiar with this subculture. Writing "TFTHAOT" is a gracious acknowledgment of future assistance ("thanks for the help ahead of time"), but your boss just may not get it if you write it as part of an e-mail message.

Text messaging is extremely popular in China, in part due to the demographics of cell phone users (young urban dwellers), and in part because of the rate structure (a text message can be cheaper than a cell phone call), but not least because a single Chinese character can represent an entire word.

What we don't know is whether text acronyms will gradually change spelling in other contexts. Language certainly evolves over time: "Hast thou responded on thine own behalf?" is grammatical, meaningful—and about 500 years out of date as a form of speech. We already see "nite" replacing "night" as a common spelling in advertisements, and more spelling changes are bound to be accepted.

informal and provides a temptation to make unprofessional comments (of the order of: "These guys are idiots"). Financial firms are required to keep copies of IM messages, and they could be embarrassing if discovered in the course of litigation. If your work group uses IM, be very careful not to use it to disparage other people, firms, or products or to discuss confidential matters.

Beyond problems of confidentiality, a bigger problem with IM is that it can be a huge distraction. Imagine having to write a term paper while your roommate is throwing a party in your dorm room—it would be hard to concentrate. Having IM running at work is not much different if you are trying to concentrate. Because many systems allow you to show multiple groups (such as "Work" and "Friends"), the temptation to waste time is even greater.

■ 5-3 SETTING UP YOUR E-MAIL ACCOUNTS

Most professional people maintain two e-mail accounts: their company e-mail account and another account for personal use. Although this is a good idea (to avoid the impression that you are using your company's resources for your social life), just be careful that your company can't see e-mails sent from your personal account when you are using your work computer and the firm's Internet connection (see *Doing the Right Thing: Use Your Company's E-mail System with Care*). However, with that in mind, most people do check their personal e-mail during the workday, ostensibly when they are on break.

When you set up your personal e-mail account, you should choose your **e-mail name** (the part that goes before the "@" symbol) with care. Although your friends may think it's amusing that you refer to yourself as:

onecrazydriver@mail.com

Doing the Right Thing: Use Your Company's E-mail System with Care

Your company e-mail system belongs to your firm, and the firm has fairly broad rights to examine and copy what you write. Even if you log off your firm's e-mail program and log on to your personal Gmail or Hotmail account, the courts have repeatedly found that the firm is not considered spying if it reads what you type and tracks which Web sites you visit if you are using the firm's Internet connection.

In practice, most professionals do a reasonable amount of social communication through their company e-mail. For example, using the company e-mail to arrange a purely social lunch meeting is likely to be considered a *de minimus* use (that is, so small that it doesn't matter). From the firm's point of view, by encouraging employees to do a certain amount of personal e-mailing using the firm's e-mail system, the firm can rely on employees to log on from home, and so they will be available by e-mail outside of regular business hours.

However, your firm may have policies against using e-mail extensively; for example, managing an after-work sports league on the firm's e-mail could get you into trouble. Certainly, you should never use company e-mail—or even a private e-mail account from a company computer—to set up a private business or to look for a new job.

as soon as you start seeking recruitment, you'll realize that you can't use this address, and you'll have to open another e-mail account. It is best to stick with something conventional, such as:

hdthoreau@mail.com.

Two things to avoid in choosing your e-mail name are *underscores* and *non-intuitive* numbers. The e-mail name

henry_thoreau@mail.com

may not be clear to recipients when it is underlined as a *hyperlink* (the underlining of the hyperlink obscures the underscore). An e-mail name that includes what might be called "personal numbers":

henry71217@mail.com

is intuitive to someone who was born at 7 o'clock on December 17, but could easily be mistyped as henry72127@mail.com by someone making an innocent error.

When you begin a new job, you can anticipate that you will be assigned an e-mail account by the company that has hired you. Your firm will likely also choose which computer program will be used to read your messages on your work computer. The firm's e-mail administrator will undoubtedly assign you your e-mail name according to a routine practice. For example, Julia Montgomery may any one of:

juliam@bigfirm.com
jmontgomery@bigfirm.com
j.montgomery@bigfirm.com

It's worth anticipating that the e-mail administrator will likely be assigning your name based on the most formal version of your legal name. So if you prefer to use another name, it's important to intervene early or you'll be stuck with an e-mail name that doesn't correspond to how people address you. For example, if William Chang invariably goes by "Bill," he can anticipate (from looking at the e-mail names assigned to his recruiter and new manager's business cards) that he's likely to be assigned:

williamc@techco.com

and he can make an effort to request:

billc@techco.com

before he's hired. Most e-mail administrators positively refuse to change an account name once it has been set up.

Once your account has been set up and you have your e-mail name, you should go into the e-mail account and edit the settings (often under "options," "preferences," or "customize") and look for the setting that allows you to show who the mail is from. In the example above, Bill Chang might enter one of these:

> Bill Chang
> Bill Chang (Contracts)

if there are several Changs at the firm.

All e-mail programs will also allow you to set up a **signature file**. This is a block of text that is placed at the end of all messages that you send. The e-mail signature should include all the ways to reach you, including a restatement of your e-mail address. (In certain e-mail programs, if a recipient prints out your message, only your name "Bill Chang" will show, not the full e-mail address.) It can be useful to have two different signature files: for internal messages (sent within the firm) and for external messages (sent outside the firm). For example, the following is an internal signature for Bill Chang:

> Bill Chang, CR2B Contracts
> billc@bigco.com
> Ext.: 2-3477
> Room 18, East Building

For these within-firm messages, Bill shows his phone extension and physical location. Note that the acronym "CR2B" means something internally but is meaningless outside the firm. So, for external messages he uses a different signature file:

> Bill Chang, *Contract Specialist*
> billc@bigco.com
> Big Company, PLC
> 3322 Scott Blvd, Mail Stop 718
> Santa Clara, CA 92120-2100
> Phone: 1+ (408) 692-3477
> www.bigcom.com/contracts

For external readers of Bill's e-mail messages, he closes by inserting the long form of his signature block, which includes his full telephone number and the firm's Web site and postal-mail address.

▪ 5-4 USING E-MAIL EFFECTIVELY

Not all subjects are suitable for e-mail. E-mail is very good for practical issues: setting times and places of meetings, handling decisions that can be made without much discussion, and posting general "FYI" (for your information) topics that don't require a response. On the other hand, e-mail is terrible for anything that involves emotional content. A message such as "I really didn't feel that you were listening to my suggestions" definitely needs to be delivered in person. If you personally meet someone later who upset or insulted you in a previous encounter, your adversary will likely sense your distress and back down and apologize. But using e-mail encourages you to engage in a one-sided, merciless tirade.

Because e-mail doesn't correctly signal the emotional subtext of a message, it is very easy to fire off an angry rant, and such e-mails have a special name: **flames.** If you find yourself typing out a "flame," you should delete the message before you send it. If you are seriously angry at someone about something, schedule a discussion with that person and talk about the issue face-to-face. Even a simple comment such as "That's *not* the way I wanted this handled!" could be very upsetting to a coworker and ruin an otherwise productive working relationship.

Friends and colleagues often forward around humorous e-mails in an attempt to enliven the workday. But there's a tremendous downside to these messages. Quite a few young professionals have been fired for forwarding jokes with racial or sexual content that violates their firm's policies. Although you may have had a chuckle at the first few lines of a forwarded joke, further down a long forward there might be something raunchy that you didn't even read. Although you might consider the following rule too extreme, it's best just to delete all humor without reading it and make a commitment to yourself *never* to forward such messages.

Remember that e-mails can be stored, copied, and forwarded. So a simple, friendly "I guess we all know who had too much to drink at dinner last night!" can look pretty awful when it's forwarded to your boss. Ask yourself, how would this look if someone printed it out and put it on the bulletin board in our break room? The message "Can we meet after work on Friday?" is pretty innocent, but "Want to catch some action with a big guy?" (however much it was intended as a joke) probably fails the bulletin board test and could land you in trouble.

Any e-mail you send can be instantly printed out or forwarded. An e-mail that begins "Just between you and me…" is an invitation to a recipient to "Fwd" the message to just the person you did *not* want to know your opinion.

Although most e-mail systems are surprisingly reliable, an e-mail sent is not necessarily an e-mail received. If you mistype a recipient's name (for example, "gbuhs@government.org" when you mean "gbush"), the e-mail may eventually come back to you (it's called a **bounce-back**) with a note from your e-mail system: "Message Undeliverable." Or it can just be lost in cyberspace (not all systems will bounce back undeliverable messages). If you don't get a reply to an e-mail, check your "sent" file and make sure you sent it to the right address. For important issues, don't be afraid to call and follow up: "I wanted to be sure you received my e-mail..."

E-mail can be useful for documenting work that you have done. For example, if you are a junior member of a team and you've asked an administrator nicely two times to reserve the conference room for your boss and no action has been taken, your "sent" e-mail files prove that you have been making the request.

On the other hand, don't copy your boss on every little e-mail (this practice is called **copying up**). It gets tiresome, and it doesn't make you look good. There's a happy medium here: You reasonably should keep your superiors informed of what you are working on and when you will be gone from the office. On the other hand, you should resist merely showboating. Don't send up copies that merely show how clever you were at handling an issue (or how unreasonable your colleagues are being).

Most e-mail systems time-stamp the date and time you send an e-mail, and records clearly show when a message was sent to you. Be careful to be truthful if you have overlooked something because e-mail is a clear documentation of just when you were informed.

■ 5-5 CHOOSE YOUR SUBJECT LINE WITH CARE

For all e-mail messages you write, put most of your effort into the Subject line, which is effectively the e-mail's title (see Figure 5-1). Indeed, if you write the Subject line with care, you should be able to convey 90 percent of the message in the title alone. "Stuck in Pittsburgh: Please reschedule meeting to Tuesday" says it all. The Subject line "You'll never guess where I am!" is more amusing but won't be as likely to get swift action.

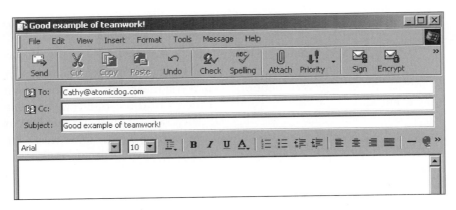

Figure 5-1   Subject Line
The title of your e-mail is the first thing a recipient sees and the most important thing to think about when you're composing it.

Remember that the person who receives your message may be reading it on a PDA or cell phone and the title may be truncated.

For the same reason, when you are *replying* to an e-mail, put new information at the beginning of a Subject line. Suppose you receive a message:

> Subject: Quarterly Results: Not due till Friday

but you really need some rough numbers to go ahead with a project you are working on. You hit the reply key and edit the beginning of the title:

> Subject: Do we have estimates? Re: Quarterly Results: Not due till Friday

One bad habit that you should be careful to avoid is thoughtlessly hitting the reply key without editing the title. The office administrator sends out a message to the work group: "New coffee machine installed" and you reply with "Re: New coffee machine installed", but your message has nothing to do with the coffee machine. This is irksome to recipients. Your message may be unread, deleted, or otherwise overlooked. Make the Subject line count.

■ 5-6 WRITING E-MAIL MESSAGES

Because many e-mails are now read on handheld devices with small screens, it's a good idea to put the most important material in an e-mail right at the beginning. However, when the recipient may not immediately recognize the sender, it may be necessary to balance the goal of "most important up front" with first providing some context:

> Sherry,
>
> This is Scott from your first-year training class. You'll remember I'm from the Auckland, NZ office.

There are many schools of thought about whether or not to use a salutation (greeting) in an e-mail. One argument is that because the recipients know who they are, they don't need a "Dear Bill" at the beginning, and it only wastes valuable screen "real estate." The counterargument is that a few words of pleasantry help the world along. E-mails sent outside the firm often begin with just the recipient's name:

> Mr. Lee,
>
> I am contacting you to see if you can arrange…

And internal messages often begin with a pleasantry, such as one might say if you ran into a colleague in the break room:

> Good morning, Sandy,
>
> Can I ask if you have the estimates…

In the same way, some people feel that an e-mail does not need a formal closing, such as "Sincerely, Sarah Brown," whereas other people experience short, quick replies as curt and rude. One solution, if the e-mail requests help or action, is to end with an expression of appreciation:

> My thanks, Tom Jones [external]
>
> With thanks, Justin [internal]

E-mails should be properly formatted, including the use of capital letters and punctuation. Using short paragraphs and more blank lines than you would in a printed letter will add to the clarity of your communication:

> Tom,
>
> Do you have the Q3 figures? I need revenue estimates for the sales meeting at noon today.
>
> Thank you, Maggie

The preceding example is much clearer (and friendlier!) than the following one:

Send the Q3 figures ASAP. I need revenue estimates at once.

Although cell-phone text messaging often uses just lowercase letters, failing to use capitalization and using text-message spelling (i need ur help on this project) will signal a lack of professionalism. ALL CAPITALS can be used sparingly to emphasize a particular term ("Sorry, I need the PURCHASE ORDER, not the invoice"), but be careful of overuse, as "all caps" can look like shouting.

Several short e-mail messages are better than one long message. When you send several messages, your recipients can reply to items one at a time or forward a "clean" message (a message on one topic) to someone else to handle. In general, with the exception of routine information (summaries of committee reports, for example), you should aim for a message that can be read on one screen without scrolling. Again, remember to put the most important information up front, as your recipient may be reading the message in a short form on a mobile device.

Even if your e-mail is only moderately long, if it is complex (for example, with several options that involve "if this, then I have an additional question" contingencies), there is a great advantage in numbering the questions "1., 2., 3.," and so on. This way, you are likely to get an answer to every one of your concerns and nothing will be overlooked.

The best endings to e-mails are either clear questions or action steps. "So, considering our options, would you prefer to meet later in the day or postpone till next week?" Or, "So I'll keep this on my desk until I see the new price list, then I'll go ahead and place your order."

■ 5-7 SENDING E-MAIL TO MANY PEOPLE AT ONCE

Aliases and **distribution lists** allow you to send a message to many people at once. Your e-mail administrator may have set up an alias so that typing the word "Marketing" in the "To:" line automatically sends your e-mail to everyone working in the Marketing Department. If you regularly write to a group of people for whom an alias doesn't exist, you can create a group name or distribution list within your own e-mail program on your computer. (You must choose a name, and you'll need to select the recipients one time, but after that, you just use the group name.)

However, if you live by the alias, you can die by the alias. If you send out too many e-mail messages to more people than you need to address, you risk becoming an **autodelete**—someone whose messages are routinely ignored by others because most of the messages from that person are irrelevant. So choose to address the smallest group of people relevant to the issue at hand (not everyone in a department).

In addition to the "To:" line for the original recipient, e-mail comes with two forms of copy: "Cc:" means a copy is sent to someone else, and "Bcc:" means a "blind copy" (see Figure 5-2). People who receive the original message ("To:") or a copy ("Cc:") won't know (are "blinded") that the message has also been sent to other recipients whose names are in the Bcc: field. When you send an e-mail to Harvey with a blind copy to Jake, Jake gets a copy of the message but Harvey does not know this. Your e-mail program may—or may not—tell the recipient of a blind copy that it's a copy of a message. This can cause confusion if the person being blind-copied thinks that the original message was for him or her. Check how your e-mail system handles this, and if it doesn't flag Bcc: messages as such, you'll have to send two messages, the first reading: "Jake, next is a Bcc to you."

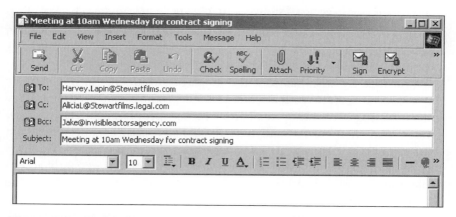

Figure 5-2   Blind Copy

This e-mail is to Harvey.Lapin@Stewartfilms.com. Harvey can see that AliciaL@Stewartfilms. legal.com also gets a copy but doesn't see that Jake@invisibleactorsagency.com gets a copy too.

Sending a copy of a message to yourself is sometimes useful if you've accessed your e-mail account over the Internet from a public computer. If you are sending an e-mail to a long list of people for whom you do not have an alias, a useful trick is to put their names into the "Bcc:" field, having addressed the e-mail to yourself. Everyone gets the message, correctly addressed to them, without a header containing dozens of other names that fill the screen.

■ 5-8 MANAGING INCOMING E-MAIL

You should be sure to always check your business e-mail account regularly. Unless you are on vacation or traveling away from your office, a *minimum* frequency would be to check your e-mail at the beginning, middle, and end of the workday. (The rule should be "morning, noon, and night.") Because business colleagues may use e-mail to send you an update overnight (in preference to waking you with a phone call), you should begin your workday with a quick review of your e-mail to see whether there have been any urgent changes in the day's planned activities.

One good tip for handling a large group of e-mails after an absence is to answer the most recent first. You'll encounter lost data that colleagues have suddenly found—"Sorry, I've got it! I realized it was in your previous e-mail!"—and "impossible" meetings that have been called off—"Sorry, I realized that next week won't work for you because you're at the sales meeting."

Prioritize by who has sent the message—your boss and customers will appreciate getting your attention at once. Some e-mail programs allow you to highlight incoming mail from certain people in different colors. Understand what turnaround time (response speed) is expected within your firm or workgroup. In some industries where executives are often on the road, a delay of a day or so in answering e-mail is perfectly acceptable. On the other hand, in some financial services firms, a 45-minute wait for a reply during the trading day would seem like eternity.

Answer e-mails selectively—not every e-mail needs an answer with your opinion. However, when an e-mail has been sent specifically to you ("Can you get me a copy of last year's brochure? I don't need it at once, but I'll need it before I go to Belgium next month"), at least briefly acknowledge receipt even if the task is pending. In the words of Mary Munter, an expert in business communication at Dartmouth College, "A nonresponse to an e-mail is a response of a kind." That is, if someone you work with makes a request, and you plan to get to it at some time in the future, but you don't acknowledge the e-mail, you may quickly earn a reputation for being unhelpful and not a team player.

When you're replying to e-mails, be very careful of the "Reply to all" function. If you have any doubt that the system you're using too easily slips into "Reply to all," it is better to start a new message by typing in the recipient's name. For example, if your office administrator sends out an e-mail to everyone in your firm noting that there's been a change in your office supplies vendor, you don't want 2,000 colleagues to get a copy of your message saying, "Thanks for telling me about the new office supplies firm. I forgot to tell you—I need a new stapler for my desk."

▪ 5-9 ORGANIZING E-MAIL

Never be afraid to delete suspicious messages: that's what the delete key is for. Delete at once unwanted **spam** (the e-mail equivalent of junk mail), such as a message sent (without much thought) to a very large group of people, or a commercial message from a firm that has "captured" your e-mail name. Delete all jokes and Fwd's (forwarded messages) from people you don't know. E-mail can contain viruses, most of which are in files attached to original messages. Even someone you know may unwittingly forward you a file that contains a virus, or a worm may get into an associate's e-mail system and send you a bogus message—with a virus attached. Many professionals won't open an e-mail attachment unless it contains information that they've been expecting (so don't be surprised if you get a phone call to confirm the authenticity of an e-mail before someone will open a file that you sent).

Messages can exist in (at least) two places: on the server—that is, the computer that handles e-mail for your firm—and on the hard drive of your computer. As part of the settings of your e-mail program, you can choose to routinely delete each message from the server as you download it onto your machine. You can set your e-mail program with different preferences on different computers that you use. For example, if you set the e-mail program on your laptop not to delete messages from the server, the next time you return to your office and log on to your desktop computer, you will be able to see new messages and also the messages you already saw on your laptop. Just one warning: Although routinely leaving messages on the server gives you the ability to retrieve old messages from anywhere (office, home, laptop), you may exceed your storage quota and your e-mail account will be blocked.

The number of old messages can become large. Your e-mail program may routinely prompt you to archive old items (you move items received during certain dates to a separate file and reduce the space needed for your inbox). But a better solution is to learn to use folders to save messages. For example, you might have one folder labeled "Admin" for routine administrative announcements and another labeled "Project X" for a new product development. Sorting into folders makes retrieving relevant information much faster.

Most e-mail programs can filter—that is, automatically move suspected spam into a separate folder. You can check the folder with less frequency than your regular messages. E-mail programs that have a "preview" allow you to look at the first few lines of a message without opening it. This feature can be a great time-saver because you can very quickly see what to delete.

You can try to "unsubscribe" to unwanted spam. The annoying message may include instructions to a Web site where you can remove your name from the list. Or you can try replying to the spam with the word "unsubscribe" in both the title and the message. Some e-mail administration programs automatically search for the word and remove your name from a large alias. However, many experts warn that merely replying to a spam only confirms that your e-mail address is active, and will expose you to even more spam. It's probable that Congress will enact some restrictions on spamming, as many corporate mail systems are now dealing with more spam than legitimate business messages.

Delete all flames that are sent to you. The person who sent such messages to you probably regretted sending them a few minutes later. Reading all the nasty things someone has to say about you will only ruin your day. If someone is really interested in working through some tough issues, talk face-to-face.

Remember, however, that many computer operating systems keep all deleted messages in a file called "trash." This feature is helpful if you decide later that you need something (you can "restore" it from trash).

But the downside is that a copy of sensitive material may be on your hard drive until you remember to "empty trash"; and even if you think you've wiped every copy of a sensitive e-mail from your computer, many computer technicians would be able to recover a supposedly deleted file.

If you learn to master all of the features on your e-mail program, you can substantially increase your efficiency in your work.

▶ ❯ ❯ PUT THIS CHAPTER INTO PRACTICE

1. Send an e-mail to yourself from one account to another (or to the account of a roommate or friend) and check how your name is displayed for the recipient.
2. Set up a distribution list for a group working on a project.
3. Take a long, rambling e-mail you have received and edit it into succinct ideas with proper formatting.

■ KEY TERMS

alias	flame
autodelete	handheld device
bounce-back	Instant Messaging (IM)
copying up	signature file
distribution list	Short Message Service (SMS)
e-mail name	spam

Multiple Choice Practice Questions: To take the review quiz for this chapter, log on to your Online Edition at www.atomicdog.com.

Chapter 6
Phone, Voice Mail, and Phone Conferencing

Often a phone call is the first opportunity to demonstrate your professionalism.

The boss comes charging out of his office, clearly in a rage: "Do you realize you just hung up on our most important client? All I asked you to do was put the call on hold and phone the trading desk to check on her order. You've been here six months and still you don't know how to use the phone system!"

There's a lot of technology in a modern office, and most of the systems have many more features than most people actually know how to use. Learning all the details of the system (how to put one call on hold while you quickly check for information on another line) will speed your workday and save you a lot of time.

You already know that the telephone is useful for getting immediate answers, but it can also be seen as an irritating interruption to most executives' workdays. A few years ago, phone systems reflected a strict hierarchy: You would call a firm's main switchboard, and if you asked for an executive by name, your call would be transferred to an assistant who would greet you with: "Mr. Entremont's office—may I help you?" You would then have to make a case for why your call should be taken, and you might eventually be switched through to the person you were calling.

These days, few executives have old-fashioned "secretaries." Instead, they have assistants who support the work of a team of people and are likely to be busy with their own duties. When you call a colleague at another firm, it's likely that the executive will answer her or his own phone and that your call may be an interruption.

In a world without secretaries, you will find yourself in control of a lot of confidential information, and you may find yourself in a situation in which a supplier or recruiter encourages you to "be a good friend" and share your company's internal phone directory. There are good reasons why you should say no (see Doing the Right Thing: Guard the Privacy of Your Company's Phone Lists*).*

Doing the Right Thing: Guard the Privacy of Your Company's Phone Lists

Companies' internal phone lists are the pot of gold at the end of the rainbow for executive recruiters, sales reps, competitors, and, sometimes even criminals. If you innocently give a photocopy of your firm's phone directory to someone outside the firm, you expose everyone on the list to, at the very least, annoying sales calls. Many of the extensions may be "unpublished" and not even be shown on managers' business cards (their published numbers may go to voice mail or to assistants first), and internal directories often list senior management's home phone numbers.

So when someone outside the firm asks you for a copy of the list, it's probably a good idea to say no. You're undoubtedly violating your firm's work rules, and you may get yourself into a lot of trouble.

▪ 6-1 ANSWERING YOUR BUSINESS PHONE

Unless you've been specifically trained during your firm's orientation to answer the phone with a standard phrase and a particular order of items, such as "Good morning, Megacorp. Trading Division, Jacqui Williams speaking," you should answer the phone with your name: "This is Jacqui Williams." You don't need to say, "This is Jacqui Williams speaking"—the caller knows what you're doing. Unless you are answering for someone else, don't use the word "office"—it's wrong to say, "Jacqui Williams's office," if you are Jacqui. It only leads to wasted time when someone has to ask: "Oh, is Jacqui there?" "Yes, this is she..." You should use that form only if you are answering someone else's phone: "Mike Wong's office; this is Jacqui Williams."

Answering with just "Hello" is definitely wrong. This also leads to wasted time. Your callers will feel awkward at the start of the call if they don't know with whom they are speaking. You can see that this violates the New Golden Rule of business protocol: You should help other people to do their jobs as easily as possible.

If answering with your name is the correct protocol, you may wonder why many Americans just answer the phone with a mumbled, "...ullo?" If you ask them, they'll tell you that they were instructed by their parents not to give out their name. Because many Americans grew up as "latchkey kids" (that is, home alone without adult supervision after school), parents feared that child molesters and potential robbers would be spurred on if they knew that little Timmy was home alone. They believed that answering the phone with any information ("Hello! This is Timmy. How can I help you?") would let bad guys know that junior was home alone. Of course, picking up the phone and saying "Hello" probably wasn't very effective at hiding the fact that an 11-year-old was home alone, but that's the history of the origination of this habit.

■ 6-2 TAKING A PHONE CALL

If you absolutely have a deadline due (for example, you have to finish a spreadsheet in time for a 2 o'clock meeting), it's reasonable within most work groups to just let all phone messages go to your voice mail. If team members need to see you on the same urgent project, presumably they will walk over to your desk.

If you decide to take a call, you can enhance your professional effectiveness by training your callers to be concise. If someone wants to ramble and tell stories, it's reasonable to interrupt and ask, "So, how can I help you today? I'm in the middle of something here." It is often helpful to restate the caller's concerns in your words: "So, if I have this right, you've seen the invoices for May and July, but you still haven't received the June invoice, and our accounting department is giving you the runaround?" Then take the concern to a reasonable action step: "I can make you a copy and send it to you. Can you give me a fax number?"

Many people confuse what is *important* with what is *urgent*. Because the telephone is a device that permits other people to interrupt you at their convenience, you should be comfortable imposing your own timetable: "I can get you a copy of that tape—but it won't be until next week. Is that all right?" Make sure you have a reliable method for managing your pending tasks. Many e-mail systems, such as Microsoft Outlook, have a "task manager," so you can note pending tasks on your personal computer. Having a good "to do" list system saves you from the anxieties associated with missing a deadline.

Most people have difficulty tactfully ending a phone call. The call goes on long after the substantive business has been transacted. When two people are speaking face-to-face, there are many nonverbal signals (stance, moving toward the door, and so on) that signal that one party wishes to end the conversation. But those cues are absent on the phone. Linguists who study human speech patterns note that toward the end of phone conversations, people tend to use shorter sentences, and indeed, short words. You can adopt those ideas, and also get into the habit of restating the purpose of a call:

> "OK, so, let's recap here: You are still interested in our technology, but you have three other vendors to see. You won't be able to make a decision until the beginning of next year. So I'll plan to call you back then."

■ 6-3 MANAGING YOUR OWN VOICE MAIL

Voice mail (automated message recording) is usually part of your firm's phone system. It is a way to digitally record messages, and it allows "random access" (that is, you don't have to listen to messages in the order they were recorded) so you can skip, delete, save, and forward messages. Voice mail can be one of your most important business tools. Using it effectively allows you to time-shift (you take your calls only when it's convenient for you) and place-shift (you can check your messages while you are away from your desk).

You should make sure that your **voice-mail greeting** sounds cheerful and fully identifies you, especially if there is any likelihood that a caller may have been looking for another employee with the same last name:

> "You've reached Albert Lee in the technology group at Purchasing. Please leave me a message at the beep."

This is a good model. Note that it does not include a ritual apology ("I'm sorry that I'm not here to take your call right now") or a promise to return the call (which is self-evident). Your callers will appreciate a short message.

In many work groups there's an option for a caller to "escape" from voice mail and reach a real person. The form for the message then would be:

> "You've reached Stephan Dreibilbis in Purchasing. If you need to talk with someone immediately, please press 03 to transfer to my assistant, Irene Kim. Or leave me a message at the beep. Thank you."

When you listen to your voice mail, your system will allow you to save or delete messages. It's worth investing some time to learn additional features such as how to listen to only new messages, how to skip forward or back, and how to forward or delegate a message to someone else. In most firms, the standard for acting on voice mail (or at least voice mail that does not indicate a panic situation requiring your immediate attention) is to respond within 24 hours. In some industries (television news reporting, for example), a 24-hour delay would be too long. Be sure to learn the accepted standard in your work group. If you have a pending item, it's worth making a quick response to let the caller know that you are not ignoring the message:

> "Terry, this is Stephan—just calling to let you know I got your call. I'm at a sales meeting in Orlando, and I'll be happy to get you those figures next Monday when I'm back in the office."

Some firms encourage all their employees to change their phone message every day:

> "Hi, this is Scott, and today, Monday, I'll be in the office most of the day, except for a meeting from 11 to noon. I'm probably on another call. Please leave me a message, and I'll get right back to you."

A message like this certainly conveys energy and immediacy, which is why this technique is popular with sales firms, such as real estate agencies. However, updating your welcome message every day takes time and, more importantly, discipline. There's nothing worse for your professional image than a message that refers to "today, Monday," on Wednesday.

You should certainly change your voice-mail message when you're going to be away for a day or more, such as when you're on vacation. Many voice-mail systems allow you to record an **alternate greeting** such as the following:

> "This is Michael Chiang in Direct Sales. I'll be traveling away from the office until the week after Labor Day and may not be able to respond to your message until Tuesday, September 9th. If you need immediate assistance, please contact Ahmed Zabolly at 555-6789."

Using the alternate greeting allows you to save your routine message and return to it when you are back at your desk.

■ 6-4 LEAVING A VOICE-MAIL MESSAGE

Whenever you phone someone else, you should anticipate that you may reach voice mail. No one wants to plow through a message like this:

> "Wow, Sheila, I was hoping to reach you...I guess you're not there. Well, I just wanted to go over some things with you...um, one was, do you know when the quarterlies will be ready? I need your figures to complete the budget planning for next fiscal year. I should've said...this is Pat in the Treasurer's office...I think we met at the off-site last year...anyway, I don't need the exact income, but I do need revenue. And there was something else I had to ask you, but I guess I'll have to call back."

The keys for voice messages that you leave are:

- Brevity
- Clarity
- Action step

The way to achieve such messages is with a moment or two of planning before you make calls (perhaps even making a few notes). Here's the revised example:

> "Hi, Sheila. This is Pat Burns in the Treasurer's office. I'm working on the budget for next year, and I need two figures from you from last quarter: revenue and head-count. If you could call me back with those, my number is 555-1621, or you could e-mail me at 'pburns'—that's all lowercase, no gap or period. Thank you."

Note that this caller gives advance notice that a phone number is coming ("my number is"), and giving the e-mail address is a way to repeat who's calling. Another way is to repeat the name and phone number at the end. If the caller heard you correctly the first time, he or she can skip the rest of the message.

When you're leaving your own phone number, remember that a number that is very familiar to you may be unfamiliar to your caller. Always pause before the number and speak quite slowly and very distinctly. Some numbers are easily confused. "Nine" and "five" can sound close, so if your phone number includes those digits, say "nine" with a heavy emphasis on the end so that it sounds closer to "niner" and say "five" short and close to "fife." For the same reason, emphasize the end of "one" and say "zero" instead of "oh." You should always leave your number. There's nothing more frustrating than a message like "Hi, it's me! Call me back—you know the number." The person you are calling may usually contact you from his or her desk, where your number is entered into the phone's speed-dial memory, but just this once, your colleague may be trying to return the call from an airport and doesn't have a phone directory along.

Finally, make sure your message has an action step. Do you really need the other person to call you back? If so, with what information? Or were you just calling to leave information? In that case, it would be polite to say, "No need to call me back, I just wanted to let you know..." This should lead you to the conclusion that, in general, phone messages shouldn't be one-sided, and you should avoid complicated "if, and, but" constructions. If you are unsure what to do about a situation, you'll need to schedule a meeting or a person-to-person phone call. In that case, the message should be something like this:

> "As you can see, it's a complicated situation, and I'm not sure how to proceed. Please, could you call me back, and if you get my voice mail, perhaps you could suggest a couple of times when I could reach you in person."

On some occasions in business, a voice message simply won't fulfill your needs, and you'll want to reach a live person(see *Business Protocol in Action: Avoiding "Voice-Mail Jail"*).

▪ 6-5 WHEN YOU REACH A PERSON AND NOT VOICE MAIL

In most business situations, you are more likely than not to reach voice mail or an assistant. But you should be prepared for what to say if you reach a "real person." It doesn't make a good first impression to say, "Oh, wow! It's actually you! I thought I'd be getting voice mail!" And don't waste time with extensive apologies and fatuous recitations about how busy the other person must be.

All this means is that, just as for voice mail, you should have your call outlined beforehand—three bullet points and an action step would be typical. Be sure to introduce yourself fully and carefully without mumbling. State the purpose of your call and aim to be both brief and strategic. The best question to ask to see if you are being "strategic" is this: If this call is successful, what will result? Suppose you know that you are but one of several hundred applicants for a great job, and you've managed to find

Business Protocol in Action: Avoiding "Voice-Mail Jail"

Figure 6-1   Reaching an Executive by Phone
One way to avoid "voice-mail jail" is to call at the beginning or end of the business day, when the phone will most likely ring through to the person you're trying to reach.
SOURCE: © 2009 Jupiterimages Corporation.

Well-designed voice-mail systems are wonderful—you can leave a message for one specific person, or if you have a question that anyone can answer, you can choose an option that switches you to a live person. But some companies seem determined to prevent you from ever reaching anything other than voice mail. All lines lead to what is jokingly called "voice-mail jail." No matter what you do, you can't seem to reach anything other than a recording.

There are some tricks that you can try to get around this problem. Even if the recorded message doesn't offer you the option to "press zero to talk to my assistant," you can try that, or "03" or the "#" key. Different systems have different transfer options, even if they do not always mention them in the recorded message. Then, if you are trying to reach an executive and you get an assistant, it's fair to ask when is a good time to reach the manager in person or if you can schedule a specific time for a phone conference.

If you are seeking recruitment, an old trick is to call at the very beginning or end of the workday (see Figure 6-1). Many managers are still at their desks at 5:45 P.M., for example. Their assistants have left for the day, and the only calls they are expecting are from family members. If you try this ruse, understand that you'll catch the person on the other end a little off-guard, so be extra polite—and brief.

out the name and phone number of the decision maker. You'll want to get across "three reasons why" you should be hired, and your goal is to make sure that you are offered an interview. If you are trying to land a new account for your business, clearly state what your firm has to offer and ask for a brief appointment to make a presentation. If you are professional and concise, few people will say no.

Don't forget to end with polite thanks to the person on the other end, but again, no great effusive outpourings of gratitude are needed: Saying, "Thank you for taking my call. I'll be sure to contact your assistant tomorrow to schedule an appointment. Goodbye" is enough. Again, avoid clichés such as, "Thank you for taking time out of your busy day."

■ 6-6 CELL PHONES

Mobile phones (cellular, or "cell," phones) produce vehement reactions: People either love them or hate them. On the positive side, they've changed communication from place-to-place to person-to-person. You no longer need to remember a list of different numbers to reach one person, and you don't have to call around and ask if someone is there. In addition, it's easy to get voice-mail service with a cell phone, so many busy professionals rely on their cell phone as their primary phone number. Indeed, cell phones are so popular in some industries that firms no longer provide "desk phones"—they assume that employees will be reachable on their mobile phones. You may even have noticed people who carry two cell phones: one for business and the other for personal matters.

If your boss carries a cell phone, you'll soon learn what the rules are for communication. A few executives expect all phone calls from team members to go to the cell phone. Others expect cell phone calls only in urgent situations, and still others use the cell phone exclusively for family contact. Your superior will let you know this, and if you are in any doubt, be sure to ask.

Cell phones are often lost or damaged—the average life of a phone is about one year. Be sure you know what happens to your stored information if your cell phone is stolen. If it's a company-issued mobile, your Information Technology (IT) Department will send a signal to deactivate it at once. But what about your "contacts," all the names and numbers that you've carefully entered into the phone? If you are using a "smart phone" (combination personal digital assistant [PDA] and phone), you undoubtedly "synch" it by dropping it into a cradle connected to your personal computer at work. This process of synchronization will back up your contacts and appointments to your computer and your firm's server. However, many people falsely assume that all their contact information is backed up by their cell phone provider. This may—or may not—be true. Make sure you find out, and have a way to keep a permanent record of your contacts for the day that you turn around and find that your phone has disappeared.

The rapid adoption of cell phones (more than 200 million are in use in the United States—about two-thirds of the population has one) has challenged the conventional rules of etiquette, which didn't anticipate a situation in which you could break off a conversation with a person who is *present* to talk to someone who is *not present*. An approach to this problem is to break it down into two parts: First, using a cell phone in a public place often means that you are ignoring the people you are with—never a good idea and almost certainly impolite (see Figure 6-2). Second, cell phones can be noisy and disruptive: The ringing is distracting in public places, and the majority of users speak much more loudly on the phone than they would to someone right next to them (referred to as "cell yell").

With those problems in mind, we can easily derive some common-sense rules for good manners when using cell phones. If you were in a casual conversation with a friend walking down the street and you saw a business colleague nearby, would you say hi? Of course you would! But if you were sitting having coffee with a friend, would you turn your back to the table and begin a long conversation with the waiter about sports scores? I hope not. So, if the setting is informal, then it's generally considered reasonable to answer a cell phone and take a brief message while speaking at a normal volume. If the call is likely to be a long one (or if the connection is bad and you are going to have to yell), you should excuse yourself and step away from the table. You can take the call in a corridor or use a phone booth. Be sensitive to the concern that speaking on the phone means that you will be ignoring the people whom you are with, so your absence should be limited.

In a semiformal meeting, you might be able to respond to a ringing cell phone by saying to the people present, "If you'll excuse me, let me just take this…" and then making it clear to the caller that you are otherwise occupied and will call back later. But as the level of formality of the

Figure 6-2   Cell Phone Etiquette
Use good judgment when interrupting a conversation to take a phone call on your cell.
Source: © 2009 Jupiterimages Corporation.

meeting increases, taking a call is unacceptable. In any formal business meeting, the intrusion of a ringing cell phone would be considered a discourtesy. At the highest level of formality—say, a job interview—even having a cell phone visible tends to signal a lack of wholehearted commitment to the meeting at hand. So, although it's certainly useful to take a cell phone with you on job interviews (to check directions or to call if you are unavoidably delayed), you should always make sure that it is turned off and put away in your briefcase or purse before your meetings begin. Most formal restaurants consider it very bad manners to use a phone at the table. Of course, what is considered "bad manners" in one culture may be considerably different in another setting. For example, in China, being interrupted by a ringing cell phone is almost a status symbol—it shows how essential your input is (see *It's Just Different: In China, Businesspeople Are Reluctant to Use Voice Mail*).

Many cell phones have a "silent" mode that replaces the ringer with a vibration, and of course, all cell phones can be turned off. You should be very careful to turn off your phone in movies, theaters, and concert halls,

It's Just Different: In China, Businesspeople Are Reluctant to Use Voice Mail

A *Wall Street Journal* article noted that business meetings in China are often interrupted by ringing cell phones. All Chinese businesspeople have cell phones ("mobiles," in British English) and many people have two or more (to take advantage of local and long-distance calling rates from different companies).

What shocks many U.S. visitors to China is that cell phone calls seem to interrupt even the most important negotiations. An exasperated visitor may be tempted to say: "Don't you guys ever use voice mail?" and the answer is, in general, "no."

The Wall Street Journal points out that this has nothing to do with a lack of technical sophistication. The problem is the strict hierarchies that exist in Asian cultures. It is considered impolite for a junior staffer to leave a message for the boss (it's as if the junior were ordering the boss around). And when the boss calls a subordinate, he expects that staffer to be instantly available. Turning off the phone in a meeting just isn't acceptable.

Knowing the culture can be helpful. A Chinese business partner may readily offer you her cell phone number. However, when you call, she may seem uninterested in your call. That's because she's in a meeting. Knowing the culture can be helpful in this situation.

and you should put the ringer on "silent" in most social settings. However, be aware that the vibration from a silent incoming call can itself be disruptive, especially if you interrupt a conversation for no apparent reason to answer your phone.

Most cell phones come with *caller ID*, so that you can recognize who is calling by looking at the phone. For that reason, most cell phone users answer the phone without identification, by just saying "Hello," or by greeting the caller when they recognize the name. That behavior is acceptable for informal social use, but in business (for example, if you are a salesperson who gives out a cell phone number to customers), it's still much better to give a full greeting when answering the phone. This principle also applies if you are in a recruiting situation. If a recruiter is calling you, just answering with a grunt doesn't get the conversation off to a good start.

One unfortunate corollary of the ability to reach anyone anywhere at any time is that all plans become tentative: "Well, we're going out to get something to eat, but we probably will go to a movie later. I'll give you a call." Although a certain amount of spontaneity is expected in social situations, you should work hard to avoid multiple to-and-fro callbacks in business. Try to think through a situation and offer a reasonable plan; then call back only if circumstances unexpectedly change.

■ 6-7 CONFERENCE CALLS

A **conference call** allows many participants to join in the same conversation. It's used commonly in certain industries, such as financial services. There are two types of conference calls. One is essentially one-way closed-circuit radio: Using your phone, you "tune in" and hear an announcement of something, such as a firm's quarterly reports. Conference calls like this can be used to connect literally thousands of people.

The second type of conference call is interactive—it's like a group meeting, in which a dozen or more people can be on the same conference call. In this case, you can talk as well as listen. These types of conference calls are useful for updating progress in long-duration projects in which team members are far distant from one another. They are more likely to work well in routine situations and when the team members have previously met and know one another well. Another good use is for a work group that comes together intermittently, such as to plan a new staff orientation program once a year. Again, conference calls work best when there is a foundation of previous face-to-face contact. Of course, the advantage of the conference call system is that you can stay at your own location and avoid having to invest perhaps a couple of days of travel to complete just one meeting.

For both types of conference calls, the system usually requires that you dial an 800 number and punch in an access code. You'll have to clear your schedule and make sure that you are not interrupted (including putting up a sign on your door if necessary). It's important to avoid distracting noises (such as background office conversations or shuffling papers), so many people use speakerphones for conference calls and use the **mute button** to silence the microphone on their phones, unless they are actually making a contribution.

Conference calls are most successful when a printed (or e-mailed) agenda is shared by the participants before the call starts. The agenda should show the name and affiliation of all the people on the call and should have an estimated time for each part of the meeting. Participants usually greet one another by identifying themselves and saying, "I'm on." One person acts as the **moderator** and has responsibility for beginning and ending the conference, watching the timing, and keeping to the planned agenda. The moderator can move the conference along by carefully summarizing discussion. The moderator should state consensus, or what she or he believes to be consensus, and then "poll" the participants to see whether everyone is in agreement. For example:

> "So, most people think the harbor cruise wasn't worth the extra expense, and we should just book an additional dinner at the hotel?"

The moderator should encourage input from everyone by referring to a list of participants. If you act as moderator and find that you are being sidetracked in a debate that appears to have no clear resolution, it's sometimes helpful just to state that and move on: "OK, so we have lots of opinions about the Friday night entertainment, and no clear plan at this point. So, we'll have to get back to you with some specific bids for the alternatives. We can send them out in writing before the next call." The moderator should try to clarify wishes and hopes ("We need a better cost estimate") and develop them into action steps with deadlines that are assigned to specific group members.

Many people find that the most difficult part of conference calls is sustaining attention (because the call may last more than an hour). You may find that you need to take a break for a few minutes and then rejoin the conversation. Taking notes may help keep you focused on the discussion.

■ 6-8 WEB MEETINGS

Web meetings (or "Web-enabled meetings") are very useful for training, such as the rollout of new products. Many large firms use them for new employee training. Using the Internet, all participants log in at a specified time and can all see the same presentation (see Figure 6-3). For a simple slide show with narration, the number of participants can be very large indeed—more than 1,000 in some cases. Some Web meeting systems require participants to watch on the Web and listen to audio using a dial-in phone conference. But it is also possible to use VOIP (voice-over

Figure 6-3   Web Meeting
Web meetings don't require special equipment and allow easy long-distance colla-
boration on projects.
SOURCE: © 2009 Jupiterimages Corporation.

Internet protocol) to run meetings if participants have the appropriate
equipment. In many Web meetings, a small video of the leader may
appear on screen if the leader has a Webcam.

Web meetings can also be used for collaborative meetings of a smaller
number of participants in a work group, especially if all of the people who
are involved in the meeting have a Webcam so it's possible to see who's
talking. For a small group, it's possible to collaboratively edit documents
and have everyone see the changes being made on-screen. Web meetings
are increasingly popular when people have to collaborate over great dis-
tances, such as between one country and another.

If you are a participant, you should prepare for a Web meeting with as
much diligence as you would for an in-person meeting. Even if you are
taking only one hour of training with hundreds of other people, give the
presentation your best attention. Don't attempt to check e-mail or your
cell phone or you may miss important points. Have a pen and pencil ready
to take notes or to jot down questions.

If you are running a training session using a Web meeting, make sure that your script (what you plan to say) will match your slides, and make sure the environment is appropriate: Turn off your phone and close your office door. If you work in a cubicle, it may be a good idea to reserve a quiet conference room for your presentation, and, of course, let your teammates know not to interrupt you.

Compared with videoconference systems (see Section 6-9), Web meetings are relatively cheap for firms to operate (they don't require much specialized equipment—at the base level, a good Web meeting can be run with a desktop computer and a telephone). They are increasingly popular and are likely to displace most corporate videoconferencing systems, which have failed to meet their promise.

6-9 VIDEOCONFERENCING

Like Web meetings, **videoconferencing** was heavily promoted as a way for firms to save on travel costs. Although many different systems have been introduced and you'll see many firms proudly show off their video-conferencing facilities, you probably won't find that many are used. Why is this so? Well, there are many reasons. Most people don't feel comfortable being on camera. In a (voice) conference call, or if you are just on the phone in a Web meeting, you can scratch yourself or move around in your chair without wondering what this looks like to other people. Looking into a camera and talking may feel pretty idiotic at first. Just seeing a picture of a colleague is actually rather odd. You are watching a TV show of someone, rather than really interacting with them. A videoconference lacks the richness of nonverbal communication that is part of a face-to-face meeting, and if the video transmission has distortion, jitteriness, or delays, the whole experience can become pretty laughable. Videoconfer-encing requires special equipment and often dedicated rooms and a tech-nician to run the system.

Like conference calls, videoconferences work best when the partici-pants have some history of a face-to-face working relationship, when there is a preannounced agenda, and when one person acts as the chairperson or moderator. It's highly unlikely that, even with a great deal of preplanning, a videoconference could substitute for a face-to-face meeting when you are proposing new business with people you haven't met before. Because there is an element of theater about videoconferencing (see Figure 6-4), you'll have to think about whether you should have some graphics made to make a particular point (such as the growth in sales of your product).

Videoconferencing has a few requirements that differ from voice conference calls. You'll probably be required to attend a specially equipped conference room that has the correct lighting and a plain background. The

Figure 6-4   Videoconference
Videoconferences take careful preparation and some effort to sustain attention.
SOURCE: © 2009 Jupiterimages Corporation.

conventional wisdom is that you should avoid wearing distracting patterns, and you probably should not wear the medium-bright blue called "French blue" for a shirt or blouse. Some systems use the TV production device called **blue screen** to overlap images, and it depends on the bright blue being used only for a background. If your firm uses videoconferencing with any regularity, the company's audiovisual specialists will undoubtedly manage the equipment. You should take some time to get their advice on how to make your appearance professional, and they will be able to arrange some practice sessions, too.

People who've been working at a firm for awhile will take the technology for granted. However, don't be shy about asking for some training. If you ask, your colleagues will likely remember that they too needed some friendly coaching to become expert with the firm's systems.

▶ > > PUT THIS CHAPTER INTO PRACTICE

1. Look at the Web sites for Microsoft Office Live Meeting or WebEx and learn about the different ways Web meetings are being used.

2. Practice leaving short, concise voice-mail messages and clearly articulating your call-back number and action steps.

3. Try to escape "voice-mail jail" on an automated phone system.

■ KEY TERMS

alternate greeting

blue screen

conference call

moderator

mute button

videoconferencing

voice mail

voice-mail greeting

Web meetings

Multiple Choice Practice Questions: To take the review quiz for this chapter, log on to your Online Edition at www.atomicdog.com.

Chapter 7
Letters, Memos, and Reports

Most firms avoid sending letters.

A few years ago, a newspaper story noted that the cost of sending a business letter had risen to more than $15. This amount seems astounding—when you think about mailing a letter, probably only the cost of the stamp comes to mind, and that's not much. But when you add in the staff time to prepare the letter (and all the overhead on the worker such as health care costs and vacation time), the cost of printing, getting the letter into the mail, filing a copy, and so on, you can see how the $15 adds up.

As a result, you are likely to find that your firm discourages you from sending a letter. Many companies respond to simple letters of inquiry with phone calls or e-mail, and the amount of business conducted by regular mail continues to drop. However, in certain circumstances you'll have to write a letter. Letters often form the basis of contracts, such as in purchasing or employment, and there are times when the officers of your firm will want to have a formal written record of what they did. These days, letters are rarely used in routine business contexts, and because they serve a purpose in nonroutine contexts, they often require quite a high level of formality.

Most firms do not provide old-fashioned secretaries who type up documents from handwritten drafts or from notes taken at dictation. Every office worker is expected to be able to produce appropriately written, carefully formatted work from his or her own computer. Because letters often serve an important business func-tion, it's reasonable to ask a colleague to check your wording when you are in a sensitive situation, most often by circulating a draft as an e-mail attachment.

■ 7-1 LAYOUT FOR BUSINESS LETTERS

Before you send a letter on behalf of your firm, look around for copies of materials recently sent by members of your work group. Your firm will have one or more types of official stationery. For example, each division may have a separate **letterhead** (preprinted paper showing the firm's

Doing the Right Thing: Don't Use Your Firm's Identity or Resources for Personal Business

Be careful never to use the company's letterhead or envelopes for personal correspondence. For instance, if in writing a letter to the editor of a business magazine to comment on a recent article you mistakenly use the firm's note-paper, your letter will be mistaken as an official pronouncement of your firm. If you write a letter of complaint for a personal transaction, it's wrong to involve your firm, and you might be embarrassed if a company replied to your firm's lawyers, rather than to you.

You should also resist the temptation to make your firm pay for postage for things that are your own expenses. Of course, you'll see this—you may observe a coworker charging express freight charges to the firm for something that you know is a gift for a family member. But at the end of the day, this is a type of theft, and you should be careful to avoid it.

name, logo, mailing address, and so on), or there may be a special letter-head for a product line or promotional campaign. Of course, you will use the company letterhead for only *company* business (see *Doing the Right Thing: Don't Use Your Firm's Identity or Resources for Personal Business*).

The firm may have a specific typeface and layout that your correspon-dence will be expected to follow. Ideally, the firm will have a written style guide that can be brief but comprehensive: Often one well-written page can improve the "public face" of a work group. However, it's quite pos-sible that you'll be given no guidance, and you'll find inconsistencies in examples from your work group. As a default, you should follow these rules.

1. Whenever possible, try to make your letter no longer than one page. Most letters that are longer either need to be broken down into two separate communications (different people are likely to work on various issues) or "deconstructed" into a letter of **transmittal** (see Table 7-1 in Section 7-4) and one or more **attachments** (an "attachment" is a term that refers to any report or document that is sent with a letter, although more often than not, it is not actually attached with a staple or clip). For example, if you are arranging a conference for several of your suppliers, you'll have a lot of infor-mation about transportation, lodging, participants, and the agenda. Each deserves a separate document, rather than all being crammed

into one letter, which can be confusing. Other overly long letters deserve to be broken into two or more separate communications.

2. Always center a letter vertically on the page. If you're writing a short note of acknowledgment, do not scrunch a paragraph at the top of the page, followed by a lot of blank space after your name. This looks unprofessional.

3. Use a *serif* font (such as Garamond, Times Roman, or Book Antiqua), not a *sans serif* font, such as Arial or Univers. Don't use a font size that is too small. Many printers default to 10 point, but 12 point will likely look better. Use single-spacing within paragraphs and double-spacing between.

4. Almost all firms use a "block" format, with all the parts of a letter beginning at the left margin. One exception is that some firms still put the date on the far right ("right justified"). There's no virtue in this placement, and you can avoid it unless it is part of your firm's house style. Use "left justification" but don't use "full justification," where both the right and left margins are flush. Full justification may seem neater but it makes sentences harder to read when spaces are added between words to block the right margin in a straight line. A "ragged right" margin is easier to read.

5. It's not necessary to indent the beginning of paragraphs—the double-space between paragraphs is a better way to show paragraph breaks and retain the "blocked left" format.

■ 7-2 PARTS OF A LETTER

Businesspeople expect information in a letter to come in a particular order. There are some differences between the accepted styles in Europe and in the United States, and you should know the standard form for American letters. The sections are as follows (see Figure 7-1).

The date comes first. This is the date you write the letter—not the date that you *meant* to write the letter. If you try to backdate a letter—put a date on it from a day before the date of the day when you are actually writing—you could run into trouble if the letter is ever used in a court case against your firm; it gives the impression that you were attempting fraud.

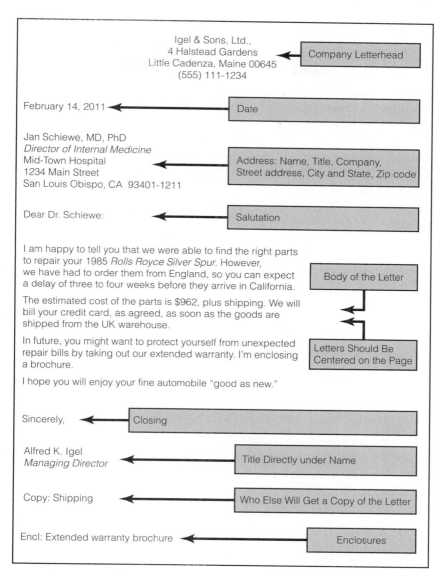

Figure 7-1   The Parts of a Business Letter

This example shows all possible parts of a formal business letter. Some letters won't need the notations for "Copy" or "Encl:" (Enclosure). Most firms have a preprinted letterhead with the company's name and logo in color. For your own formal purposes, such as recruiting, you can print a letterhead for each letter you write using your computer printer.

The format for the date in U.S. commerce is:

September 15, 2006

You also may see this format: September 15th, 2006 (although that would be less common). Note that you don't use the day of the week, as in "Wednesday, September 15th...," which might be used in a social letter between friends or family.

The format *month, day, year* is uniquely American. (One suggestion is that it was a symbol of separation from Great Britain after the signing of the Declaration of Independence, but because the U.S. national holiday is always referred to as "the Fourth of July," that explanation hardly makes sense.) In Europe and most other parts of the world, you'll see the following format:

15 September 2006

This logical "small, medium, large" ordering is quite common among U.S. computer companies, so you should feel free to follow it if it is acceptable to your firm.

The address comes next. The line-by-line format is name, title, firm name, street address, as in this example:

Jan Schiewe, MD, PhD
Director of Internal Medicine
Mid-Town Hospital
1234 Main Street
San Luis Obispo, CA 93401-1211

Note that you usually don't use an honorific in the address, but do include a degree that is used professionally. Using the form "Attn.: Jan Schiewe" is old-fashioned. In most cases, the word "Attention" doesn't add any value. If a **recipient**—the person to whom you are sending the letter—says, "Mark it to my attention, or it'll never get to me," the format is:

Medical Staff Office: Attn.: Jan Schiewe, MD, PhD
Mid-Town Hospital
1234 Main Street
San Luis Obispo, CA 93401-1211

Never, ever put "Attention" and then a name on the last line of an address. Most mail is sorted automatically, and the sorting machines "look" for the last line of the address to machine-read the ZIP code. It's always best to look up the extended ZIP code (ZIP + four numerals separated by a hyphen) because it really does speed delivery. Use the two-letter postal abbreviation for the state. In the United States, the city name is not in all capital letters as it is in parts of Europe.

You begin a letter with a **salutation**, which has a conventional form:

Dear Jan,

or

Dear Dr. Schiewe:

If you use the informal first name, end the greeting with a comma; if you use the formal title with honorific (in this example, "Dr."), then the salutation ends with a colon. You'll see many letters addressed by first name only, even when the correspondent doesn't know the recipient. Such a greeting may seem jarring, as it presumes a low level of formality. A reasonable rule would be to use the "Dear Tom" form only when you've met the recipient in person and would address him or her by a first name.

The form "Dear Dr. Jan Schiewe" (with both first and last names) is wrong in most cases and shouldn't be used. It should be either "Dear Jan" or "Dear Dr. Schiewe." In general, for people whom you don't know, you should use the honorific "Mr." for all men. For women, use "Ms." unless you know specifically that the recipient prefers to be addressed as "Mrs." (For example, the former U.S. secretary of state was always referred to as "Mrs. Madeleine Albright.") You will have problems if you don't know whether the recipient is male or female. If the letter is important (for example, if you are applying for a job), you'll need to make a phone call. An executive with the name "Dana Leath" would be impressed that you called to say, "May I ask, is 'Dana Leath' Ms. Leath?"

In the rare circumstance in which you are confronted with a name you cannot understand and it is impossible to call for clarification, it's probably better to begin a letter with "Dear Phat Quach" rather than "Dear Ms. Phat" when in fact Mr. Quach is male and is called "Phat" by his friends. Lastly, the general form "To Whom It May Concern" is one you should always avoid (see *Business Protocol in Action: To Whom It May Concern*).

Many business letters have a Subject line—you can see why. Some pairs of firms have hundreds of pieces of correspondence going between them every week, all on different topics. The form for a subject line is either two lines above the salutation, left justified (the most common American form), or centered and two lines after the greeting. The line is introduced with either the word "Subject:" or the word "Re.:" ("Re" is

Business Protocol in Action: To Whom It May Concern

You may come across a letter written by someone else with the strange salutation "To Whom It May Concern." This salutation is a very old-fashioned form of address that was used when a letter was sent to a recipient that the writer could not identify by name. It was common for letters of reference given to departing household servants such as butlers and maids. They would carry this general recommendation with them as they looked for a new job. This anonymous salutation was also used when someone was writing to a company but did not know who would actually be handling the letter.

This outdated salutation violates just about every rule of Plain English, so you should avoid it. The reaction of most modern businesspeople is: "Well, it doesn't concern me!" That is, your letter can easily be ignored. "To whom" is a very high level of formality, so it begins in a rather stiff manner—unlikely to engage the reader. And "may concern" implies some doubt—perhaps it concerns you, perhaps it doesn't.

These days, with cheap long-distance phone rates and universal access to the Internet, you should easily be able to find the correct name, spelling, address, and mail code of the person who will handle your request. But in some circumstances, you'll have to write to a company when you have been unable to find a personal name. In that case, address the envelope and letter to the correct department, such as "Human Resources Department" or "Accounts Payable: Student Loans," with as much detail as possible so that your letter lands on the right desk. Then, for the salutation, invent a nice, slightly flattering title such as

Dear Human Resources Professionals:

or

Dear Student Loan Officer:

a contraction of "In re," Latin for "In the matter of.") Because your work group may need to correspond with another firm about several different topics and each letter will be answered by someone different, you can see why aiming for one-page letters—even if you have to write two or three— is better than sending a long letter on several subjects at once.

Turning now to the body of your letter, you should quickly get to the point. If you have chosen not to use a subject line, your first sentence should indicate your purpose:

"I am writing in reply to your request for a new quotation for insurance on your boat."

It's Just Different: What Goes in a Letter

In Japan, it's unthinkable to come straight to the point in a business letter. Executives often spend a long time crafting an introductory sentence, such as: "The cherry blossoms are just coming into bloom and we are all having happy thoughts of Spring. I hope the weather is getting warmer in Boston and your colleagues are enjoying the longer evenings."

In Europe, there is a great deal of attention paid to the end of the letter. Anyone who writes on the firm's letterhead is considered to be acting in a rather formal way on behalf of the firm. European letters are likely to end with wording such as: "For and on behalf of the Container Company, by Gerhard Schmidt, Assistant Accounting Supervisor," and then there is a typed line, for Herr Schmidt's full signature.

Although these practices may strike you as odd, remember that they are just manifestations of different cultures and histories, and your American letters will look odd to them, too!

Other cultures find the American habit of getting right down to business without any pleasantries to be rather jarring (see *It's Just Different: What Goes in a Letter*).

It pays to be as precise as possible. For example, if you write: "We provide free shipping," a customer might interpret this statement as a promise to always ship at your firm's expense. If you are offering free shipping only under certain conditions, then it's best to say precisely: "As this is your first order, we will provide free shipping one time."

If you're having difficulty in formulating a letter to address a complicated business situation, try this simple framework:

- What's this letter about?
- Briefly, what's the history of the situation?
- What has been done so far?
- What decisions have you or your firm made?
- What action step or response do you want from the other party?

Most letters should end with an action step: either what you or your firm will do next or what you expect the recipient to do. For example, "If you can send me copies of your receipts for the purchases in question, I will be able to research the problem." If you are just giving people information that they requested, you might have nothing further to say. However, as a general rule, if you can't think what the action step should be, perhaps you needn't send a letter at all.

In some business disputes, you may need to write a letter to document your side of the story. In that case, using the term "to document" may be helpful. An experienced businessperson will read this as signaling that you are very serious and may move toward litigation (suing the other firm or person). You should never threaten, no matter how unreasonable the person to whom you are writing has been. If you think the situation may end up in court (for example, when your firm is owed money), you may need to foreshadow the possibility of legal action, but do so with regret: "I'm sure you'll agree that neither of us wants this dispute to result in litigation…" If you are seriously considering a court action, then you should carefully consult with your firm's attorneys (who may be referred to as "counsel" or "the legal department") and have them review the wording of every letter.

The **closing** for a letter has a set form. Historically, letters written in English ended with profuse expressions of fealty, such as "I have the honor to remain your grace's most humble servant." This form was gradually contracted to "Yours sincerely," although most Americans now end with the single word "Sincerely," as in this example:

Sincerely,

Harriet J. Makepeace
Corporate Counsel

Some people still use "Yours sincerely," but because it is a sentence fragment, the "s" on "sincerely" is not capitalized. In countries that use British English, you'll see "Yours truly," from people who've not met each other, and "Yours faithfully" if a high level of formality is intended. In American English, "Sincerely" is the most formal term, followed by "Cordially" (a word that means both "sincerely" and "warmly") and "Best regards" or "Best wishes." Abbreviating either of these forms to a single word, "Best," is meaningless; don't use this ending. Be careful about ending with "Best personal regards" or "Warm regards" in business. This is certainly appropriate to use in social correspondence with a friend, but in business it might be misinterpreted as implying that you want a business relationship to develop into something more intimate.

There should be three or more lines between the closing word(s) and your typed name to provide the space where you sign. You should use the same typed form of your name as written on your business card, although when you sign, a more informal name is acceptable. For example, the printed words might be "Charles W. Ford," with "Chuck Ford" signed above. It's a good idea to sign letters (and contracts) in blue ink (or some other color if your firm has a distinctive color scheme to its printed material). The color signals that this is an original document. This is especially important in two circumstances: First, in contract negotiation, it may matter which of a set of documents is the original (and who has the original and who has copies). Second, when you are sending out a mass mailing (for example, sending résumés to many employers or sending a letter to many different customers), a blue-ink signature shows a more personal touch, whereas signing in black ink makes the letter look generic.

After your name, you should indicate your job title and either whom you work for or the title of your work group, as in these examples:

Condor Nell	Jack Wei
Assistant to Mr. Eisner	*Intern, Marketing Group*

If you're expecting a mail reply, and your company uses an internal **mail code**, you could mention that fact in the body of your letter ("If you'll mark your letter Mail Code 1900, it'll reach me directly"), or you could add this information under your name, as follows:

Ellen Dobie
Associate Director
Mail Code 1900, Millennial Building

Next, some firms indicate who will be getting copies. For example, if you are writing to a client and also sending a copy of the same letter to your Accounting Department, you would indicate:

Cc: Accounting

"Cc" is an abbreviation that derives from "carbon copy." Because no firm uses carbon paper anymore, it's probably better just to write:

Copy: Accounting

but follow your firm's house style.

Next, you can indicate any enclosures. If they are self-evident within the context of the letter, you will likely omit this line. For example, you don't need to add:

Encl.: Résumé

when you are writing a cover letter to apply for a job, and you would not need to add an enclosure line for a letter of transmittal sending a report or brochure. However, when someone else will complete the process of stuffing the envelope and mailing your materials, this is a very useful line, for example:

> Encl.: Our check for $982.18
> Copy of your invoice dated 15 May 2004

Finally, many firms still use initials to indicate who actually typed a letter. It's hard to see what purpose this serves except, perhaps, when executives really do write out letters by hand and have them typed. If there is an error in the typing, the executive knows whom to talk to. But the form

> DOR/jb

indicating that Jeanie Bell typed a letter for David Robinson doesn't seem to add much value and looks fussy. Because most people type their own work these days, the form "DOR/dor" looks positively ridiculous.

If you've had any experience with formal business correspondence from another country, you'll know that each culture has its own rules. Something that is "just a routine letter" in the United States might look rather odd in Japan or Europe, as noted earlier in *It's Just Different: What Goes in a Letter.*

■ 7-3 WRITING AND SIGNING FOR OTHER PEOPLE

Often in business, superiors will ask you to write on their behalf (see Figure 7-2). This may be a request that you prepare a draft of a letter and send it to your boss by e-mail for completion; or it may mean that you are to prepare a nearly final version of the letter, ready for your superior to sign; or finally, the leader's intention may be for you to write a letter and sign it yourself. So it follows that you should always respond to such requests by seeking clarification: "Do you want it to go out in my name—or would you prefer to sign it?" Don't worry about writing something that someone else signs—this isn't school homework and is fairly routine in business.

On occasion, your supervisor may instruct you: "Just sign the letter for me." For example, a busy CEO may wish to appear to have responded personally to a request for a company brochure but simply doesn't have

Figure 7-2   Signing Documents
There will be many instances in business when superiors ask you to write on their behalf.
SOURCE: © 2009 Jupiterimages Corporation.

time to sign all such letters. You can handle this situation in many ways. The best is to send out letters over your own signature while mentioning your boss, as in this form:

"Ms. Stewart has asked me to reply to your request."

However, if you are really supposed to sign *for* the boss, you'll have to ask people in your work group and try to determine the consensus of how your colleagues handle this situation. In some firms, you'll find that people just write the boss's name in their own handwriting (this doesn't seem to be a good idea and implies fraud). Many firms use the form where the manager's name is written out by an assistant, who then adds his or her own initials: "Fred Smith/jw." You may also see this form: "Fred Smith by Jacqui Williams" (all written out). If you can't determine a consensus by talking to other people on your team, this would be a great topic to bring up at a regular staff meeting, as many other people may have wondered how best to handle this problem.

■ 7-4 SOME COMMON TYPES OF BUSINESS LETTERS

Although there are many reasons why a company would send out a letter to a customer, supplier, or partner firm, they all fall into one of the types of communication introduced in Section 4-2. Your firm may have particular wording that you are expected to follow, and you may even hear the term **boilerplate**. (This term refers to certain blocks of text that are routinely added for legal protection—although no one expects people to read them in detail.) When you are new to a position, one way to orient yourself is to look through the files for some recent examples of the firm's correspondence, and ask your boss or a friendly colleague about terms that are unfamiliar.

Aside from industry-specific letters, business letters in general can be classified as one of the seven types described in Table 7-1.

Here are some details on the content that might be appropriate in each case. A *letter of acknowledgment* is often brief—even to the point of seeming curt. Your purpose is just to let someone know that you have received something without indicating what your firm's actions will be. In most cases, you'll avoid writing this type of letter and just respond with a phone call. However, you will encounter some situations in which you are expected to document that your firm received the material by providing a specific, written response.

A *letter of transmittal* accompanies one or more other documents such as a brochure, a bid, a contract, or a check. The form is simple. Say what you are sending and why, and carefully list the contents on the enclosure line. A letter of transmittal might have a simple action step, such as "Please call me when you've had a chance to read this."

The purpose of the *letter of thanks* is self-evident. The protocol here is to write quickly to acknowledge assistance that someone has given you, especially when it is beyond the ordinary. Making reference to

Table 7-1 Types of Business Letters

Type of Letter	Purpose
Acknowledgment	Lets people know that you have received material they sent
Transmittal	Accompanies something that you are sending; says to whom the material is directed, what's enclosed, and its purpose
Thanks	Expresses gratitude to a business associate for special consideration or effort
Informational	Gives the recipient news or instructions, such as a place to meet, directions to your firm, or details about a product
Contractual	Forms the basis of a business agreement, such as bidding, ordering, or offering employment
Good news	Tells the recipient something positive, such as a new product announcement or a price cut
Bad news	Denies a request or announces something the recipient won't like, such as a product discontinuation or price increase

some specific aspect of the kindness will show that your letter is not boilerplate.

In an *informational letter,* make sure you provide all the information necessary (for example, instructions for a career fair might include information on parking as well as the location). It might be a good idea to give yourself some time to develop such a letter over a few days, making notes as you go along, and have the draft checked by interested colleagues to see whether you've left out anything. An informational letter should always end with contact information in case the recipient has needs that weren't covered in your letter.

The most important aspect of a *contractual letter* is to recognize when you are in a situation in which what you write will commit the firm. If you are unsure about such situations, check with your boss or, if necessary, the firm's Legal Department. Employment, bids, and counteroffers are common situations, but many others may be specific to your company and its industry. The language will be precise and quite formal. For example, writing "Harry, I *loved* the new bid!" could arguably read as an acceptance, but what you meant to say was: "Harry, I wanted to acknowledge that we've received your carefully prepared bid. We are now in the process of giving all the bids careful review and hope to make a decision by early next week."

Pretty much all other business correspondence can be determined as either "good news" or "bad news." Being able to identify such situations is important, especially concerning the order of ideas. In a *good-news letter,* you can choose to begin with your main point, such as "I have exciting news; we've just cut prices on our entire model line by 30 percent." Or you could lead in gradually and announce the good news as a "surprise" toward the end.

■ 7-5 BAD-NEWS LETTERS ARE ANYTHING BUT ROUTINE

You've probably been taught that "the customer is always right," but there are many times when you will be asked to communicate bad news to other people, customers included. For example, a replacement part that a customer really needs may be out of stock, or a customer's transaction may not be eligible for a rebate that she had hoped for. And there are times when things have gone wrong and you will need to deal with something unpleasant.

The key to approaching a bad-news letter is to understand that this type of letter is subject to specific conventions, the most important of which is the *order of ideas.* If you start with the main news up front, your recipient may ignore the rest of what you have to say. On the other hand, if you bury your point at the end, the person reading the letter may never get to it. So, the usual order is as follows:

- Begin with a "gentle lead" that acknowledges some positive aspect such as valued patronage ("I was pleased that you've enjoyed more than 40 years of successful photography with your Photomatic-50").

- Next, clearly state the bad news in unequivocal terms with some reasonable justification or explanation ("We cannot replace the switch on your camera as it's out of warranty").

- Don't "catastrophize" ("I realize this means you are going to have to buy a whole new camera"). And don't overexplain ("If we repaired all 1955 models for free, we'd be bankrupt").

- Seek to ameliorate or sweeten the situation in some reasonable way ("I'm enclosing a packet of lens cleaners," or "The new models don't have this switch, so I'm sure you'll get long use out of a replacement").

- Don't indulge in what's called "doing and undoing" ("We can't give you a new camera, but here's a check for $50").

- Finally, close with a few positive words about the future, such as: "We are always happy to hear from customers who have been such longtime users of our products and we hope you get many years of enjoyment from one of the new models."

The good news about bad-news letters is that in your particular line of business, you can anticipate that common problems will come up many times (for example, Human Resources executives often have to tell candidates that they didn't get a job), so you'll develop both some expertise and some preferred phrases for handling most situations you encounter.

■ 7-6 KNOW HOW YOUR FIRM HANDLES MAIL

At your home and in a small office, mail arrives each day in one pile. However, large corporations may have one address at which mail is received for thousands of people. You'll soon get to know how your mailroom works.

To identify your specific location, you may be known by your office number, work group, or a code that will be called a "mail code" or a **mail drop**. If you can give this specific code to people who are writing to you, you are likely to receive your incoming mail up to one day earlier than you would otherwise. Most of the mail received by large corporations consists of invitations, conference brochures, and magazines. Firms have established routines: Mailroom staff will probably sort code-addressed mail first and then during the workday try to identify first-class or priority mail identified by name but not mail code. Lastly, as much as there's time available, they'll sort through the advertising material.

It's important to know your mailroom's routine for both incoming and outgoing mail. For material sent to you, your firm may schedule deliveries to your office twice or more per day. On the other hand, you may have a mail slot in a central mailroom where you are supposed to check regularly for your mail. You should know what happens to express (overnight) packages. Does the courier (for example, Federal Express [FedEx]) bring them to your desk? Are they received by the mailroom and brought to you at once? Will your mailroom or front desk call you when a package arrives? Or is it subject to the routine sorting and interoffice delivery schedule?

You can also increase your effectiveness by understanding your company's outgoing mail procedures. Letters you have written may be collected from your department and taken to a central mailroom for postage to be applied and then taken by van to a main post office sorting facility. On the other hand, your mail could be subject to one or two days' delay as your firm processes it before it even leaves the building. If you know the routines and the time deadlines (for example, mail leaves your department at 3 P.M., but you can still make the same day's mailing if you take it by hand to the mailroom by 4 P.M.), you can achieve optimum results.

Because mailrooms can be cluttered with advertising material and their personnel sometimes overwhelmed by the volume of incoming mail, the sorting and delivery process for regular mail imposes many delays. So a lot of business executives rely—indeed *over-rely*—on express (overnight) delivery such as FedEx or United Parcel Service. You may find that almost every document in your business seems to go out by an express courier. You should try to resist this temptation. First, avoiding such deliveries will show your boss that you are cost-conscious. Second, using express delivery for routine documents may give your customers or business associates the impression that you are a spendthrift or that you don't have good judgment.

Many busy executives rely on catalog or Internet shopping for personal items. Having packages delivered to your work is often convenient because you know that someone will always be there to accept delivery and sign for them, and you know that your goods will be safely kept. Some firms positively encourage this practice as a way to reward employees for working long hours. But other firms have found that the volume of personal packages has become too great and is a distraction to the main purpose of the firm, so they've instituted a strict ban on accepting personal packages.

Of course, you would never put a personal letter or bills into your company's mail system to attempt to get the company to pay postage. However, even if you are using your own stamps, you might want to find a mailbox on your lunch hour. Your personal mail could likely be delayed for one or two days if you use your company's mailroom.

Your firm is likely to have some system for internal mail. It may be rapid, secure, confidential, and sophisticated. Pickups may be twice a day, or more often. On the other hand, you may encounter a system that is prone to misdeliveries and is treated as an afterthought, to be addressed only when incoming U.S. Mail is being handled. So it pays to quietly evaluate the system and to understand whether that system is useful in your firm. You may well identify occasions when it's worth your while to deliver time-sensitive material to other departments in person.

■ 7-7 MEMORANDUMS, OR "MEMOS"

Memorandums (see Figure 7-3) (memoranda, memos) are rarely used in business, as they have been almost entirely replaced by e-mail. They are used to send out information that recipients are likely to refer to over a long period of time. For example, if a work group agrees on a schedule for vacations (so that there is always coverage in the office), the plan might have been distributed as a memo. Memorandums are also used to provide a written record of a meeting, phone call, or conference for a firm's internal records.

As written records, memos have serious limitations—the style tends to be bureaucratic and stilted, and there is no place to sign, so it's often unclear whether memos are original or, indeed, authentic.

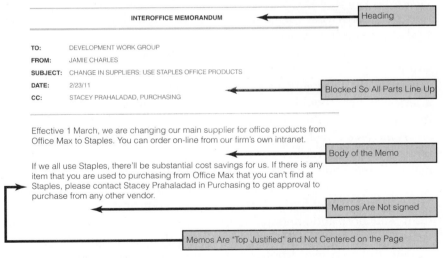

Figure 7-3   The Memo Format
Most memorandums have been replaced by e-mails, but if you are asked to write a memo, look around for examples of your "house style." In this example, the heading is in "all capitals" but that's just one possible style. Note that memos are unsigned and, unlike letters, they are "top justified" and not centered vertically on the page.

The form for a memo is as follows. There is invariably a "Memorandum" heading at the top. This format comes from the memo's use in legal situations and at least serves the purpose of indicating that it is a semiformal document, not just an odd piece of paper. A memo is always laid out "top justified," that is, beginning at the top of the page and using up only the amount of paper necessary. Unlike a letter, it's not vertically centered on the page.

After the title "Memorandum," there are four or five lines of identifying information:

Date:	1 July 1776
Subject:	Draft Declaration of Independence
From:	Thomas Jefferson
To:	Ben Franklin
Copy:	Col. Washington

(The "Copy" or "Copies" line is optional.) Many different styles of headings are acceptable. For example, the captions may be double-spaced or not, the "To" might come before the date and before or after the "From." However, you should always double-space after the heading before beginning the text of your memo, and notice that you should always tab over so that the specific names and dates line up in a block.

The text should be formatted the same as a letter: single-spaced within paragraphs, double-spaced between; left justified with a ragged right margin, and using a serif font of about 12 points. However, unlike a letter (which should be vertically centered on the page), memos are invariably top justified, with white space below.

A memo has neither a salutation ("Dear Tom,") nor a closing ("Yours faithfully,"). This means that there is no place for the author to add a signature. Some memo writers write their initials next to their names. As you can see, someone else can fairly easily generate a fraudulent memo. For example, if you find a typed memo on your desk appearing to come from your boss and announcing that you are now eligible for 16 weeks' vacation each year, you would most likely think it is a prank from a co-worker. But an e-mail from your supervisor's e-mail account telling you that the firm is granting a pay raise to all employees might be more believable.

It's important to recognize that memos can be in a number of different formats, and before you write one, you should look around at examples in your workplace and try to follow the preferred style. If you detect inconsistencies, at least ask your supervisor which format is preferred. If there doesn't seem to be a standard and you really do have to write a formal memo instead of an e-mail, use one of the templates that exist in your word processing software.

Memos tend to stay around for a long time and may be read by people outside of your work group. So you should choose a moderately high level of formality and avoid casual comments. For example, the following could look really unprofessional:

> After no end of fighting and backstabbing, we all agreed to take the Friday after the Fourth of July off. Try not to drink too much!!

A better alternative would be this example:

> At the team meeting this week, the group members agreed that the office will be closed on 5 July, and we will all take this day as a vacation day.

■ 7-8 FAXES

The advantage of a fax—short for "facsimile transmission"—is that it takes just moments to transmit. You can send a letter from Jacksonville to Jakarta in seconds, rather than the *days* that even airmail would take. However, faxes have some limitations and disadvantages. Because the fax will likely be printed out in black and white, you'll lose the impression of formality provided by your firm's color letterhead or shade of paper. Many work groups share a central fax machine, and it's very easy for your important document to be mistakenly included with someone else's material at the recipient's firm. Or your fax could be received and mislaid by someone who didn't know you were expecting it. Finally, although your fax machine may indicate correct transmission, a paper jam at the other end can mean that your document never printed out.

Make sure, then, that you know this rule: A fax sent is not necessarily a fax received.

To address the problems outlined in this section, you should send a "cover sheet" that clearly indicates the intended recipient (with details such as mail code or specific office location), the number of pages that follow, and the call-back number for any problems in transmission. Most businesspeople phone recipients to alert them that a fax is coming and to ask for a confirmation phone call that all pages have been received.

In general, faxing very many pages at once (say, more than a dozen) is not a good idea, as this may exceed the capacity of the recipient's machine. An alternative is to send a long document by overnight delivery or perhaps as a file attached to an e-mail message.

The use of faxes varies considerably within an industry. In some companies, it's a primary method of communicating. All the executives may have their own fax machines (sometimes referred to as "my desk fax" to indicate that your message won't be lost in a mailroom), or they may be able to "read" faxes on their personal computers. In some circumstances, a faxed signature will be treated as a legal binding contract, and in others only the signed original document is acceptable. However, in many firms, faxing has largely been replaced by scanning materials into computer files and then shipping them around as e-mail attachments.

■ 7-9 REPORTS

If your job requires you to write reports designed either for your own company or for publication outside the firm, there's no doubt that your firm will have a specific format that you are expected to follow. It's possible that most firms in your industry will use a specific order of sections—for example, for bids or for financial analyst reports.

To learn the house style, you can ask your supervisor whether your firm has a style guide (or similarly named document). If it doesn't, ask your boss to show you one or two good reports, and—if possible—one or more reports that he or she did not like. You can then analyze the documents and generate your own idea of an acceptable style.

Here are some things to look for:

1. How are graphics (tables and graphs) handled? Are they integrated with the text or placed at the end? If so, are they called "exhibits," "figures," or "appendices"? Are they usually numbered or lettered?

2. Do good reports use the first person "I" and "we," or is a lot of effort taken to write reports in an impersonal style?

3. Does the house style use subheadings following a colon (like *Business Protocol in Action: To Whom It May Concern*) or headings written in a broad left margin?

4. How are references handled? By inclusion in brackets in the text (FDA Annual Report, 1997), by **footnotes** at the bottom of each page, by footnotes within graphs and tables, or by **endnotes** (at the end of the text)?

The style in which you will write will be very different from the style expected for many liberal arts college papers, or indeed from the style you may have used for lab reports in engineering school. Again, try to find what people consider to be "good" and learn from it. Business writing is concise and direct. The writing style of *The Economist* and *The Wall Street Journal* are good models to follow.

If you're working for a start-up firm or writing a report for a team that has no good models for you to work from, word processing software programs, such as Microsoft (MS) Word, contain good templates that can guide you through the sections and format for a generic report. You should be able to adapt them to your purpose.

You may well find that all reports in your firm come with an *executive summary*. This is different from an abstract, which is found at the beginning of a scientific or academic paper. The executive summary may be quite long (two or more pages at the beginning of a long report), although it's always good to keep it to one page if you can. Unlike an abstract, it should repeat almost verbatim the specific recommendations from the end of your report.

The executive summary serves two functions. First, it serves in place of the main report for people (such as board members) who need to know about your process, options you considered, and your conclusions but who don't have time to read your whole report. Second, for people who are going to read the whole report, your summary should lead them into the main body of the work and should foreshadow your main points. You are not writing great literature, and you won't be spoiling a surprise ending.

■ 7-10 WORKING WITH EDITORS

In a large firm, you may be surprised to find that although you write the first draft of the words in a report, and it may indeed be printed with your name on it, many other people will work on the project. You may be assigned to a technical writer who will act as your editor. The editor may "tighten up" your prose and may ask you for clarification in places.

Don't be afraid to stand up for yourself if you feel the editor is making you say something that you don't mean. However, on the other hand, try not to be defensive, and don't experience editing as criticism. Remember, major writers from Charles Dickens to F. Scott Fitzgerald relied on professional editors at their publishers. For major reports, you'll find yourself involved with a large team of editors, graphic artists, and designers, and many business reports are not the product of a sole author, but rather a team of coworkers, a situation addressed next in Section 7-11.

■ 7-11 WRITING AS A GROUP

When you find yourself assigned to write up a report as a member of a team of several people who have been working on the same project, you'll likely be in an unfamiliar situation. If you've ever tried this team approach, you may have found that it seems like an almost impossible task if you gather as a group and try to write sentence by sentence. Many groups try to solve this problem by breaking the task into parts and assembling them at the end ("You do the financials, and I'll write the introduction..."). The result invariably looks like Frankenstein's monster: stitched together and quite ugly as a whole.

The solution is to work from an agreed-upon **outline**. You get the group to meet together and agree, in general terms, about what the report will say. Turn on the outliner in your word processing software. (In MS Word, open the Format menu, choose "Bullets and Numbering," then choose the "Outline Numbered" tab, select the style you want, and click "OK.") Type in your main points first, for example:

1. Group met three times over 6 months

2. Three possibilities, only one is feasible

3. Need $100,000 budget to complete project

Then you can expand each main point by pressing the tab key to successive levels of subdetail and sub-subdetail:

1. Group met three times over 6 months

    a. Team members from Marketing, Engineering, and Manufacturing

        i. Finance promised to send a rep, but no one attended

2. Three possibilities, only one is feasible

    a. Switch production to factory in Singapore

        i. Shipping would be too expensive

    b. Outsource production to supplier

        i. Quality control problems in the past

        ii. Their bid is very high

    c. Run our factory on overtime

        i. Feasible if we can start within the next month

3. Need $100,000 budget to complete project

    a. Covers the cost of overtime

    b. Project will be done by the end of the quarter

At this point, you can have the group members review the outline. Perhaps you need to add some details, explanation, or additional justification. Or perhaps you can omit some minor points. Using an outliner on the computer, you can easily "promote" or "demote" subpoints to major points and vice versa, just by adding additional tabs.

Once the group members agree on the outline, it's best to acknowledge that because only one person's fingers can hit the keyboard at a time, the best use of group members' time is to have one person write the report, sticking closely to the outline. If the outline has been well prepared, the report will almost write itself, with each line of the outline becoming a complete sentence. It's a good idea to have another team member act as editor, and on a long, complicated report, other team members can be working on appendices and exhibits.

▶ ⟩ ⟩ PUT THIS CHAPTER INTO PRACTICE

1. Practice writing a "bad-news letter" by writing the perfect "turn down" letter that you'd appreciate receiving if you thought you'd interviewed well but weren't offered a job.

2. On visits or interviews at firms, ask for copies of reports and ask managers what they liked and didn't like about each report.

3. Interview professionals who make on-campus visits to career fairs and firm nights and ask them if they agree that memos have been completely replaced by e-mail.

KEY TERMS

attachment	mail code, mail drop
boilerplate	outline
closing	recipient
endnote	salutation
footnote	transmittal
letterhead	

Multiple Choice Practice Questions: To take the review quiz for this chapter, log on to your Online Edition at www.atomicdog.com.

Chapter 8

Effective Presentations

You can't say, "I'm no good at public speaking."

Sooner than you think, you'll be asked to make a formal presentation as part of your job. You can't work in American business and hide behind, "I'm just no good at public speaking." Whether you're good at it or not, you'll be required to do it. But effective public speaking is much easier than you may think.

Very few people have to give formal speeches to large groups of many thousands of people. You'll most likely be facing a friendly audience of at most a few dozen colleagues or customers who are interested in what you have to say. If you are well prepared and follow some simple rules, you'll be successful. There are many different styles of effective public speaking, and you don't have to copy a style that doesn't fit your personality. Yes, some people are charismatic; some people are highly amusing. Your ultimate goal, however, should be that when you sit down, your boss will turn to you and say, "Thank you. That was thoroughly professional!"

8-1 KEEP IT SHORT

Former Cuban president Fidel Castro was famous for giving speeches that were four hours in length. It's hard to imagine how his audiences managed to sustain attention for that length of time. In contemporary U.S. business, even 45 minutes is very long for a speech. When financial professionals are pitching a multibillion-dollar takeover, or when consultants are reporting the results of a six-month investigation, you may well see an initial presentation that's just 20 minutes long, followed by a period for **questions and answers (Q&A).** You'll note that you rarely see the President of the United States giving long speeches using *formal rhetoric* (in general, the science of writing or speaking, but often used to mean a grand style of declamation). Most often, what you see are press conferences, where the president may make an opening announcement, often no more than five minutes long, followed by more than an hour of questions.

At a business meeting, when you see that several hours are allotted to a particular topic, it's most likely that some of the time will be spent on a presentation, some on Q&A, and some on a general discussion. It's very unlikely that you will be expected to speak for hours at a time unless you are running a training session (for example, explaining a new software program that your company has adopted). Because the attention span of even well-rested, highly motivated adults is rarely more than 45 minutes, you should make an effort to break up long training sessions into lectures, practice sessions, discussions, and so on. If you are presenting during a long meeting and you notice audience members nodding off or beginning to talk among themselves, it's reasonable to say, "I think we're all getting a little tired here. Let's take a five-minute break, stretch our legs, and get some fresh air. Then we can come back and give this our full attention."

8-2 RECOGNIZE DIFFERENT SETTINGS

Although pictures of high-technology CEOs announcing new products often show them addressing a convention crowd of thousands, you are unlikely to be addressing more than a few dozen people at one time. There are several different formats that you will encounter in business when you are expected to make presentations. You'll need to be able to identify the three types of public speaking formats based on the size of audience: small, medium, or large. Based on each type, your approach will be a little different.

To begin with presentations to *small audiences,* many presentations today are given to customers, or within a firm, across a desk in an executive's office. One or two people will be listening to you, and you are likely to remain seated. However, you will want to be specifically prepared and clear in your mind about the transition from when you are just chatting pleasantly to when you have started your presentation. You could mark the shift by saying, "Well, let me get started with…" and announce your topic.

Some in-office presentations use **visual aids** in the form of brochures, flip charts, or a PowerPoint® graphics presentation on a laptop computer. In this setting, you should aim for an informal style (see Figure 8-1). That in no way precludes your being professional and authoritative; however, you should expect to be interrupted. Because the situation is informal, you will be asked to skip over a series of background slides or to jump back to a previous topic.

The most common audience size is *medium*—that is, a group of from 6 to 24 people who gather to hear a report. The typical setting is in a

Figure 8-1   Visual Aids
Many important presentations involve just a few participants in an office setting.
Source: © 2009 Jupiterimages Corporation.

conference room where your audience sits around a single table. You are likely to use some visual aids, although not necessarily projected media like PowerPoint. Some type of handout is common in this situation. Although the audience will sit, you should always stand (even if you are not at the head of the table) to signal the beginning of your presentation and the end of general discussion.

You should anticipate a few questions as you go along. In most business settings, there is an unwritten rule that audience members can ask questions that require further definition or restatement of something that was unclear during your talk; however, substantive questions should be left until the end of the talk. (Bear this point in mind when you are among the audience. Try to let the speaker get through the presentation before interrupting with questions that challenge the proposed strategy or underlying analysis.) Although you can announce that you would prefer to take questions at the end, it may sound a little defensive; it's probably better to graciously answer a few questions briefly as they come up and deflect long, complicated questions until the end. "Perhaps you could hold that question until we're through?" is a polite way to phrase this.

We can call the third audience type *large,* although the most you will encounter in typical large business situations will be from 24 to 70 people—still small enough for you to address in a well-designed small lecture hall without using a microphone, amplifier, and loudspeakers. There's a probability that you'll have some kind of visual aid, and you should be quite formal in making a clear start and a clear end to your talk. That is, don't chat to audience members in a way that makes it unclear when you've started your presentation. Most likely you'll indicate the end of your prepared remarks by calling for questions. Again, if someone interrupts with a question as you are going along, you can answer if it's brief ("You're right—that was the fiscal year, not the calendar year"), but if you can, you'll most likely want to defer most questions to the end. The reason for this is to give the best coherence to the logic of your speech.

Once you know the setting for your talk, you can begin to plan the content of the speech and what medium you will use for any visual aids.

■ 8-3 UNDERSTAND YOUR PURPOSE

Any presentation has to be governed by the rule "Begin with the end in mind" (see Chapter 3). Simply ask yourself, "What will be the end result if this talk goes even better than I expect?" In Chapter 3, we were introduced to the idea that the purpose of any business communication is to *inform, persuade, or remind.* As a practical matter, though, few people would give a formal presentation to *remind,* so there are two main types of speeches: informative and persuasive. The distinction between informative and persuasive speeches is important. The preparation for your presentation will be different, as will be the words that you use. If you hear a speech that someone else gives and you feel that it was not very effective, one of the most common reasons is that the speaker was unclear as to whether the task was to inform or persuade. You can be clear about your purpose by asking yourself whether a beginning such as "I'd like to tell you about…" or "I'd like to convince you that…" is most appropriate for the start of your talk. Only one of these choices should fit.

You may be wondering where the traditional jovial "after dinner" speech fits in—the type of speech that you hear after a business dinner or at a wedding reception. Although *inform* and *persuade* are the two main types of business speech, you might argue that there is this third type of speech where the goal is solely to *entertain*. As you begin to learn about public speaking, don't worry too much about this type of *special occasion* speech. You won't be required to give one very often, and the conventional format is to tell a series of weakly connected jokes about the honoree. Just try to keep the jokes clean and avoid using the speech as an excuse to settle old scores.

In planning your speech, be thoughtful about cultural differences. American businesspeople tend to be very direct and to the point—a style that can seem positively rude to many people in Asia. And Americans' loud heartiness can seem abrasive in Europe (see *It's Just Different: Please Don't Give Us a "W"*).

As you begin the planning for a business speech, you can make some notes and begin to organize the material as an *outline* (Microsoft [MS] Word has an automatic outline feature under the tab where paragraphs and fonts are formatted; look for "Bullets and Numbering," "Outline Numbered," or "Multilevel List"). You should use an outline to make sure that your speech has a good structure. Your speech can have any logical structure that makes sense to you and that you think will be appealing to the audience.

It's Just Different: Please Don't Give Us a "W"

The boisterous enthusiasm of college "pep rallies" is not unusual in American companies. Organized cheering and chanting of slogans is often part of corporate sales meetings. However, jubilant group expressions of camaraderie aren't universally welcome.

Walmart is widely regarded as one of the most successful retailers in the world—in addition to its 2,500 stores in the United States, it has nearly 1,000 stores in China and is one of the biggest retailers in Canada and Mexico. But Walmart tripped up in Germany. The firm tried to motivate workers with presentations from top management that began with the famous Walmart cheer: "Give me a W!" (to which the crowd of workers was supposed to respond: "W!"). Culturally, Germans detested the forced cheeriness, and worse, the ritualistic chanting gave many employees unhappy memories of political rallies. Relations between American managers and German workers went from bad to worse. In 2006, Walmart abandoned Germany completely and no longer retains stores there.

Once you've made your list of all the ideas that you'd like to get across, you will probably have more than a dozen points written down. Now, think back to the last major speech, sermon, or presentation you heard—think of one that you thought at the time was really good. Now, write down what you think the speaker's main points were. Most likely, you found it hard to come up with more than three or four points. Yes, it's true—whether you speak for 5 minutes or 45 minutes, attentive audience members will probably be able to grasp and remember only three or four main points. With that in mind, you should plan your speech to make about three major points. Then think of an effective, attention-getting opening, and finally, plan how you are going to make a strong conclusion.

■ 8-4 PLANNING YOUR VISUAL AIDS

You may—or may not—use one or more visual aids when talking to all audience sizes, but the description of the three audience sizes and settings implies that some aids are more likely to be expected than others. The decision whether to use visual aids at all—and if so, which—will depend on the nature of your talk, the equipment available, and your careful assessment of the good and bad side ("pros and cons") of each type of aid (see Table 8-1).

Perhaps the simplest form of illustration for your speech is a handout. It is cheap to prepare, and people can take notes as you are going along. Written handouts are essential when many facts and figures are involved, especially when audience members will need something to take away with them. This is true for budget meetings, quarterly financial reports, and times when you are announcing new policies and procedures. However, if you hand out materials at the beginning or during your speech, there's inevitably some distraction in large meetings as materials are passed around from one row to another. And in meetings of any size, there is always a tendency for audience members to look down at printed materials, rather than seeing the expression of your face and your gestures. So an ideal plan is to announce that you are presenting an overview, and the detailed information will be on handouts on the way out.

A simple **prop** (something you can hold up for the audience to see) can be very effective for gaining attention. For example, in small meetings, holding up a photograph can lead into a compelling story. If you are

Table 8-1   The Types of Visual Aids for Presentations

Type of Visual Aid	Pros	Cons
Handouts 	Useful, indeed essential, for presenting long lists of numbers, such as financial reports and budgets. A permanent memorandum of your speech.	Most people stop listening to what you are saying and start to read as soon as they are given a handout. The "rustle factor" as people turn pages can be very annoying.
Props 	Great for getting attention or making a compelling visual point.	If you pass something around so that everyone can examine it, the "stage business" of passing from one row to another can distract from your talk.
Overhead transparencies 	Can be projected with the room lights on in most cases. Can show fine detail from photographs.	May be hard for people at the back of the room to see, and the projector is invariably quite noisy.
PowerPoint 	Very flexible, permitting color and graphics. Gives a professional, polished look to any speech.	PowerPoint special effects such as motion have a tendency to overwhelm your speech, and people always focus on the screen, not the speaker, so you lose the value of your expression and gesture.

(Continued)

Type of Visual Aid	Pros	Cons
PowerPoint		The room lights need to be at least dimmed, which can lead the audience to snooze if you are not careful.
Video	Highly attention getting. A short video clip is often the only way to show a product in use. Video clips are a good way to break up a speech that is getting too long.	The room lights have to be fully off. Making sure the equipment, especially the sound, works well adds anxiety to a presentation.
35-mm slides	Compelling color and detail.	Expensive to produce and impossible to change at the last minute if you discover a mistake. Slide projectors can be noisy and usually require an assistant to operate them well. Slides can jam.

describing a piece of miniature technology that is smaller than a dime, holding up a coin as you make your closing can bring the point home. Props often work well when they are hidden (for example, in a bag or beneath a table), but you shouldn't delay too long, or your audience will feel that you are playing games with them. In all but the smallest meetings, don't rely on passing something around. For example, if you pass around two sample fabrics in a medium-sized meeting of just 12 people, 24 transactions will take place (plus some back and forth!) while you are speaking, and this can be very distracting.

Overhead transparencies once were the most common form of visual aid, although they are increasingly being replaced by projected computer-driven displays. When you use overheads, you almost never need to dim lights, and you can manage your own media. An overhead projector can be noisy, so it's best to turn it off whenever possible—and while it is on, speak loudly. It's important to have the projector properly placed and focused before you begin. There's a trick to this, which avoids your giving away any possible surprise on your first slide. Place a pen or a paper clip gently on the flat surface of the projector. When you have adjusted the projector so that the outline of your object is clear, turn off the projector and put on your first transparency (it goes "right way up" facing you), and when you turn on the projector, your slides will be shown in perfect focus. Overhead projectors have the advantage that you can read your own slides without turning back to the screen. They can show color, but the hues are some-what washed out (especially compared with projected PowerPoint slides), and you cannot show very fine detail on an overhead.

Projected computer-driven displays using programs such as PowerPoint and Keynote® have achieved overwhelming popularity. Almost any desktop or laptop computer can create a presentation that just a few years ago would have cost thousands of dollars in graphic designer fees. The slides can be shown directly on a computer screen or projected to make a large, bright image. PowerPoint presentations can include graphs, spreadsheets, photos, and even sound and video clips. The elements of each slide can be animated, and slides and elements can change either on a mouse click or automatically on a preset timer. However, the visual imagery is so compelling that audience members may not pay attention to the speaker, and some experts feel that flashy PowerPoint slides can sometimes hide a poorly structured argument. You can check your pre-sentation for an excess of special effects over content by asking yourself: If the projector broke and I had to speak from just my notes, how good would this talk be? Indeed, there are some times when you should plan *not* to use PowerPoint at all (see *Doing the Right Thing: Sometimes PowerPoint Is Dead Wrong*).

There is no set number of slides that can be shown in a talk of a given length. Some experts recommend one slide per minute of speaking. How-ever, in college lecturing, 12 to 20 slides (admittedly, with each explained in some detail) are enough for a 50-minute lecture. If you find that you are rushing slides during a run-through of your talk, you probably have too many slides. Consider reserving some slides as backups to use during Q&A. It's a good idea to have a blank slide at the end of your presentation

Doing the Right Thing: Sometimes PowerPoint Is Dead Wrong

PowerPoint and similar computer-based presentation programs are extremely common in business. A presentation accompanied by PowerPoint slides gives an appearance of professionalism, of thinking ahead, and of thinking through the issues at hand.

But there are times when PowerPoint can be dead wrong. Imagine a top executive arriving at a branch office and calling an "all hands" meeting. Workers are assembled and the executive says: "My first slide, please." The first slide is headed "An Apology" and below are the bullet points:

- Senior management doesn't listen.
- We run things "top down."
- Input from branch offices isn't welcomed.

No matter what the executive says in the words of his speech, he has already communicated that he knows all the problems and he isn't really interested in hearing what workers at the branch have to say. Even if his speech is well crafted and eloquent, few people in the branch office are going to believe that his apology is sincere.

So before you open up PowerPoint, stop and think if it's really going to fit with the purpose of your presentation. Sometimes it is better to do without the fancy graphics and speak from the heart.

so that the screen goes dark (rather than reverting to an ugly "slide sorter" view in the program).

Your slides don't need to have complete sentences, such as "We need to move aggressively to enter the Japanese market." Just use simple bullet points:

- Enter Japan in 2010
- First product, handheld

Then with these bullet points on the projected slide, you would expand on these ideas in natural speech: "We are very enthusiastic about Japan as the best opportunity for growth in the next planning year. Our recommendation is that we make a strong push to enter the market with our time-tested handheld line." Note that natural speech has a structure that is quite different from how the same ideas would be written in a report (see Section 9-6).

Video clips can be very compelling. They can tell a short story, conveniently demonstrate a product in action, or show more detail than any amount of verbal description. Most meeting rooms have DVD players, or you can play a DVD through your laptop computer. In most settings, you'll need the lights almost completely off for video, so you should plan for the lighting to be up both before and after the show to stop people from nodding off.

Unless you work in an artistic environment, such as a museum or design firm, or a scientific environment, such as a research medical school, you are unlikely to encounter 35-millimeter projected slides. The level of detail and the richness of color are compelling. But 35-mm projectors are noisy and almost always need an attendant (at least to turn them on and off, if not to focus and to change slides). The room needs to be completely dark, and this makes it difficult to give a talk; instead, you are left to merely comment on the slides.

Whenever you are speaking with any type of equipment—and this is especially true with PowerPoint—you have to ask yourself, "What could possibly go wrong?" (The answer is: "A lot!") Travel with a second copy of your presentation on a different disk or on a flash-memory drive for "mission-critical" presentations (such as winning a big order). Many professionals have duplicate sets of computer or projection equipment on hand to switch over to quickly in the event of an equipment failure. You should plan in advance what you will do if projection equipment fails: In a training session or course, you can probably move some material around ("I'll show you that video after the lunch break"). But in most situations, you'll have to decide whether to go ahead without your visual aids or to reschedule the talk.

■ 8-5 KNOWING YOUR AUDIENCE

When you know the purpose and format of your talk, the setting, and the approximate size of the audience, you'll want to find out as much as you can about the audience members. Consider a simple example where you have to give a routine quarterly report about a project. Who will be in the audience? Are these people familiar with the current status (because they've been working on aspects of the project or because they've already seen written reports)? Will what you say come as a surprise? What functional areas (accounting, marketing, production, etc.) are the audience members from? What is their attitude toward this project?

You can get this information from a knowledgeable (and friendly!) insider. It helps to be forewarned when people are likely to be initially hostile to what you are going to say: "Finance opposed this project from day one, so they're going to have a field day when you tell them we're over budget and behind schedule." If you are appointed to present to another firm (for example, a supplier), you can also do some research to find out about the audience. You might make a specific visit to the person who you think can most help you, or you might phone a few contacts at the firm. You'll be asking: Who is likely to be invited to hear me? What are their backgrounds? What do you know about their level of interest? Do they have any preconceived attitudes about the topic, and if they disagree, what's the basis of this disagreement?

You may feel as if you've been given an impossible task: Some of the people are engineers with graduate degrees who know more about the underlying science of your project than you do, and some of the people barely understand the nature of the project in its most general terms. Reassure yourself! You are dealing with a very common problem called **audience heterogeneity.** *All* audiences are heterogeneous—that is, they vary from member to member in terms of interest, expertise, and predetermined attitude toward your speech. Your task is to identify the range of each parameter and address the majority of your remarks to the middle 75 percent. In general, then, you will choose the level of detail and how technical to be in such a way as to appeal to the middle part of the group. Then, from time to time, you should acknowledge the presence of others in your audience. For example, you might say:

> "Now, I know that a few of you don't have a background in biochemistry, so before I go into the reaction, let me just summarize that this is how we synthesize the new drug—you don't need to follow the details."

At the other end of the spectrum, you acknowledge the experts by saying something like this:

> "Now, I know that many of you will realize that this description is going to be quite a simplification of the process..."

■ 8-6 STRUCTURE OF AN INFORMATIVE SPEECH

Let's begin by planning an informative speech, and then we'll show that persuasive speech needs certain modifications of structure and word usage.

At the very beginning of your speech, as you rise to begin, in all but the small in-office setting, you will start by identifying yourself. If the chairperson of a meeting says, "OK, here's Nick with the financials," you would begin by saying, "Good morning. I'm Nicholas Chang, financial analyst with the Advanced Projects group." Although all the people in the room may be familiar faces, not everyone may be sure of your full name or your role. It's professional to make a self-introduction in all cases when you haven't been fully introduced by someone else. One variant of this format in a well-structured speech might be to begin with your attention-getting lead-in, and then do your self-introduction.

The introduction to your speech should accomplish two objectives. First, it should get the attention of people in the audience, and second, it should show them where you plan to go. Old-fashioned public speaking experts used to suggest you start with a joke to break the ice. But the form of telling one or two irrelevant jokes and then saying, "Well, that has nothing to do with microprocessors!" is viewed by most businesspeople as merely time wasting. More to the point, it's hard to come up with jokes that don't depend on disrespecting some racial, ethnic, or religious group or that don't have a sexual undertone. Any of these will get you into trouble, so it's a good idea not to start with a joke.

Your attention-getting opening should be designed to *motivate* audience members to be eager to hear what you have to say. If we set aside jokes, you are left with:

- A remarkable fact
- An engaging story
- A demonstration with a prop

Two beginnings that are likely to fail are *rhetorical questions* and *ancient history*. When a speaker begins with a question: "How many of you have been to Europe?", it's not clear to the audience if the speaker wants a head-count ("OK, 14 out of 35") or is going to make a joke by picking on one person ("OK, well, you probably drank too much!"). In short, the rhetorical-question opening leads to a muddled and ineffective start. A recitation of "ancient history" (too much background on the topic) merely signals that your speech is going to be boring ("As you know, we've been working on the new market entry strategy since spring of last year. The task force initially included people from another division, but, as you know, that's been closed down").

Once you have the audience members' attention, you should clearly set out the structure of your speech. This is a process of **signposting.**

> "As I describe our market entry strategy, I want to begin by showing you the size of the opportunity, and then I'll describe the competitive market environment. Lastly, I want to give you the details of our entry execution, including the proposed promotional campaign."

As you see, the three main points of the speech are specifically articulated. As you begin your speech, you'll remind the audience of your structure and where you are by making a good **transition** from one topic to the next.

> "Now that I've reviewed how weak the domestic competitors are, I want to talk about our specific market entry plans."

Carefully crafted transitions are a mark of an expert public speaker. Whenever you are planning to introduce a concept that the audience may not have heard before, such as a technical term or proper name (of a firm or person), you should plan to immediately repeat the term, as naturally as possible, as in this example: "These workers experience carpal tunnel syndrome. Now, carpal tunnel syndrome has been identified as a chief cause of worker's compensation claims." Note that the potentially unfamiliar term "carpal tunnel syndrome" was naturally stated twice in quick succession, enabling audience members to grasp it.

In your conclusion, you will briefly restate your main points. As best you can, try to paraphrase, rather than use exactly the same words—it will make your speech more interesting. An ideal conclusion nicely summarizes what you've just said and also moves work forward. For example, if you're giving a report on project status, in addition to summarizing the work done so far, you might draw some conclusions about how future projects should be tackled.

■ 8-7 STRUCTURE OF A PERSUASIVE SPEECH

When your task is to persuade your audience, rather than just inform them, preparation will be more important than ever. In addition to knowing who will be in your audience and their background, you'll need to assess how and why they agree or disagree with the position you're going to present. At one extreme, if the audience is in total agreement (you are speaking to Disney executives about the need to produce wholesome family entertainment), there's really no need for a persuasive speech. At the other extreme, if your audience is in complete opposition to you (you are trying to persuade a group of executives to make a business decision that will eliminate their annual bonuses), then a persuasive speech of any length or form is unlikely to be of much use.[1]

However, in most situations you will face in business, you will confront an audience whose members have a broad range of opinions: Some audience members may already be close to agreement with what you have to say, some haven't considered the issue and are in a neutral frame of mind, and others are opposed to you before you've started. For example, let's suppose you have to persuade a group of managers to cut back on travel expenses. Because many managers will likely own stock in your firm, they may be ready to keep control of expenses. Most of the audience will expect some belt-tightening and will grumble and go along with it, but a few managers may consider the anticipated proposal to be an interference with their right to run their business units as they wish, including deciding how much to spend on travel.

Interestingly, the best approach when you are facing a range of opinion is not to begin by pointing out how many people are in agreement with you. Instead, you should begin by reaching out to your adversaries. In this instance, people in the audience will probably have a good idea of the topic before you start to speak (everyone in the firm knows there's a big push for cost containment). Moreover, people can likely anticipate that you are going to call for reductions (there's zero chance that you'd be there to say, "I want more of you to fly first-class instead of economy"). So, to persuade, you'll start by acknowledging the importance of face-to-face

---

[1] Where persuasive speech is not sufficient, communications experts recommend that rather than a single speech, the officers of a firm consider a major campaign to change strategic direction. This might involve many speeches and many other forms of communication over several months.

meetings, how important they are to the firm's sales effort, and how business-class travel reduces the stress of long intercontinental flights. This beginning might surprise those in the audience who are "with you" on the need for cost containment but will engage those who were prepared to dismiss anything you had to say. You can then move into your persuasive thrust. You can show how one full-fare business-class ticket costs more than four trips to the same destination bought as advanced-purchase coach-class tickets. You could demonstrate that if each department in the firm could cut just one trip per quarter, the whole company would save $1 million in this fiscal year.

This example is an introduction to **persuasive reasoning.** When you are trying to persuade people, your speech will include comparisons and analogies to help people grasp the size or the seriousness of what you're proposing. In this example, the cost of one airline trip alone is not as compelling as when you show what the total cost becomes over all the firm's units for a whole year. As you speak, you'll plan to use round numbers such as "less than $500" or "more than four times as much." If you give exact comparisons, such as "This alternative costs 3.52 times as much as…," your audience will wonder whether they are to pay attention to the decimal places because another example will be 3.53 or 3.51.

Sometimes you have to get people to care about something that may seem too small to worry about or is a low-probability problem. Without distorting or exaggerating a problem (that is, without making up statistics), you can make your point. One technique is to *multiply*. For example, the statistic that one in five U.S. high school graduates has problems with reading is alarming. But to state: "This year, more than 1 million students will complete high school without the ability to read a daily newspaper" is truly compelling.

A second technique is to *aggregate* (add up a number of small occurrences)—for example, "If each department can cut just one out-of-town trip, we'll be able to report our target 10 percent growth in profit." For low-probability events (for example, the chances of your house burning down), you should go into detail of the consequences of the event, no matter how rare. "While it's true that only 1 in 500 houses experiences a fire each year, the average loss to homeowners for each fire is more than $35,000."

Careful selection of your words can make your speech powerful. For example, instead of just describing convention travel as "wasteful," you could say that it has "little—if any—direct contribution to the bottom line." As you search for strong language to make your point, be careful to avoid hyperbole (exaggeration or extreme wording), such as saying, "Let's face it: Going to conventions is just money down the drain!" The extreme tone of your speech may provoke listeners to ignore what you have to say.

When you've done some research and have facts at your fingertips, you are making a *rational* appeal. For thousands of years, experts in rhetoric have identified three common appeals:

- Rational
- Emotional
- Moral

For example, if you are selling toothpaste and you say that your brand has twice as much fluoride as the competitor's product, then you've made a rational appeal. An emotional appeal encourages people to imagine how good they'll feel about a decision or an action, such as bathroom cleanser advertisements that say: "Because you care about your family's health…" Moral appeals are less common in business but are based on the notion "It's the right thing to do." For example, most business won't suddenly achieve higher profits by adopting environmentally responsible packaging, but most executives would agree that eliminating unnecessary waste is a good idea from the perspective of society as a whole.

As part of your planning for a persuasive speech, you must anticipate the arguments that someone who disagrees with you will have. Think of the reasons why other people will say you are wrong—anticipate objections. In your speech, you must identify and then refute these objections by disproving or rejecting them through clear, solid arguments. For example, "I'm sure many of you feel that restricting business-class travel may make some of our salespeople defect to the competition. But most of them have lived through downturns like this before and they understand that a little belt-tightening is necessary for us to get back to profitability."

If it's true that you can get across only three main points in an *informative* speech, you should aim for no more three or four main positive points in a *persuasive* speech. Then, you should also think of two or three likely objections and refute them. Note that you must address the most compelling objections to your proposal. You can't make a persuasive case by setting up trivial objections to defeat while ignoring the serious drawbacks to your position.

As you craft your speech, make sure that your arguments actually prove your point (and achieve a desired result). One model for persuasive reasoning is "problem, complication, solution." This is rather trite—it assumes that every problem has a complication, and indeed that every complex business situation has a single, credible solution. But there is a grain of truth to the model. If you can't show that you have a viable solution, either you haven't correctly identified the problem or you haven't worked long enough to consider the options. As you identify problems and solutions, make sure you have accurate research to make your case. For example, instead of saying, "Most homes now have Internet access," be able to quote that "for middle-income families, more than 85 percent of homes have Internet access, and of these, more than 25 percent have broadband connections."

Logic flow is important in persuasive reasoning. If you begin with a touching story about one small example (Ronald Reagan grew up in rural Illinois), you should move toward the underlying principle or general lesson (even someone from a humble background has the potential to be president). Conversely, if you decide to begin with a broad description of the problem (secondary education in the United States is ineffective), then be sure to make the general statistics compelling by including some individual examples (young Thomas won't be able to go to college because his high school couldn't afford new math books).

The conventional wisdom is that a persuasive speech should end with a call to action: "Vote Democrat!" or "Buy War Bonds!" However, in business, when managers are trying to influence attitudes and beliefs, the desired end may not be a specific action. In essence, you want to be able to conclude: "I'll hope you'll agree with me that..." Sometimes when a speech is part of a broader initiative to change long-held points of view, it is reasonable to end by hoping that you've at least encouraged your listeners to think about your alternative. As in an informative speech, a persuasive speech should end with a recapitulation, preferably one that doesn't just recite the same words. Make use of the moment to reemphasize the positive results of what you have to say.

When you've researched and planned out your speech, you may want to give it a run-through for practice. Be warned, however, that most people practice too much (see *Business Protocol in Action: How Do You Get to Carnegie Hall?*).

Business Protocol in Action: How Do You Get to Carnegie Hall?

There's an old joke concerning the famous concert hall in New York City that runs: "How do you get to Carnegie Hall?" The punch line is: "Practice! Practice! Practice!"

Most beginning public speakers tend to overpractice their speeches, with the result that the delivered speech sounds more like a recitation of something someone else wrote, rather than a natural conversation with the audience. However, if you are unfamiliar with public speaking, it's understandable that you'll want some rehearsal of your speech. And you may wonder: How much is too much?

Public speaking expert Gene Zelazny, who coaches presenters at one of the world's leading strategy consulting firms, recommends no more than three run-throughs. The first should be on your own, and the second can be in front of a friendly audience such as your immediate coworkers. If you can, save the third rehearsal for the room where you are going to speak.

As you give your practice speeches, observe unnecessary repetitions (for example, "Many of you have many concerns..." when "A number of you have several concerns..." would be better) and think of places in which altering your word choice will make your speech more compelling. Check your timing. If you are running over the allotted time, cut some material rather than try to speed up. Practice taking a slight pause before important terms and clearly enunciate any technical terms or proper names.

▷ ▷ ▷ PUT THIS CHAPTER INTO PRACTICE

1. Practice using persuasive language and reasoning by using multiplying, aggregation, and showing the consequences of a rare event.

2. Listen to a speech given by someone else and try to deconstruct it: What were the main points? What was the supporting evidence? Did the speaker give signposts, and how were transitions handled? Was the conclusion compelling, or was it just a restatement?

3. Tune in to a radio talk show and analyze the callers. Are they informative or persuasive—or is the message confused?

KEY TERMS

audience heterogeneity

persuasive reasoning

prop

questions and answers (Q&A)

signposting

transition

visual aid

Multiple Choice Practice Questions: To take the review quiz for this chapter, log on to your Online Edition at www.atomicdog.com.

Chapter 9
Giving Effective Presentations

If you are well prepared, you won't have to worry about "nerves."

When you watch other people present, you'll be surprised to notice that some of the best public speakers can be people who are quite shy in personal conversation; conversely, there are some people who are the "life of the party" in an informal setting, but who are stumbling and tongue-tied in front of an audience.

Public speaking is simply a skill, like riding a bicycle. You may not have done it much before, but anyone can learn to do it well. The single most important part of public speaking is to adopt a good attitude: If you start with the attitude "This is going to be fantastic!", you'll have a successful result.

In Chapter 8, you learned about planning a speech. Now we turn to specific recommendations for how to present your material in the most effective way. You won't need to rely on luck. There are several concrete steps you can take to make sure that your speech goes well.

■ 9-1 MANAGING THE ROOM

To put yourself at ease, you should become as familiar as possible with the room where you are to speak, either by visiting the location or by researching it beforehand. If possible, practice your speech in the location, paying attention to how your voice sounds in the acoustics of the room and planning ahead where you can use movement for emphasis without tripping up. (See *Business Protocol in Action: How Do You Get to Carnegie Hall?* in Chapter 8.)

Before you begin, make sure that there are no distracting sounds that can be eliminated. For example, in many hotel function rooms there is background music (such as Muzak) that doesn't seem noticeable when people are gathering and chatting but is completely distracting when you are giving a speech. You should make every effort to eliminate this distraction by finding the volume control or a hotel manager who can help you. If you are called on to speak and you notice this problem, politely ask someone else to go and have it turned off. Similarly, if there's noise from an open window, you could say, "It's a little hot in here, but I wonder if we could close the windows for a few minutes; I think it'll be easier for us all to hear."

Checking out the equipment that you'll be using takes only a few moments—and this step should be completed well in advance. Nothing will destroy your professional image faster than plugging and unplugging cords into laptops and portable projectors while an audience waits for you to get set up.

Some conference rooms have computers built into the podium. In others, you may be working from a laptop. To avoid uncertainties and the risk of incompatibility, many consulting firms plan to bring their own computer and portable projector. In most PowerPoint presentations, the presenters use the keyboard to pull up the next slide, but some presenters prefer to use a radio mouse. This is a matter of personal preference, but you need to make sure the equipment works reliably, or stick to the keyboard.

If you are giving a group presentation, some teams choose to designate one individual to manage the computer while the others give the talk. Typically, this approach guarantees a smooth presentation of the visual aids at the expense of giving the appearance that at least one group member was "out of the loop." One good option is for the team members to take turns being in charge of the computer. Of course, this must be rehearsed ahead of time, or confusion is bound to result. The alternative is to choose a speaking position so that the speaker also controls the computer-projected presentation. This method guarantees that the next slide appears at just the right moment, but it has the disadvantage that the speaker is tied to the podium and cannot use movement to emphasize speaking points.

When using a projected presentation, don't dim the room lights too low. This is one detail you can investigate if you are able to check the room ahead of time. Adjusting window shades and reducing room lighting to about half the normal working level will usually be about right. And with rooms that are well designed, it's possible to have quite bright lights for the audience (for note-taking), while leaving the projection screen relatively dark. Running a presentation in the dark is a mistake: Even the most attentive audience will get sleepy, and they will miss the facial expressions and gestures of the speaker(s).

You should be careful and thoughtful about how the light from the projector will strike the speaker. In general, you should stay out of the way of the projected image. In a few meeting rooms, it is impossible to move sufficiently far to the side. In that case, it's better to take a position in the light and keep it. The worst situation is when a speaker's face is half-lit, or if the speaker bobs in and out of the image, shading his or her eyes. So that you can manage this possibility, it's best to begin with the projector turned off or the computer screen blank,[1] introduce yourself and your topic, and then begin the presentation and the main part of your talk.

■ 9-2 WHERE TO STAND AND HOW TO TAKE A CORRECT STANCE

If you are giving a speech by yourself, how you give your presentation will be determined by the audience size—small, medium, or large, as described in the Chapter 8. For small audiences, you'll probably be sitting—so, all you need to worry about is making sure that your desk is uncluttered (put the empty coffee cups in the trash before you begin!) and that you are sitting up straight. If you are using a laptop, make sure it's in a place where everyone can see the screen clearly.

For medium-sized groups, you will likely be at a conference room table. It's a good idea to stand up at the beginning of your talk—this helps to focus attention on you and to signal that you are about to start your speech. If there is a podium at the front of the room, you can consider using it based on your comfort level, what you've seen other speakers do, and the level of formality you wish to signal (standing behind the podium would indicate a high level of formality).

In a large-audience setting, there will undoubtedly be a lectern or at least a table at the front of the room. You should stand and probably begin behind the podium. An exception would be where you particularly want to signal informality. For example, suppose you have a meeting of everyone in your department and your task is to get everyone to agree to work over a holiday weekend to meet a deadline. In that case, you would probably want to stand away from the podium to signal that you are "one" with your audience and not lecturing at them.

Practice a **stance** (how you are standing) at the podium that is comfortable for you. For most people, that involves resting your hands on, but not gripping, the sides of the lectern. If you aren't standing behind a podium, you may have notecards or a prop in one hand or on a table in

---

[1] In MS PowerPoint in "Slide Show" view, press the "B" key on the keyboard to toggle a blank screen on and off.

front of you. Some people hold their hands behind their backs (although this stance can look uncomfortable and limits your ability to make gestures), whereas others lightly catch the thumbs of each hand on their pants pockets. However, you should resist the temptation to stuff your hands into your pockets—it looks too informal and can be distracting for the audience. Serious debaters keep their arms straight down, with the fingers slightly curled in (about one quarter of the way to making a fist), absolutely motionless. If you can do this without paying too much attention to yourself, the effect is dramatic when you move from this stance to making a gesture. The exact position of your hands at rest will depend on your height, your personal style, and what you like to wear. Practice and find a solution that is comfortable for you, and remember to implement it. Your goal is to look confident and unflustered. Make sure that your hands never fidget with your notes or your clothing—if you are in any doubt about this, videotape a practice speech and watch yourself.

Make an entrance, even if you are sitting at a conference table and merely rise to speak. Make it clear from your body language when you are taking control of the room. If you are walking up to a podium, stride purposefully, and immediately take a strong, stable stance. The trick for how to do this is to stand with your feet about 6 inches farther apart than usual (that is, a little wider than when you are standing in conversation with someone). This position will feel weird at first. But you will look rock-solid, like a lighthouse, and this will eliminate any temptation to bob and weave backward and forward. You need to make sure that you do not pace back and forth or side-to-side. If you are unfamiliar with public speaking, you may find that a certain amount of pacing feels natural and helps you keep the rhythm of your speech. However, it is extremely distracting.

Now that we have you immobile and frozen, it's time to add some movement and gestures. If you've adopted a nice, professional stance, a small amount of movement can be a compelling addition to your public speaking. If you are calling for cooperation from the audience, you can step out from the podium and take one or two steps forward. You don't have to be very close—often a half-step forward and a half-step back to continue your speech can be very effective. In a long talk where you are not tied to the podium, it's a good idea to change your position as you change topics. Be careful not to speak as you are walking, and indicate the transition:

> "Now that we've covered the financials [move a few paces], I'd like to turn to the long-term benefits for our division."

You can develop a small vocabulary of hand gestures: reaching out, emphasizing, dismissing a weak idea, and so on. These gestures can be accompanied by a lively expression on your face—a bit exaggerated, but not clownish. The gestures that work for you will be part of your personal style, and you shouldn't adopt a set formula. However, as you are developing your public speaking abilities, you can carefully watch how other speakers—and even performers on stage—use hand gestures. You don't want to look like a rock musician, but you can get some good ideas. For example, you can use a horizontal, semicircular sweeping movement of your arm to accompany, "I'd like to welcome you *all*...," with the gesture signaling inclusiveness. Be careful about clenched-fist gestures and banging the podium—you don't want to come across as a third-world dictator! Of course, the meanings of gestures are culturally determined, so you should be careful if you are speaking to an international audience (see *It's Just Different: The Meaning of Gestures*).

Eye contact is culturally determined and is a sensitive issue. In American business culture, if you never look people in the eye, you'll be seen at best as someone who is lacking in confidence, at worst as someone who has something to hide. On the other hand, if your gaze fixes on one person for too long, you'll make that person uncomfortable. Because it's important to engage all of your audience, you should shift your gaze, from front to back and from right to left. The best way to study this behavior is to think of

It's Just Different: The Meaning of Gestures

In America, if you stand with your arms folded across your chest, it's a gesture of defiance (imagine a naughty child being lectured by an angry parent). However, in Viet Nam, the same position means "I am waiting quietly and submissively," so it's a stance people sometimes use in church.

You might think that most gestures must be universal. After all, everyone smiles and frowns in the same way throughout the world. But many simple gestures have different meanings in different cultures. The U.S. "OK" sign (index finger touching thumb to make a circle) has vulgar sexual meanings in much of Europe. In many parts of the world, pointing directly with an extended index finger at someone (for example, at someone who is going to ask a question) is considered very rude.

Consequently, if you are welcoming guests from another country or if your work takes you overseas, it's a good idea to consult an international business protocol book for some quick do's and don'ts.

someone you think is a good speaker and watch specifically what she or he does. Practice this, have yourself videotaped, and ask friends for feedback.

9-3 MANAGING GROUP PRESENTATIONS

When a team has worked together on a project, one possibility is to use one team member as a spokesperson who will deliver a presentation on behalf of the group. But this approach has liabilities. When the team is made up of professionals from different functional groups (say, finance, marketing, and manufacturing), a presentation by one person inevitably is seen as partisan: "This is the Finance position on this proposal."

Group presentations take some effort, but getting four to six people to work on a presentation together can produce a very professional and persuasive result. It takes some skill to give several different speakers a chance to participate, to keep to time, and to rotate answers to questions. But the result is a powerful demonstration that the project team has thought through the issues carefully, and their proposed solution represents a consensus.

When four people give a 20-minute presentation, four 5-minute speeches are fine. But an even better approach is to have one person both open and close the talk. The first speaker should outline the presentation and, on the second appearance, draw a value-added conclusion, emphasizing the main points made by the middle three speakers, not merely restating them.

In every group, there will be some variation in the talent of individual group members for public speaking. You should aim to end with your best speaker and begin with your second-best. If someone clearly has difficulties of language or articulation, that speaker should come in the middle of the group. A weak speaker should probably have a smaller percentage of the total presentation time and should practice thoroughly to do the small part well.

As a group presentation develops, each team member will develop an expertise in a specific area, so who will speak about what will begin to become apparent. But you should work to make sure that your whole presentation appears integrated. It is invariably a mistake to assign the "financials" to one person. If so, you will have a presentation that reaches a low spot after three of four team members have talked about strategy and then, without proper integration into the strategy, one unlucky team member is introduced with the phrase "Here's Peter to do the numbers." When financial information is presented in isolation rather than being properly integrated into the presentation as a whole, the audience is likely to become completely lost.

■ 9-4 WHERE GROUP MEMBERS STAND

A team can take several possible positions of where to stand, depending on the shape of the room and whether there is a table or podium for notes. In all but the smallest meetings, all team members should stand for a presentation, even when they are not presenting or controlling the visual aids.

The key success factor is the professional stance of the people who are not presenting. Once you've said your part of a speech, it's tempting to sigh, exchange "Glad that's over!" expressions with other team members, and relax. The most effective teams don't do this. Instead, every member who is not speaking turns to the speaker and watches the presentation as if it were the most fascinating talk he'd ever heard. Almost military discipline in standing still can have an impressive effect.

Figure 9-1 illustrates a typical positioning for four people when speaking from a podium. In this case, the group has chosen to have the speaker control the appearance of the next PowerPoint slide. This

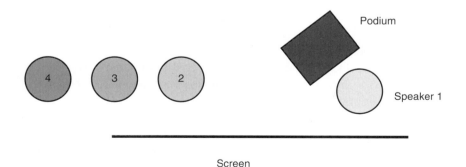

Figure 9-1 Basic Group Format
This is the basic position for team members during a group presentation.

arrangement needs careful rehearsal—Speaker 2 may collide with Speaker 1 as they exchange places at the podium. In any case, Speaker 1 should join the end of the line (next to Speaker 4) when her turn is complete.

If the speaker doesn't control the PowerPoint presentation, a well-rehearsed presentation should not require: "Next slide, please." However, if the slides are lagging, a simple request can be made to appear professional. For example, you can start talking about the next topic with a clear indication that you are moving on: "Now, let's turn to the implementation plan…" (this should make it clear to the computer operator that you are ready for the next slide). Angry debates with teammates ("Not that one! Go back to the other slide!") seriously detract from the presentation, and the only sure preventative is plenty of practice. When the team chooses to have someone other than the speaker control the computer, it's also important that other team members not huddle around the keyboard. For example, an improvement on the basic form seen in Figure 9-1 is to have the waiting speakers line up at a slight angle with an independent Power-Point operator, as shown in Figure 9-2.

Once again, changing from one speaker to the next without making it look like slapstick comedy will take some practice, especially when the space is constrained by the seating and desks for the audience.

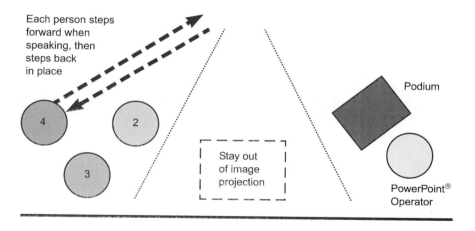

Screen

Figure 9-2   Improved Group Format
Based on the basic group format, here is an improved position for team presentations with the speaker not controlling the computer.

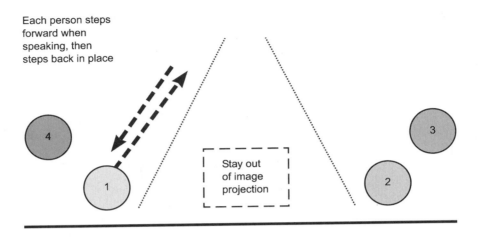

Each person steps forward when speaking, then steps back in place

Stay out of image projection

Screen

Figure 9-3   Butterfly Format
The butterfly format works well for team presentations on a large stage—note that each team member moves forward to speak.

When the team is large enough to have four speakers and a visual aid manager, and particularly when there is a stage or large space in front of the audience, the *butterfly format* is very effective for four speakers (see Figure 9-3).

In this format, Speakers 1 and 2 take a few steps forward when it's their turn to speak, and Speakers 3 and 4 step forward and to the middle (remaining out of the line of the projected image). When finished, each speaker calmly walks back to his or her original position and pays close attention to the next speaker.

■ 9-5 SPEAKING WITH VISUAL AIDS

Even if you are giving a solo speech, you'll need to decide where you are going to stand with respect to your media if you are using some sort of projected visual aids. If your audience size is small, your media may be a laptop with a slide show. In a medium or large audience setting, you will probably use a projected PowerPoint presentation. Your first decision will be whether to have someone else control the changing of slides or to control the computer or projector yourself. If you have help, you should print an out-line of your slides and give the assistant a brief overview of the presentation. This will avoid endless repetitions of: "Next slide, please." When you are projecting media onto a screen, you should stand as close as possible to the screen, but avoid getting light from the projector on your face.

If at all possible, avoid blocking the view of the screen for any audi-ence members. In some small meeting rooms, some blocking of the screen may be inevitable; handle this problem one of two ways. The first option is to stand your ground (hold one position)—people whose view is blocked will soon figure it out and lean around you. The alternative, if you are talking for quite a while about each slide, is to make half of your com-ments, then move to a new position and conclude what you have to say. The one thing to avoid is interrupting yourself with questions such as "Can you see back there?" and bobbing around from side to side in a way that robs you of your professional demeanor.

If you are using visual aids, you may want to draw attention to specific parts of a graphic using a laser pointer. This technique can be very effec-tive if you use the pointer in moderation and can avoid any fiddling with it. If you are not using a pointer, you should gesture toward a point you are discussing. For example, with a PowerPoint slide of bullet points pro-jected on a large screen, turn and extend your arm toward each bullet point as you move through your explanations of them. You don't need to actually reach the specific bullet with your hand (it may be several feet above and behind you in a large room)—the goal is just to acknowledge your own slides. Gestures can help you achieve this objective.

Although it's very easy to add compelling graphics to almost any PowerPoint presentation, make sure you don't claim someone else's work as your own—be sure to add a footnote on each slide (see *Doing the Right Thing: Acknowledge Your Sources*).

■ 9-6 USING NOTES OR A SCRIPT

If you are speaking with PowerPoint slides as your visual aid, you should be able to speak naturally using what is on the screen as your notes. For other speeches, you should be prepared to work from notes, either typed on a sheet of paper in front of you or handwritten on index cards. However, you should almost always avoid a word-for-word script. When you write out every

Doing the Right Thing: Acknowledge Your Sources

In the early years of the Internet, many speakers were so excited by the instant access to knowledge that they let their standards of attribution slip, failing to acknowledge where material they used came from. They got in the habit of clipping and pasting information without indicating that they were using someone else's graphic or data. Although not attributing sources will rarely get you into trouble for violating copyright, you should always have notes on your slides or handouts as to where the information was obtained. An exception to this guideline is if you are quoting a commonly believed fact such as "there is roughly an equal number of men and women in the United States." A common standard for this exception is that if a fact can be found in at least three readily available sources, it doesn't need to be footnoted.

You may come across the opposite situation—where you risk losing control of your own work. For example, suppose you have spent three weeks of professional effort to make an incisive analysis of competitive trends in an industry, and a good customer says, "Say, why don't you e-mail me a copy of your slides?" You might be reluctant to do that if you consider the work to be your own intellectual property and you are worried that your work might not be properly acknowledged. It's appropriate to agree and then send a *printout* of the slides later. You are being responsive to the customer without shipping her a PowerPoint file that can be cloned into someone else's presentation.

Lastly, if you are giving a presentation on behalf of a team, or if a team member cannot be present, it is a good idea to begin your talk by acknowledging how other people contributed to your speech.

sentence of your speech before you give your talk, you'll use a sentence structure that is inappropriate for spoken delivery (most likely too long with too many complicated subordinate clauses). Worse, you will speak with your head down, without making eye contact with your audience.

Many people mistakenly use a script to protect against the possibility of losing their place. Of course, once they've lost their place, there's no hope of finding it again from the many words on a script, but a glance a note cards will soon get a speech back on track.

In a very few circumstances, your talk will be written out in full ahead of time. First, if you have a legal responsibility—for example, announcing layoffs—the exact wording of what you say may have important consequences. Your speech may have been written by other people and reviewed by your firm's lawyers and outsiders, and you'll have no option but to stick to the script. A famous example of the need to have the wording exactly right occurred in the swearing in of President Barack Obama. Although the presidential oath of office is just 35 words long, Chief Justice John Roberts tripped up over the words. Because President Obama repeated what Justice Roberts had said, he hadn't quite taken the oath of office spelled out in the U.S. Constitution. Later that day, the president had a "do over" and repeated the oath to the chief justice in front of a small group of reporters. In retrospect, this would have been an occasion at which having the words written out in front of Justice Roberts would have been a good idea.

A second circumstance where you would need to rely on a script would be if you are asked to give a speech in a language in which you have some speaking abilities but not fluency. You would want to make sure that both your choice of vocabulary and your use of grammar would not cause offense to your audience. Thirdly, you might be asked to deliver a speech for someone who can't be present at the last minute. In any situation in which you are reluctantly forced to read from a script, make sure that you look up and make eye contact with your audience right before you start and from time to time during your talk (about once each paragraph).

If you practice speaking from notes, you'll soon find that natural turns of phrase occur to you better when you're on your feet delivering your talk, rather than when you're sitting at your desk typing. Unless you make formal speeches every day as a routine part of your job, you should plan to rehearse your speech. For a "mission-critical" speech (such as to an audience that'll be hard to win over, or to an unfamiliar and rather large audience), you should try to rehearse in the actual room where you'll be speaking. But don't over-rehearse your speech. If you try to memorize every line, you may completely lose your train of thought if there are interruptions or distractions, and have difficulty in restarting.

After you have prepared, you may have plenty of time before you are due to speak. Make use of the time to do some **wordsmithing** (carefully editing what you have to say to achieve a harmonious talk). Ask yourself: Which technical terms need to be repeated and defined? Are there any phrases that have been used too often, and is it possible to add some variety? Make sure you've avoided **clichés**—common expressions that, although true, are trite and overused, such as: "In this modern world of ours, change is always with us." Clichés rarely add any value to your talk and could mark you as an unoriginal, boring speaker. Then work on transitions: An eloquent summary of one section and an appealing "lead" into the next section will show your expertise.

■ 9-7 DELIVERY

No matter how carefully you prepare your talk, it won't be effective if people can't hear you! Yes, when you are speaking in public, you must speak somewhat louder than you do in conversation. However, you don't have to shout. The key is to enunciate clearly. You can do this by slowing down (that is, reducing your **rate of speech**, the number of words per minute that you speak) and by taking pauses between phrases. If you are doing this right, you may feel as if your speech is very unnatural. Try watching yourself on videotape: A pause that felt like an eternity when you were speaking looks like a tiny moment when you yourself are part of the audience. You should heavily emphasize consonants. For example, in conversation, we often pronounce the word "technology" almost as "teh-nolgy"; but in a speech, it has to come out as "teCK-no-lo-GY." In sum, although you need to be loud enough, speaking slowly and clearly beats shouting.

Once you become experienced in public speaking, you will find that it is quite easy to speak without amplification to medium-sized groups (up to about 40 people). For larger groups, you'll need a microphone, and with a few tips you can speak naturally and be heard clearly (see *Business Protocol in Action: Speaking with a Microphone*).

Plan to keep your talk interesting by varying the tone and rate of speech. That is, although in general you should not speak too rapidly, you can say some familiar phrases or expressions quickly, although you must introduce new terms carefully and slowly. In addition to a slight increase in volume (you'll already be speaking medium-loud, so you don't have too much room to adjust your sound without shouting), you can emphasize important terms by preceding them with a slight pause. If you listen to radio commercials, you'll hear experienced announcers doing this:

"...and that's just [pause] 99 cents a day!"

You can practice this by saying "pause, pause" silently to yourself right before the words you want to emphasize.

Business Protocol in Action: Speaking with a Microphone

For most business meetings with up to three dozen people in the audience, you really don't need amplification for your voice. Remember that Roman senators in the Forum and medieval bishops preaching in large cathedrals managed just fine without modern electronics. But where you are a guest or invited speaker, you may be under some pressure to use the setup that is provided by your hosts or that other speakers are using. Of course, speaking to large groups (hundreds of people) invariably involves microphones. Here's how to use amplification well.

Types of microphones.   There are many different types of microphones that you will encounter. For all of them, avoid banging them or having clothing rub up against them (remember, they are designed to pick up the smallest vibration of air). You will demonstrate your professionalism if you make sure the microphone is properly placed and test it before you start, and then ignore it.

The best type of microphone is a "radio mike," a small microphone that clips to your tie, jacket, shirt, or blouse and that feeds to a small radio transmitter that you can clip on a belt or put in a jacket pocket. If you anticipate using this type of equipment, dress accordingly—don't wear pants or a dress with no pockets. The microphone itself needs to be directly below your mouth at about the level of your breastbone. (Be careful if you clip the microphone to a coat collar—it may face away from your mouth and give a poor sound quality.) It's the responsibility of your hosts or technicians to adjust the level of amplification so your voice sounds good when the microphone is correctly placed. If the sound is not loud enough, ask the technician to raise the volume level a bit rather than unclipping and moving the microphone. With a radio mike, you have complete freedom of movement, and the sound quality is usually good. The only thing you have to worry about is making sure the microphone is turned off when you are not speaking—you can easily get caught making private comments if you don't realize it's on.

A handheld microphone (the type used by sports reporters) is probably the second-best choice of microphone. Although there are some radio handheld microphones, most will have a cord or cable, and the rules for effective use are the same for both. You need to position the mike at about chin level and about 6 inches in front of your face. Don't hold it closer to your mouth, or amplified "p" sounds will sound like an explosive "pop." A handheld microphone should have an on and off switch—make sure it's turned on before you start to speak.

If it is a microphone on a stand or at a podium, take a moment when you first step up to adjust the microphone to the correct height for you (just below the level of your chin). Never duck down to speak into a mike that is adjusted

(Continued)

too short for you, as this destroys your professional stance. If you are especially short, arrange for a small stool to stand on behind a podium so you can be seen.

In some conference settings, you'll be seated at a table with a desk microphone on a stand in front of you. These mikes rarely work well. If there's only one mike, it gets banged around as it's passed from one speaker to another. Even if there's a microphone in front of each speaker, it is often hard to adjust the volume so that each speaker can be heard equally well. As much as you can, make sure the microphone is placed squarely in front of you, and again, try not to duck down to speak into it. Speak clearly and to the audience and hope that the technicians will do a good job of adjusting the level for each mike.

Probably the worst kind of microphone is the *lavaliere:* a microphone with a cable that attaches to a cord and hangs around your neck coming at mid-chest. This old-fashioned type of equipment doesn't work very well. It doesn't pick up speech clearly but does get a lot of extraneous noise from clothing. Try to adjust the cord so the microphone is a little higher up, clear of your jacket, and then try to ignore it (don't look down at it). If the lavaliere comes with a long cable, try to have some slack on the floor just to your side before you start to speak so you can use some movement, and be careful to avoid getting tangled when you step back to your regular position.

Testing the microphone.   Whichever type of microphone you are using, your public speaking will go much better if you have tested it before you start to speak. Don't tap the microphone with your hands (it's a sensitive device designed to pick up small vibrations of the air, and thumping it won't do it any good) and don't say, "Is this thing on...?", which appears tremendously unprofessional. At stage shows, you've probably noticed that the setup crew usually just counts into the microphone: "One...two...three," etc. But probably as good a line is to say, "Good morning! This is a mike check on the podium mike...," and so on. Try to test the mike before the meeting starts or during a break, and the start of your speech will look much more professional.

Interference.   When radio mikes work, they work wonderfully well. Occasionally, they suffer from brief interference from police or taxi radios. If you have a single interruption, you can handle it with humor ("If there's anyone here from Car 96, please respond to that call"). But if interference happens repeatedly during your presentation, all that people will remember about your talk is the interruptions. So if you experience this problem, or bad static in the radio reception, the only way to handle it is to turn off the microphone. "Clearly, this is not working for us today" is what you'd say. Then speak a little more slowly, very distinctly, and loudly enough to fill the whole room. Remember that public speaking went on for centuries before the invention of electric amplification. Your audience will be grateful.

A more common type of problem—which can affect any of the microphone types—is the howl and screech called "feedback." This occurs when the

(*Continued*)

volume of the amplifier is turned up too loudly. A small sound is amplified and played by the speakers, and is then picked up by your microphone and reamplified. A nasty squeal results. If your microphone has an on/off switch, turn it off as quickly as possible to stop the howl. Before you turn it back on, quietly ask your hosts or the technicians, "Can you take the level down a bit, please? We're getting bad feedback here." If the people running the meeting can't fix the problem, then once again, it's better to dispense with the amplification completely and do your speech "unplugged." A screeching microphone is so aversive to members of the audience that no one will be able to concentrate on your content.

If your talk is going to be more than 5 minutes long, vary the lighting as much as you can. For example, if you are the third speaker in a row and the previous two speakers have set the lights low to show slides, take a few moments of introduction with the lights fully on to wake up your audience. If you have a long, complicated presentation (for example, financial material), break it up in the middle by blanking the projection and raising the lights while you make some narrative comments.

When you're speaking, work very hard to eliminate **placeholders** in conversation, such as "um, err, you know." One or two are acceptable, but if you have a severe problem with this, your audience will become irritated. One way to cure yourself of a bad "um" habit is to take a stack of quarters (or dollar bills, depending on your income level) and practice giving a talk with a friend playing the role of audience. For each time you say "um," your friend gets a quarter. You'll find that although you may still use placeholders in casual conversation or phone calls, your public speaking will be greatly improved.

If you make a mistake, correct yourself quickly and naturally as soon as you notice it. For example, "I just said Panama and, of course, I should've said Patagonia." And then move right along. Don't make your mistakes worse than they are: "Argh! I'm completely stupid! Of course it's not *Panama!*" We call this **catastrophizing**—treating a small slip as if it were a catastrophe. Most people don't like to listen to people who are completely stupid, so you shouldn't label yourself that way. The same advice applies if you show the wrong slide or have some other technical problem. The correct approach is to acknowledge an error, correct it, and continue with confidence. If you carefully watch star athletes (especially ice skaters), you'll notice that they all make small errors—but the winners are the ones who can recover well.

■ 9-8 QUESTION AND ANSWER PERIODS

The key to a successful question and answer (Q&A) session is to manage, or control, the situation. Your host may choose which audience member can ask each question, but you should not allow one person in the audience to dominate the discussion with several follow-up questions or attempts to engage you in debate. You can handle this by saying, "Perhaps I could take some other questions before my time is up?" while pointedly turning to face other parts of the audience, which is a polite but firm way to terminate the situation.

It's always good to restate a question. All members of the audience may not have been able to hear the questioner, and restating gives you a moment to collect your thoughts. You verify that you are about to address the questioner's chief concern, and you can edit a question to your advantage:

> "Well, I heard a number of concerns, but if I can summarize, your question is: How can we propose a major capital expenditure at a time when operating budgets are being cut?"

If a questioner points out something you haven't considered, don't try to dismiss the question as unimportant. "Thank you—that's an aspect of this proposal I didn't address today" is gracious and sufficient. If a questioner points out that there's an error in your reasoning or in your math, it may be very hard for you to think through the correct solution on your feet. Responding, "You're right, those numbers don't add to 100 percent; clearly, I'm going to have to check that" would be a good way to handle a potential embarrassment. If you've worked hard, you'll actually enjoy defending your ideas, but you should never appear defensive.

■ 9-9 HANDLING Q&A FOR A GROUP PRESENTATION

Almost all group presentations end with a Q&A session. The goals that a team should aim for in a Q&A session is for all questions to be answered succinctly, each team member to take turns in answering, and the selection of who should answer which topic to occur naturally. Of course, it is very hard for this rotation of speakers to happen seamlessly, and only the highest-functioning groups who've worked together for a long time can achieve this. Sometimes a smooth Q&A session depends on having good luck in the order of questions posed by the audience.

In an ideal situation, when each question is posed, one member will step forward and take on the task of replying on behalf of the team. However, waiting for one person to self-select may cause an embarrassing delay; so many teams appoint one group member to be the "master of ceremonies" for the Q&A part of the talk. Many democratically organized groups may dislike the idea of choosing one person to be in charge, as this gives the appearance of one person being the team captain, but the alternative is time-wasting silences, or two or more team members interrupting one another as they both try to answer one question.

Most answers offered by speakers in Q&A sessions are 90 percent correct—it's simply very hard to be complete and perfect when you are answering on your feet in front of an audience. So it's naturally very tempting for the remaining team members to jump in and add the last 10 percent. Resist this temptation. In most instances, the second speaker either contradicts the first or goes over old ground, wasting time. Most often, the hidden message is: "My colleague is a fool! Here, let me save him from himself!" In short, routinely having more than one person pile on an answer usually detracts from your group's professional image. When a group member has made a clear mistake that needs correction, be brief and gracious:

> "I believe Taylor just said the fixed costs are $400—of course, that's $400 million."

Try to prevent audience members from giving a speech of their own when they should be asking questions. A gentle interruption (signaled by taking two steps smartly toward the questioner) is appropriate: "So, if I can form that as a question, your concern is that…" When one of the audience appears to be "drilling" by asking several questions in a row pointedly directed to only one of the team members, the team member under fire should try to gracefully engage other team members: "I believe Leslie can give more details on that…," and other team members should be prepared to draw hostile fire. At the limit when one line of questioning has gone on too long, it's best to get the discussion going again by moving on:

> "Well, it's clear we have some more thinking to do on that topic… I wonder, does anyone else have a question we could take in the remaining time?"

High-functioning groups spend as much time planning and practicing questions as rehearsing the main part of their presentation.

■ 9-10 ON THE WAY TO BECOMING AN EXPERT PUBLIC SPEAKER

Before you give a speech, you may be eager to do well, and you'll want to know what you can do to make sure that it is a success. Of course, practice is helpful. But be careful about overpracticing a single speech (it may only add to your anxieties). Instead of going over and over your talk, put some effort into some of the subtasks, such as experimenting with a variety of gestures or with different speaking positions.

A better way to develop your speech-giving skills is to have a lot of practice with many different speeches in many different settings. You can get more practice by volunteering at work to be the person in your group who'll speak on behalf of your colleagues. Many professionals have bene-fited by participating in Toastmasters, a nationwide association that exists solely to give its members regular and varied public speaking opportunities. In addition, you can find many opportunities in social settings to practice giving a short speech. For example, if you and your cousins are attending your grandmother's 80th birthday, instead of joining in when someone says, "It's time to say Happy birthday, Grandma!", make it into an oppor-tunity for a brief informative speech. Gather your facts (Grandma immi-grated to America at age 7, went to work at age 14, has 10 grandchildren and 4 great-grandchildren, etc.), make a few notes, step to the center of the gathering, take a powerful stance, pause, and then begin, "If I could have your attention…I'd like to say a few words on behalf of my cousins…"

Videotaping yourself giving a speech can be helpful, as you are able to see annoying habits such as fidgeting and pacing. But while you are learning public speaking, the presence of a camera could make you more nervous than you otherwise would be. So consider videotaping an actual speech once you feel you are doing pretty well at public speaking and you want to become expert.

You may be wondering when we are going to address "nerves," fear of public speaking, and stage fright. The answer is: We don't. Although you'll hear all sorts of anecdotes about how professional speech coaches encourage you to overcome nerves, the best solution is simply to concentrate on the technical aspects of your talk: being clear about your goal, doing adequate research, the points you are going to make and the most appealing logical order, what visual aids to use, your stance, gestures, and so on. By the time you've reviewed all these, you won't have time for anxieties and you'll be surprised that you'll do much better than you ever imagined.

▶ ⟩ ⟩ PUT THIS CHAPTER INTO PRACTICE

1. Look for a DVD of "Great Speeches" at your library, and make an analysis of the gestures used in one speech.

2. At a social event, take the initiative to deliver a short speech such as welcoming a guest on behalf of the group.

3. If you feel that you are already expert at public speaking, discuss with a group of friends how you would handle "disasters" such as:

   • A PowerPoint file refuses to open.

   • You spill coffee on yourself right when it's your turn to speak.

   • The power goes out while you are speaking.

▌ KEY TERMS

catastrophizing	rate of speech
cliché	stance
placeholder	wordsmithing

Multiple Choice Practice Questions: To take the review quiz for this chapter, log on to your Online Edition at www.atomicdog.com.

Chapter 10

Business Dining

Let's do lunch!

The American attitude to food is shockingly casual to many visitors to the USA. They are surprised to find that many office workers don't leave their desks for lunch and to see many American workers eating while walking down the street during lunchtime, so-called "eating on the run" (see Figure 10-1). Meals just don't have as much significance in American business as in other countries. Mealtimes are simply an occasion to get food, and because Americans are universally friendly and outgoing, they often eat with coworkers, superiors, and business partners without assigning a great deal of significance to the occasion.

Figure 10-1   Eating on the Go
Americans have a very casual attitude toward food and often eat while doing something else.
Source: © 2009 Jupiterimages Corporation.

However, there are other occasions where business dining is used as a formal device, a sort of miniature ceremony. This can be to mark the beginning or end of a project or of employment, to recognize a promotion, or to set the stage for harmonious business negotiation.

10-1 WHAT TO EAT

Americans have a super-abundance of excellent food perpetually available—the finest steaks, fish, fruits, and vegetables are to be found in all seasons. In general, office workers eat lightly (perhaps too lightly) at breakfast and lunch, and in consequence, dinners are heavy with huge portions—some restaurants serve more meat on a single plate than an individual would eat over the course of a week in many other countries.

You should never feel under any obligation to eat anything that by religion, habit, or personal preference you choose not to eat. When you receive an invitation, it's polite to give your hosts pre-warning of your restrictions. For example, you might say, "Yes, I'd love to come, but I should mention—I'm a vegetarian." This forewarning will save your hosts from the embarrassment of taking you to their favorite steakhouse. But even in the worst circumstances, menus of American restaurants are quite eclectic, and you should be able to find something acceptable to eat. For example, even a steakhouse will have a salad.

If you are encouraged to try something that you don't want to eat, politely declining ("Actually, I don't eat pork") won't cause offense— your hosts would likely acknowledge that there are probably some things that they don't eat themselves. No polite host would insist that you eat something against your will.

If you are really uncomfortable with the items offered on a menu, you can probably get a good restaurant to make a substitution. For example, you could ask if you could have two (vegetarian) appetizers instead of a main course, or if rice could be served instead of potatoes. Don't be afraid to ask.

10-2 HANDLING ALCOHOL

In many social situations it's the cultural norm to drink alcohol, or even to drink too much alcohol (such as at wedding receptions). However, in business you probably don't want your associates to see your silly side, and indeed, you may have a personal or religious reason not to drink alcohol.

In American business dining, offering beer or wine at dinner is common, whereas most people would expect to go through lunch without an alcoholic beverage. This is in contrast to Europe, where wine would be common at both meals, and to Asia, where bottled beer is often served.

If you are asked to select a wine, you shouldn't worry too much about choosing something impressive or about which wine goes with what type of food. For example, the old rule about always drinking white wine with fish and chicken has definitely been discarded. Drink what you like. You may encounter some people ordering mixed drinks (for example, scotch, bourbon, or gin mixed with soda) either before a meal or at the table. This is more common in the generation that started work in the 1950s, and in most business situations today it is probably a good idea to avoid these hard drinks and stick with wine or beer.

Even if the meal is part of a celebration, you don't want to build a reputation as a heavy drinker, and if you are driving home after the meal, you need to be very cautious about how much you consume. If you are not driving, a glass of wine before the meal and one with the main course is about right, and if you're drinking beer, two medium glasses of beer is enough.

You should never be embarrassed to refuse to drink alcohol (see Figure 10-2). Nor should you worry about stopping drinking when you've had enough. People who are heavy drinkers may try to encourage you, and might even make fun of you. But you should be confident that, by their insistence, they are only making themselves look bad.

Having some socially acceptable excuses may help you to avoid drinking or drinking too much. "I should stop now; I have a heavy day tomorrow" is one possibility to limit the amount you drink. Because drunk-driving laws are strictly enforced, one socially acceptable reason to avoid drinking at all is: "Better not—I'm driving."

If your associates are still pressuring you, all you need to say is: "No, really. I choose not to drink." If you can do this with grace and a cheerful attitude, everyone will respect you. Your only responsibility is to be courteous in your refusal and not "preach" to those who do choose to drink.

Figure 10-2   Drinking and Business
Don't feel compelled to drink alcohol just because everyone else is.
SOURCE: © 2009 Jupiterimages Corporation.

■ 10-3 WHO WILL PAY?

In general, companies pay for meals that involve entertaining a client or job candidate. When a meal involves only members within the firm, the occasion must usually be special, such as honoring a longtime worker's retirement. When a dinner marks the closing of a deal between two firms, the party that's making a profit (the seller or banker usually) will propose the meal and pick up the bill. In general, when you are invited to a meal, you can assume that the person who invited you will pay. There's no need to go through a ritual offer to pay for the meal that you know will be refused (as is commonly expected in many countries). If you are being treated to the meal, offer your thanks at the beginning and then while your host is paying for the bill: "Thank you again for a great lunch."

When colleagues from the same firm go to lunch together, the expectation is that they will **split the bill,** also colloquially called the "tab." There is some protocol about this procedure. First, when the bill is presented, it's reasonable to say: "Let's split this." Because many people like to pay for meals by credit card, you may get the response, "No, let me get this one, and you can pay next time." You should graciously accept but keep track of who in your office you owe meals to, or over time you'll get a very bad reputation as a freeloader. Conversely, if you think you've paid too many times in a row, you can cheerfully announce at the beginning of the next meal, "Great! This one's on you!" You'll occasionally run into a situation where the other person insists on paying every time you eat together. This is rarely as good as it seems (see *Doing the Right Thing: When It's Never Your Turn to Pay*).

If a restaurant is unwilling to provide separate checks for each diner in a large group of people (for example, when a team decides to go to lunch together to celebrate the end-of-the-month payday), you may run into a

Doing the Right Thing: When It's Never Your Turn to Pay

You may find yourself in an odd situation if a business acquaintance always insists on paying. At first you are flattered that as a low-level new hire you are being treated to the fanciest restaurant in town and your host insists that you order a whole lobster at lunch, saying, "Don't worry, it's all on the expense account."

Your common sense will make you wonder what is expected in return. Sure enough, sooner or later, your generous host asks you to pass a copy of the firm's confidential phone directory (see Chapter 6) or to leak the terms of a competitor's bid for your firm's business. You'll feel put on the spot by being placed in an awkward situation, but you will just have to say no.

Of course, it's best to never find yourself in this situation. If you work for a group that has the power and money to award contracts, you and your team members may find it easier to simply refuse entertainment and meals (however sincerely offered) from potential suppliers.

You can also find yourself put on the spot by well-meaning colleagues who always insist on paying. Although you can routinely allow your boss to pay for meals (she's making much more money than you!), if it's a peer who won't follow the rule of either splitting bills or taking turns, you can use these tricks: When a lunch date is set, arrive early and make sure your credit card is in the waiter's hand before you are seated; or before the bill comes to the table, make a "bathroom" excuse and give your credit card to the waiter on the way. Some people curiously like the power of always paying, but they'll probably be relieved when you say, "Oh, I think it's so much better to take turns, don't you?"

common problem of how to split the bill. The calculation of who owes what often leads to hurt feelings. Someone orders a $6.95 sandwich and puts $6 into "the pot." Of course the true cost of their lunch is $6.95 plus $1.75 for an iced tea. That's $9.42 including tax, or $10.72 including tip! Common practice is to total up the bill plus tip, announce the total to the group, and divide the sum equally among all people who attend. Haggling over who had the $6.95 sandwich or the $16.00 salad is considered petty and poor form.

■ 10-4 WHEN YOU ARE THE HOST

Even if you consider yourself to be the junior member of a team, you will soon find yourself responsible for making arrangements to host clients or visiting colleagues. Begin by making clear who should be invited. In general, spouses aren't invited to business meetings, unless the setting is a conference away from home where all participants may be accompanied. Next, make a decision about the level of meal that is expected: Are you just providing nourishment while a project is in progress, or does the meal have an important symbolic function?

For most restaurants, especially for large groups of people (more than six), you'll need reservations. Calling a restaurant a week in advance is typical, but for very popular restaurants or for large groups of people, you may have to book a month or more in advance. You don't need to tip the person who makes the reservation, and the idea of tipping the restaurant's maitre d' (host or greeter) in the hope of getting a prestigious location is amusingly antiquated. Unless you're Bill Gates, you'll be seated wherever the staff can accommodate you (see *Business Protocol in Action: Becoming a "Regular Customer"*).

Most restaurants won't seat incomplete parties; that is, if you've reserved a table for six people, you won't be seated until all six people have arrived. Although you do have to be prompt to keep your reservation (many restaurants cancel a reservation after 15 minutes' delay), there may be an occasion when you and your guests are all present but the table isn't ready. Take this situation in stride—a restaurateur is at the mercy of other diners finishing their meals, especially if you have a large party requiring several tables. If you are hosting a dinner, offer to buy your guests a glass

Business Protocol in Action: Becoming a "Regular Customer"

You may have noticed that some people seem to get preferential treatment at restaurants: They are seated promptly, always seem to have the best tables, and receive attentive service from the waitperson and the restaurant management. That's because they are considered "good, regular customers." Regular customers are the mainstay of a restaurant's business. They are not necessarily the people who run up the biggest bills—they are patrons who understand how the restaurant works and who are considerate of its operational constraints. You should always aim to be considered a "good customer"—here's how:

1. Develop a "portfolio" of three or four preferred restaurants, and concentrate your repeat business on them. You could include a cheap, quick place for lunch; a more expensive place where you know you can linger; a place that accommodates large groups; and one more expensive, very good restaurant where you take your most important clients. Try to include one restaurant that is unique to your city. Giving regular business to a few restaurants, rather than trying every new place that opens, will have a big payoff.

2. Always make reservations, and learn about how far in advance each restaurant takes reservations.

3. If you are going to be late, or if the number of guests changes at the last minute, be sure to call the restaurant, apologize, and explain.

4. Learn the names of the owner or managers, so you can address them with courtesy and hint to them that they remember you from previous visits.

5. Explain ahead of time if the meal has a special purpose, or if you need any special arrangements, such as how the meal will be paid for.

6. Get to know the size of group each restaurant can routinely accommodate and what sizes of tables they offer. If you have a very large group, you should probably rent a function room from a local hotel or arrange to have a meal catered at another venue.

7. Understand the restaurant's peak hours and try to work around them. For example, if a restaurant gets busy by 7 P.M., you can often arrange a group meal at 5:30 that works well with plans for theater, sports, or tours later in the evening. If you are dining at off-peak hours, the restaurant may offer you a small group discount.

8. If you have budget limitations, especially for a group meal, work cooperatively with the restaurant. The managers may well be able to suggest a special menu to suit your price point.

(Continued)

9. For a group dinner, decide in advance whether your firm is going to cover the costs of guests' alcoholic drinks. Make sure your guests understand if they are paying, and arrange for the restaurant to charge people separately.

10. If you know your group is going to be noisy, take a private room. If your group becomes unexpectedly boisterous, encourage the group to move on from the restaurant to a bar or other social setting.

11. And, of course, tip generously. Almost all restaurants will add a 15 percent service charge to the bill for a large group. It's a good idea to personally give a few dollars more in cash, especially for special accommodations or particularly good service.

of wine while they are waiting. But you'll impress no one by insisting on your reservation or your importance.

Most invitations are issued informally, by word of mouth, phone, or e-mail. But if the event has some specific significance, you may issue a written invitation. The form of a printed card bearing a flowery phrase such as "...request the honor of your presence at..." is only used for weddings. The wording you should use can be simple and direct:

> I'd like to invite you to attend a small dinner party in honor of Mariette Fourmeaux, who is joining us as Director of Strategic Planning. We're planning a dinner at Max's next Thursday, the 30th, at 6 P.M. Please let me know if you'll be able to come.

This example uses simple wording to ask for a reply. On invitations you receive, you may see the letters **RSVP** ("répondez s'il vous plait," the French for "Please reply"); it is mandatory that you let the host know whether you are coming or not. However, even when an invitation doesn't say "RSVP," it is good manners to reply whenever you receive an invitation.

If you cannot attend a function, the conventional wording is to express your **regrets** and perhaps mention that you have a prior commitment. You don't have to be specific as to what the commitment is. This is often abbreviated: "I'm afraid I'm going to have to send my regrets—I have a prior commitment." Even when invitations ask for a reply, Americans can be exasperatingly casual about complying with this simple courtesy. So if you are organizing an affair, you should anticipate that you'll need to make follow-up phone calls to be sure who's actually attending.

▪ 10-5 AT THE TABLE

When your group is seated, the waiter will bring menus for each member of the group but possibly only one wine list for the person who most looks like the host. In some subcultures (particularly in California and other winegrowing regions of the United States), one or two people in the group may consider themselves wine experts and may care a great deal about what is ordered. It's not a bad idea to defer to them if they have some preferences, but you should be careful because some bottles of wine can be very expensive and may cost more than the meal itself. If you choose not to drink alcohol, you can politely refuse with a comment such as: "I'll stick to just water for now" (see Section 10-2).

If you are a guest, you'll be asked to order first. The old-fashioned etiquette advice that you should avoid ordering particularly expensive items is still good advice. Even if someone else is paying, appearing respectful of that person's wallet is prudent. It's typical to begin by selecting your main course and then waiting to see whether other people are having soup, salad, or another first course (often called an "appetizer"). You can always pile on at the end, "I'd like a salad too." However, no one would be expected to give an order for dessert at this point in the meal.

In business dining, you should avoid anything unfamiliar or exotic. When you are conducting negotiations, or when the meal is part of a job interview, you should avoid all messy foods such as lobster (which must be cracked and eaten with the hands) or spaghetti dishes (which tend to dribble sauce over whatever you are wearing). If the food seems to all look strange and unusual to you, you're bound to find a safe choice buried somewhere in the menu. If all else fails, you can choose to eat a salad.

If you are not particularly hungry, as may happen if you've traveled far and you are jet-lagged, then there's no offense caused by eating lightly. Even if your host insists: "These are the best steaks outside Kansas City!", you can reasonably say, "I'm upside down because of the time change. I think I'll have something really light." People will respect you, and doing this is much better than ordering a large dish that you don't eat.

Most restaurants make a great effort to bring out the meals of all the people at one table at the same time. But if your dish should arrive first, whether you are the guest or the host, you should wait until everyone else has been served to begin eating. If your guests have been served before you and there appears to be a delay in your meal, you should encourage your guests not to wait for you: "Please, go ahead and start." A good rule to follow is that when the host picks up his or her utensils and begins to eat, you can also start. In family dining and very informal social situations among friends, people may offer samples of their dishes to one another around the table. But this behavior wouldn't be acceptable in most business situations.

Americans love the cuisine of other countries, and some **ethnic foods** come with different courses. For example, Italian meals often include an antipasto (first course), a pasta course, and then a separate meat and vegetable course, before finally reaching "dolce" (sweets or dessert). If you are unfamiliar with the fare, there's no offense in saying, "This is my first time eating (name of the country) food. Tell me what I should be doing here." Your host will guide you and be happy to explain the particular routine. The same applies to restaurants that encourage you to use anything other than a knife and fork. For example, Afghan and some Indian food is eaten with the hand—and strictly only the right hand. If you aren't familiar with this custom, just ask your colleagues how to go about it.

Old-fashioned European cuisine came with multiple courses and enormous numbers of utensils: knives, forks, and spoons (see Figure 10-3). Knowing that one blunt-shaped knife was the butter knife—to be used only for transferring butter from a communal dish to a side plate—was one of innumerable little pieces of protocol that were used to determine who really was a "gentleman." Most Americans would agree that this is silly and that often they are confused about which fork to use. In general, the simple rule for utensils is that where there are multiple courses, you begin with the utensils on the outside (farthest from your plate) and move in as each course goes along. But if you've made a mistake and used a utensil meant for a later course, just say to the server, "And I need another knife..." For many dishes that you order, the waiter will bring additional utensils, such as a soup spoon or (sharp) steak knife.

If you usually use chopsticks at home, the protocol for a knife and fork is pretty simple. In the European style, the knife is always held in the right hand, the fork in the left. Meat and vegetables are cut a little bit at a time, and you use the fork in your left hand to put the food in your mouth. A knife should never enter your mouth, and it's unacceptable to pick up a large piece of food and take bites from it (which is routine in Asian eating). In the American-style use of cutlery, diners cut several pieces of food first (with knife in the right hand, and the left hand using the fork to position the meat or other food), set the knife down, and then switch the fork to the right hand to eat. The knife and fork should be placed resting on the plate,

Figure 10-3   A Formal Place Setting
This is a typical place setting for a formal meal.

never on the table, when not in use. You'll see U.S. businesspeople using both the American and the European style of eating interchangeably.

You'll find that side plates (for bread, for example) are placed to your left, and wine and water glasses are placed to your right, at about the 1 o'clock position relative to your plate. There should be a napkin at your place that you should put on your lap before ordering. If you leave the table during the meal, you should place your loosely folded napkin on the table to indicate that you'll be returning.

In theory, strict etiquette requires that you not talk while you are eating—although in practice, you'll see that most people do talk while eating. In Asian cultures, people cover their mouths if talking or laughing at the table but don't necessarily keep their mouths closed while actually eating. This is a big difference from Western culture, and an important one to learn. Americans may laugh or talk while eating, but otherwise, lips are firmly sealed shut while chewing. Chomping with an open mouth would be considered a distinct lack of manners.

It's considered impolite to lean on your elbows at the table, and your hands should be kept on your lap unless you are handling utensils or

It's Just Different: Leaving the Leftovers

In many Asian cultures, it is common for every scrap of leftovers from a restaurant meal to be boxed and bagged and presented to the host, a practice that has transferred to Chinese restaurants in the United States. The belief is: "It's your food—you've paid for it." Although it's true that some diners of Western cuisine will ask for leftover food to be boxed up for later consumption at home, it's not common in all subcultures.

Carrying out leftovers would be polite only at a family outing. In most business situations, you don't want to be carrying cooked food around with you after dinner or lunch, and hoarding a few morsels from any meal might make you look cheap.

glassware. One common nightmare for the inexperienced business diner is how to handle bread rolls. Don't attempt to saw the roll in half with your knife. Using two hands, break the roll into pieces with the thumb of one hand and butter a small piece at a time.

When you've finished eating, indicate that you are ready for a course to be cleared by placing your knife and fork together in either the "4 o'clock" (U.S. style) or "6 o'clock" (European style) position on your plate. A good server should not have to ask, "Are you finished?" To many international visitors to the United States, the amount of food cleared away uneaten from tables is a scandalous waste. However, it also seems to be a part of the American culture that signals the overall wealth of the economy. In general, it's not customary to take the leftovers from business dining (see *It's Just Different: Leaving the Leftovers*).

10-6 WHEN YOUR MEAL ISN'T RIGHT

If the server brings you the wrong dish, it's probably best to bring the matter to the attention of the server as soon as possible. For example, if you are served something you didn't order, assert the positive: "Ah, mine was the grilled sea bass!" A more difficult situation comes up if your meal isn't prepared correctly (perhaps something is undercooked or tastes strange). In a very formal business setting, you may decide to work around this situation and just avoid eating the offending item. However, if you are the guest, this causes the risk that your host may detect that you are unhappy with your food, and then the whole issue will become escalated. So it is generally better to attract the waiter's attention and quietly explain the problem and propose a solution ("Could you ask the cook to grill it a little longer?" or "Perhaps you could just bring me a hamburger instead?"). You should do so in a way that feigns that the problem is yours, that of course you are asking too much, and that you in no way want to criticize the cook, the cuisine, or your host for selecting this restaurant.

If you detect a lump of gristle or something else inedible in food that's already in your mouth, you will have to discreetly get it out of your mouth and onto your plate, putting it to one side. You can use your fork for this, but an alternative is to bring your napkin up to your mouth, pretend to cough or clear your throat, and take the offending object away. Of course, at this point, you have a lump of something nasty in the napkin on your lap, and it becomes very hard to discreetly dispose of it. But many people would recommend that maneuver.

■ 10-7 GETTING THE ATTENTION OF YOUR SERVER

American waiters are usually readily available throughout a meal, so you should have no difficulty contacting them if you have any request. Indeed, most Europeans visiting the United States find the habit of waiters checking back and asking, "And how is everything?" to be intrusive. But if your waiter is absent, or busy with other tables, there's always a problem of how to attract his or her attention. Perhaps your guest's meal is not cooked correctly, or you really need the bill quickly so you can settle and go on to a meeting.

Don't worry—getting a waiter's attention is something that many people find difficult. The problem is that in liberal, democratic America, any term of address that implies a master/servant relationship is bound to cause offense. So, although "Excuse me, waiter!" is technically correct, most people aren't comfortable using it. Almost no one addresses a waitress as "Waitress!" and "Hey, Miss" is even worse (most women no longer use "Miss" as a title). Quite possibly, your server began the meal with an introduction: "Hi! I'm Gerry, and I'll be your server this evening." (Again, Europeans object to this behavior because they don't want to know wait staff on a first-name basis.) If you've remembered the server's name, then you can call out, "Gerry, when you have a moment..." In most circumstances, you won't remember the server's name. The steps then are to try first to make eye contact, then to exaggeratedly turn in your chair to make eye contact; and if you're still being ignored, the simple phrase "Excuse me!" will usually work.

In Europe, if a server presents a bill before the customer is ready, this could be taken as discourteous haste on the part of the restaurant to get rid of the guest. But in the United States, it's not unusual for the server to place the bill on the table in the middle of the meal, especially at breakfast or lunch. It's just a matter of efficiency, and no one is trying to get you to rush your meal. But most people have experienced the opposite problem at one time or other. The meal is finished, and no bill has appeared. What to do? Some etiquette experts feel that pantomiming writing a bill is poor form, but it's what most people do to signal quietly that they need the bill.

If you are on a tight schedule, it's best to anticipate a long wait for a check at the end of a meal—and avoid it. Alert the server at the beginning of the meal. Saying, "Gerry, just to let you know, we're on a 7 o'clock flight, so we need to be out of here pretty quickly" is acceptable and helpful to the server, who can't guess which guests want to linger at the table.

10-8 UNIVERSAL TERMS OF REFERENCE

After you've mastered how to address your waitperson, you can demonstrate "polish" to your manners by the way you refer to other people at the table. This may seem courtly and perhaps rather old-fashioned, but you'll observe people who have a good understanding of business protocol using these forms of speech.

When you have to refer to someone else while addressing the waiter, it's considered impolite to use the personal pronouns "he," "she," and "they." So the form "She needs more coffee" is technically impolite in formal manners because you are referring to an associate as an unnamed person, "she." It's as if you don't care about her name. But the alternative—"Dawn needs more coffee"—also seems out of place because you won't want to be on first-name terms with the wait staff.

The solution is a group of polite terms that are called **universal terms of reference** (a way to indicate that you are referring to someone else without using a personal name or pronoun). In this example, you would say, "And my colleague [gesture with hand] would like some more coffee." In essence, you are referring to people by their social titles: "my friend," "my mother-in-law," etc.

Although this arcane piece of etiquette probably won't mean much to your waiter, referring to a boss as your "colleague" or someone from another firm as "my colleague" is a subtle pleasantry that may be well appreciated.

■ 10-9 DINNER WITH THE BOSS

The first time you are invited to dinner (or a party) at your boss's house, you are bound to be anxious. With a little research and planning, you can put yourself in a position to enjoy the event and perhaps enhance your career. Before you go, you'll want to have some idea of the level of formality of the function, which may depend on the time of day and on its size, location, and purpose. For example, an annual holiday party in December, scheduled for 8 o'clock in the evening, would usually mean that the menu would be drinks and some snack food, but probably not dinner. The cultural norm determines that you would be dressed in your very best clothes—considerably more smartly dressed than you would usually be at the office. Women at such an event would be wearing very glamorous outfits, appropriate only for evening wear.

On the other hand, if you were invited to your boss's home at 3 P.M. on a summer weekend, you would be way out of place if you turned up in a suit and tie or a dress and high-heeled shoes. You might find that everyone else would be in beach attire, playing at the side of the pool. So it is entirely reasonable to do a little bit of checking around beforehand to see what's expected at an event. Some of your colleagues may have been to similar events before and will be happy to give you some guidance on what to wear and what to expect. If they can't help you, you might feel too embarrassed to ask a senior manager, "What should I wear on Saturday?", but you could certainly ask the manager's assistant: "I'm not really sure about this event on Saturday...Could you give me some hints? How formal is it, and do you know roughly how many people are invited?"

For most large functions, it's expected that you'll bring your spouse or significant other. A **significant other** is the person whom you are sharing your life with, including a spouse, fiancée, partner, or longtime girlfriend or boyfriend. When the invitation encourages you to bring your significant other, you should not bring a casual date—your coworkers will be embarrassed if they make an effort to get to know someone who isn't really part of your life. Invitations should explicitly say who is invited to come with you, and whether children are invited too (for daytime summer functions). Again, if the invitation doesn't make this clear, you should check and make sure—ask your colleagues or the personal assistant of the manager whose name is on the invitation.

Some social functions organized by senior members of a firm are quite large and are a routine part of the firm's annual calendar. For example, in many law firms, all interns may be invited to a barbecue at the end of the summer, held at one of the senior partners' homes. Such a function is likely to be catered (that is, a professional firm will do the cooking and provide waiters), and it will be common knowledge that this lavish event is actually paid for by the firm. For that reason, social custom does not require that you bring a gift for your host (the host is nominal—it's really the whole firm that is hosting the event). However, a "thank you" note after the event (see Section 11-5) would be a good idea.

No matter how routine or how large such an event may be, you should be sensitive to office politics. Are there any people in the firm whom you've wanted to meet? Are there departments with which you'd like to have a better working relationship? And, darkly, are there departments that have been causing your boss trouble? You don't want to be seen cozying up to them. Don't slip in to the event late and leave quietly so that no one knows you were even there—you will miss the opportunity to make use of the social gathering. Out of courtesy, seek out and greet your immediate supervisor first, and ask her or him to introduce you to senior managers. If the event is large, your host may not know your name or your position in the firm, so you should try to be introduced. If no one is around to introduce you, don't hesitate to introduce yourself and describe your position and, in a general way, the work you've been doing for the firm. However, you should avoid detailed discussion of business issues at such a social gathering. Spouses and other guests who don't work at the firm will be bored by endless discussions of work projects, and there's also a danger that you'll violate the firm's confidentiality.

What are acceptable topics of conversation, then? The conventional wisdom is that you should not talk about sex, politics, or religion in polite society. But this is probably a bit out of date—indeed, you may think that Americans talk of nothing else! (In practice, much social talk is also about sports.) Freedom of speech is a fundamental American value, so of course, you can express any opinion you want about any political person, issue, or position. Common sense will dictate that you do so with tact (don't refer to the president as "an idiot," for example). It's perfectly acceptable to make comments about the differences between U.S. customs and those of other cultures, as long as you are politically correct (see Section 15-9).

10-10 DINING AT HOME WITH YOUR COWORKERS

If you get along well with your coworkers, the time will soon come when you are invited for a meal at a colleague's home. Just as in social functions with your superiors, you'll be most comfortable if you have a reasonable idea of how big the function is going to be, whether it is for some specific purpose (for example, a birthday party or to celebrate a promotion), and what level of formality to expect. This will give you some idea of what to wear, whether to bring a gift, what food will be served, and how long you'll stay. In most cases you would be expected to bring a spouse or significant other, although again, you might want to check on that if the invitation doesn't make this clear.

There is a wide range of possibilities concerning whether you should bring some food, drink, or a gift. The expectation will depend on both the broad cultural context of your firm (for example, whether the firm is located in Manhattan or in Silicon Valley) and the specific company culture. Because there is quite a bit of variation in what is accepted and expected, you'll have to do some specific research into your firm's protocol to be confident of the correct approach.

At one end of the scale, for example, a spontaneous party suggested by one of the junior—and hence lowest-paid—members of your work group, you may be expected to contribute substantially to the food at the event. This is explicitly so if the event is designated as a **potluck** (a social gathering where everyone invited is expected to bring a dish of food for others to eat). For many parties among peers, it's expected that you just bring some alcohol to contribute—either wine, beer, or a bottle of liquor, roughly equivalent to the amount you and your guest will drink during the event. The way to handle this uncertainty is to ask the host directly when you accept the invitation, "And may I bring something?" You should take the answer "No, just bring yourself" at its face value. At the other end of the scale, there are some events where attempting to bring something would be positively wrong. There are few things more embarrassing than turning up at a party with a casserole dish in hand, only to find that the event is being professionally catered.

▶ > > PUT THIS CHAPTER INTO PRACTICE

1. Next time you are out dining with friends or family, practice getting the attention of your waiter in a professional manner. For example, ask for the water glasses to be refilled or for some plates to be cleared.

2. Select three restaurants in your community that would serve for different kinds of business meals discussed in this chapter.

3. Practice graciously splitting the check after a meal with a friend. Use the phrase "I'm working on splitting all checks."

■ KEY TERMS

ethnic food

potluck

regrets

RSVP

significant other

split the bill, split the tab

universal terms of reference

Multiple Choice Practice Questions: To take the review quiz for this chapter, log on to your Online Edition at www.atomicdog.com.

Chapter 11

Social Skills

Not all business is "strictly business"—social conventions play an important role.

Abhijit really liked his first job at a prestigious Silicon Valley high-technology firm, and he was anxious to make a good impression in every way. Each day, he was one of the first to arrive at work. One day, shortly after Thanksgiving, he came in early as usual and saw a box wrapped in red and green paper on his desk. His mind began to race—he'd heard about Christmas presents, but he wasn't really sure how they worked. Although Abhijit was a U.S. native, his parents had immigrated to the United States and had avoided any family practice of religion. So even though he thought he had a pretty good handle on business protocol, he'd never experienced holiday gift giving. Now here was someone else in the work group who'd beaten him at something by being the first person to buy gifts for everyone on the team. He quickly drove to the nearest shopping center, and finding the office supply store open, he bought wallets, fancy pens—even a nice leather briefcase for his boss. He wrapped the gifts in appropriate festive paper, added cards, and was back in the office in time to place his presents on the desk of every member of his team.

Later that day, he was at dinner with a friend who worked in a different industry and who had been celebrating Christmas for many years. "Good heavens! You weren't supposed to do that!" his friend said as Abhijit related the story of his early morning panic and the huge unplanned expenditure on gifts.

"Well, that's the point of the story," continued Abhijit. "The box that was on my desk was just a cheap box of chocolates from my boss. Everyone seemed terribly embarrassed to be opening gifts from me, and of course, they had no gifts to exchange. The whole thing was a total disaster, and I was left with a box of chocolates and a boss looking very uncomfortable with a leather briefcase."

"What's worse, you know," added the friend, "those cheap chocolates were just charged to the firm—your boss didn't even pay for them."

All cultures are full of unspoken rules about social interaction, and it's impossible to try to stick to just doing your job and hoping that you won't have to make any judgments about complex social situations.

As you make the transition from college to the working world, or from doing business outside the United States to working in America, you'll soon see that professionalism involves much more than simply doing the tasks of your job. Although the protocol for handling business dining discussed in the previous chapter is fairly straightforward, business often presents more complex situations that involve the interface of professional and personal conduct.

■ 11-1 CEREMONIES MARKING LIFE EVENTS

In the casual American culture, the boundary between business and friendship is often blurred, but the boundary between what is considered "business" and what belongs to "family" is much clearer. Unless you have developed a personal friendship with a coworker, there is little requirement that you attend or even acknowledge many of the ceremonies that mark the major life events for a coworker. Weddings, engagements, births, baptisms, first communions, graduations, and funerals of family members may go completely unremarked by coworkers. This is in contrast with the culture in Latin America, where coworkers might be invited (and expected to attend) important family celebrations, and in Japan, where the presence of a company official at a worker's funeral is considered essential.

Even though your presence isn't going to be required at any of these rites of passage, you may well receive an invitation to one of these events. Here are some examples of events that you might be invited to by coworkers, beginning with the happy events. When a coworker becomes pregnant, people in the same work group might get together and hold a small party, called a "shower" (for showering the recipient with gifts), and each guest may be expected to bring some modest baby-related gift (for example, an item of clothing), or the whole group might join together to get a more substantial item (such as a car seat or stroller). If it's possible, it'll be less work for you if you can join in the "from all of us" gift.

A shower might also be held for a colleague who is getting married, although by custom usually only for the bride. The gifts have traditionally been items for the home, but because many couples now live together before marriage, or may be merging two existing households, there is less need for basic household items such as pots and pans. If you have received a personal invitation to a wedding, whether you plan to accept or not, you will be sending a personal gift so you can opt out of any group gift at the office. The couple who are about to get married will likely let you know where they are registered—they'll give guests the name of one or two stores where they have set up their "wish list" for gifts. You go to the store and choose something on their list in the price range of what you are prepared to pay.

How large a gift you should send is a complex function of your wealth and how well you know one or both of the bridal party. It's not wrong to bring a gift with you to a wedding, but because you'll have to balance it on your knees during the ceremony, and the bride and groom will be busy welcoming guests at the reception, it's preferable to send the gift ahead of time. By tradition, gifts were always sent to the bride, but if you know only the groom, sending the gift to the groom, with both names on the accompanying card, would be acceptable.

It's most unlikely that you would be invited to a baptism or first communion—the separation of church and state is reflected in keeping most religious beliefs separate from the workplace. However, if you decide that the personal relationship is strong enough that you want to attend, you may be at a loss to know what is expected of you. Because the United States is a pluralistic society, no one will expect you to be familiar with the protocol details of all faiths. However, before attending you'll need to know what clothing is appropriate and what you'll be expected to do and not do. Don't be afraid to ask before the event, and then carefully follow the behavior of other people.

Sometimes proud parents send out a graduation announcement when their child finishes high school or college. It's a protocol error to send out such announcements to people at work, because it implies that a congratulatory gift is expected. Don't allow yourself to feel obligated to send a gift—the obligation falls on only direct family members.

If a coworker suffers the death of an immediate family member, you probably would be expected neither to turn up at the funeral nor to send flowers. However, most people would express their concern with a personal or group card. More importantly, the work group would make a practical expression of concern and support by temporarily taking on the colleague's duties. When the coworker returns to work, the cultural norm would be to make the briefest mention of the bereavement, something like, "I'm sure this has been a tough time for you," and then not go much further into personal details. Similarly, if a coworker has a parent, spouse, or child who is seriously ill, you can express your concern and think about the help that you can offer in the workplace to support your colleague.

A different situation exists when a colleague dies. If a coworker is in an accident, either while traveling or at the workplace, the entire work group may close the office and attend the funeral, while also contributing flowers. If a colleague dies of natural causes (say, a heart attack), the work group would probably send a fairly extravagant floral display to the funeral ("from all of us at XYZ Corp"), but whether to attend a funeral is not as clear. The funeral may be held according to a religious rite with which you are unfamiliar, or it may be considered a strictly family affair. So your presence, no matter how well intentioned, might be perceived as an intrusion into a period of private grief. On the other hand, having no representatives from the work group might be considered disrespectful ("They worked him into the ground, and this is all the thanks we get!"). It may take some very tactful negotiation with the survivors, ideally with the member of the work group who knows the family members best. Be guided by their wishes.

In general, senior managers don't make an appearance at the funerals of people who didn't work directly for them. However, an exception to this is when there is an on-the-job accident resulting in death, when the highest company official (such as the CEO) would be required to attend the funeral. In such circumstances, a token appearance at the religious service is sufficient, and the official might leave before any graveside services or other function where only the family would be expected to be present.

▪ 11-2 OTHER PEOPLE'S BUSINESS

Avoiding gossip is one of the cardinal tenets of professionalism discussed in Chapter 1. Of course, when you work closely with a group of people over several months, you'll get to know some details of what is going on in their lives, and you are bound to become aware of your coworkers' personal problems. Although you may want to appear concerned or even sympathetic, you don't want to cross the line between business and family life and become overinvolved in someone else's problems. In general, if you feel you're being drawn into the role of confidant in some hopeless domestic drama, you will have to use some tact to indicate that while you are concerned, you cannot play the role of counselor. It is appropriate to extricate yourself if you feel that you are becoming overinvolved by emphasizing a group response. For example, instead of being a reliable shoulder to cry on for a colleague who is going through a divorce, you could acknowledge the topic when your coworker brings it up and say: "This must be a very difficult time for you. If you need a few days off to move into your new place, I'm sure all the people on the team can help to cover for you here at work."

If a colleague appears to have a personal problem that is affecting his or her ability to function at work, your first inclination may be to ignore the situation and hope that it gets better. But if marital discord, spousal abuse, or alcohol or drug dependence is involved, the situation is very unlikely to resolve itself. No matter how tempting it is to offer your advice, you should not become overinvolved with someone else's difficulties. Most firms have an **Employee Assistance Program (EAP)** (you can find out about it from the Human Resources Department) that has trained professionals who can direct your colleague to appropriate resources. If you allow someone to share too much information about personal pro-blems, returning the relationship to a well-functioning business rapport later may become very difficult for you.

If a colleague is away for an extended period due to serious illness, family bereavement, or maternity leave, most work groups will reassign duties and will "cover" for the absent team members. How long the team continues to cover the workload will depend on how long the absence is expected to continue, the nature of the work, and the company culture. You may be provided with quite a bit of information about an ailing col-league's health status, hospitalizations, recovery, and so on. However, you shouldn't be too intrusive when questioning if information isn't offered to you. For example, if you are told that a colleague has been hospitalized, it is considered impolite to ask, "Oh, what for?" Leave it up to the person involved to decide how much information to share. We'll return to the issue of illness later in Section 11-7 when we think about what to do if you become ill yourself.

11-3 GIFT GIVING

The customs of gift giving differ more strikingly from one culture to another than any other behavioral marker. In most Asian cultures, it is unthinkable for a businessperson to make a first contact with another company without bringing or sending in advance a substantial gift. At the other end of the scale, a Scandinavian businessperson would be shocked to receive a gift in a business setting and might simply send it back.

In American culture, firms and executives almost never exchange ceremonial gifts. However, there are a few occasions when it is appropriate to bring a small gift, especially if you are the recipient of a social invitation that you are unlikely to reciprocate. For example, if your boss invites you and a few coworkers to her house for dinner, you probably don't plan to invite everyone else to your house in the near future. On these occasions, the cultural expectation is that you will arrive with a small gift—there's a very good word for this in German, a **mitbringsel** (something *brought with*). The gift is not an attempt to provide equal value to the hospitality you are going to receive, but merely a token of appreciation.

Traditional *mitbringsels* are cut flowers or a bottle of wine. But they are by no means riskless choices. If your host is welcoming quite a large group of guests, or if the setting is a formal dinner party, thrusting a bunch of flowers into her hands on the doorstep requires her to stop preparations to go find a vase. Moreover, in subcultures (see Chapter 1) where a well-trained host would be expected to have already thought about appropriate flower arrangements (Chicago and Manhattan would be examples), arriving with flowers in hand subtly implies that you expect that your hosts will be deficient in this area. The same can be true for arriving with food. Although in Asian American circles, arriving with an elaborate dessert in hand would be customary politeness, in many other U.S. homes it would be taken as an implication that the hosts couldn't be expected to plan a complete meal, and hence it is an unintended insult to their menu-planning abilities.

A good choice for a *mitbringsel* is a small gourmet item of food that demonstrably is not meant to be part of the actual meal. Choose something modest but interesting that doesn't involve special handling. Unlike bringing a permanent object (like a vase), where you have to guess at your hosts' decorating preferences, this type of gift is something that doesn't require much knowledge of your hosts' tastes.

If you are confident of your wines, or if you recently took a trip to a wine-growing region, a bottle of wine is an acceptable *mitbringsel* in most cases. Don't be surprised if your wine is not served at the meal—your hosts may already have selected something else. If you have any reason to suspect that your hosts are expert oenophiles (wine lovers) and you know very little about wine, don't embarrass yourself by picking up a bottle of nonvintage wine at the supermarket—come up with another gift idea instead.

Unlike in Asian cultures, in which the wrapping is sometimes more important than the gift itself, most people in America don't pay too much attention to wrapping. You may well see people hand over a bottle of wine unwrapped or in a brown paper bag. However, some small effort in wrapping your *mitbringsel* would always be appreciated and would signal that you thought about this in advance. The one setback is to make sure that you have removed the price tag from whatever you bring, as this is probably true in all cultures in the world. You don't want to seem to be either bragging or "cheap."

A reasonable alternative to arriving with a gift in hand is to send a gift afterward. For example, if you were on a business trip, and to your surprise a business dinner turned out to be an invitation to an associate's house, you would probably have little chance to repay the hospitality at the time. So a particularly gracious gesture would be to send a small souvenir from your home office, or perhaps an arrangement of flowers to your hosts a week or so after you return. This is also a good way to demonstrate your thanks when you've been a houseguest (stayed overnight at someone else's house).

In general, only close personal friends exchange birthday gifts beyond childhood years. However, it may be the custom in your office for everyone to get together to buy a single gift to acknowledge the birthday of a team member. This piece of subculture often begins when several managers depend on the work of one support person who should be recognized—and there's no better time than a birthday to say "thank you" for months of loyal service. But you may come across a situation that has escalated to the point where there is a group gift for every birthday, engagement, promotion, retirement, anniversary, and so on. Before long, it seems that every other day there is a solicitation for someone or other. The burden falls unequally on lower-paid staff: The $5 to $10 that is "pocket change" for executives represents a significant amount of money for hourly paid support staff. You may end up giving money toward a gift for people you don't know very well or don't particularly like. So if you are a manager or have an opportunity to influence the culture, try to minimize gift giving and limit celebration of personal events to a card and some modest token of appreciation such as a cake for the whole work group. If you become responsible for buying a gift on behalf of a group, try to avoid "gag" gifts (such as a bottle of aspirin, implying that someone's job is a big headache) and anything that is overly personal (such as lingerie).

Most American firms don't arrange for elaborate gifts for business associates from other firms. Indeed, presenting a purchasing officer with any gift of value, such as an expensive bottle of scotch, might be seen as an attempt at a bribe. Gifts of money are definitely unacceptable (see *It's Just Different: Gifts of Money Are Frowned on in U.S. Business*). With the possible exception of the Hollywood movie industry, firms do not go to elaborate efforts to send gifts to individuals. Usually, gifts are limited to little **tchotchkes** (pronounced "CHOCH-kees") (literally "trinkets," that is, souvenirs of little real value), especially promotional items that are printed with your firm's name and logo (see Figure 11-1). Note that it's illegal to give anything of significant value (even tickets to sporting or cultural events) to a procurement officer of the military or government. So if your firm is selling to institutional buyers, make sure you are trained carefully on the rules.

It's Just Different: Gifts of Money Are Frowned on in U.S. Business

Gifts of money are common in most Asian cultures. In Western cultures, within families, people may give cash gifts to close younger relatives such as nephews or nieces, often with a specific designated purpose. However, you should be careful with simple cash gifts in all U.S. business settings. They could look like bribes. In almost all cases in which you are expected to give a gift to a colleague, a cash gift would look out of place and might cause embarrassment.

When a group of employees is giving a gift (such as at a senior colleague's retirement), and they really don't know what the recipient would like, then a gift certificate issued by a retail store is reasonable. An exception to the "no cash gifts" rule would be when your group is giving a gift to a low-paid service worker such as a janitor or cafeteria worker. In the case of a very low paid worker, cash might be welcome—but for a worker paid on salary, such as your secretary or assistant, a cash gift would at best look as if you didn't care enough to think of something suitable to give. When you decide that a cash gift is best, choose a round number such as $50 or $100, go to the bank and get a nice, crisp new bill, and enclose it in a card with a note acknowledging something personal about the work that the employee has done. As you may have experienced yourself, a thoughtful card is often more valuable than the gift itself.

Figure 11-1   Company Gift
In U.S. companies, gifts are often limited to small items, especially those that are printed with your firm's name and logo.

You will encounter a great deal of variation in the practice of gift giving at the holiday season at the end of the year. In general, no gifts are distributed at Thanksgiving, although mining, manufacturing, and retail firms often used to supply their workers with free turkeys. The practice is fading away as workers are better paid, may be dining with family, may prefer cash, and so on. Being invited to attend Thanksgiving dinner with a colleague would be a special honor because this meal is traditionally a gathering for extended family only. You certainly would want to acknowledge this kindness with a small gift.

Your firm or supervisor may give you a small gift in late December, although it likely won't specifically mention Christmas, as many employees may celebrate other religious or cultural holidays. The gift will likely be small and impersonal—for example, something edible or a desk calendar. You should not respond with a similar gift to your boss. You are not expected to reciprocate, and in any case, your firm probably paid for the gifts. Within the work environment, most companies discourage people from exchanging gifts among peers. The reasons are that someone invariably gets left out, and inevitably there are disparities in the values of the gifts and consequent hurt feelings.

There are two exceptions to this rule. Some firms organize a gift exchange as part of a holiday party. Often this is done by a system called "Secret Santa," in which coworkers draw names for other people in their work group so that each person receives one gift without knowing whom it was from. You will be given some guidance on the price range and should stay within that range. You can choose something thoughtfully to match the coworker's interests and hobbies (such as a book), but again you should try to stay away from overly personal items such as lingerie or joke gifts.

The second exception occurs when a support person does work for a whole group and receives little recognition for an extraordinary effort. For example, a mailperson or custodian may deserve a reward at the holidays. If this seems like a good idea, try to make the gift from the whole work group so that you don't look like you are trying to show off or to gain special favors.

■ 11-4 RECEIVING GIFTS

If a visitor to your firm brings a gift that is more than just a token *tchotchke*, you are faced with a difficult situation. Unless you're working on a government contract, you can reasonably accept the gift as long as it is of moderate value (say less than $25), whether or not your firm has something of equivalent value to offer in return. If the donor is from another country, you can both accept and simultaneously indicate that a gift really isn't necessary.

In some cultures, it is considered unseemly to hastily unwrap a gift at once—but in U.S. culture, it is always acceptable to unwrap a gift as soon as it is presented. If an international visitor hands you a beautifully wrapped gift, the polite response would be to comment on the wrapping and ask, "May I open it now?" If the gift is too generous, or too personal, you should decline with great tact. For example, instead of a plain vase, you are presented with a complete set of crystal. You'll have to be both gracious and clear in your refusal: "Oh, it's lovely, but I'm afraid I simply can't accept!" You can explain your firm's strict rules or, ultimately, state the truth: "It's a cultural difference...We usually don't give and receive such generous gifts at work. I sincerely appreciate the thought, but I'm afraid I can't accept this." Beware that in some cultures, every gift that is accepted is preceded by at least three ritual refusals and reoffering of the gift. So anticipate that you may have to repeat your firm, gracious refusal.

If you receive a gift for a social occasion (for example, your birthday) and it's accompanied by a card, the polite protocol is to carefully open and read the card first before opening the gift (etiquette teaches that the kind thoughts expressed are more valuable than the gift).

■ 11-5 "THANK YOU" NOTES

Is it almost impossible to write too many "thank you" notes? Well, a beautiful card with the following message clearly diminishes the value of all the other thank you notes that you write:

> Dear Melissa,
>
> I want to thank you for loaning me your stapler this morning when I couldn't find mine.
>
> Sincerely, Adrian

But a card left on a colleague's desk with the following message might have a big impact:

> Hairi,
>
> Just a note to thank you for the extra effort on the presentation materials for this weekend's sales force team meeting. You caught that we had omitted page 13, and stayed late on Friday to reprint the packets. Thank you for your dedication to the team and for helping make the meeting a success.
>
> Barbara

You should send a **"thank you" note** for any gift you've received and for any event that had a specific invitation, unless you are really sure that it was a big corporate event paid for by your firm (and even then, a brief note to someone who made the arrangements isn't a bad idea). It's a good idea to keep on hand some small greeting cards with generic scenes (for example, landscapes) that you can use for such notes; you don't need to buy cards that specifically say "Thank you" on the front. A handwritten note on plain paper is also fine, but in strict etiquette, the formal style is to use a **correspondence card**—a nice piece of stationery with your own name printed in calligraphy or a stylish script.

As a general rule, all thank you notes should be handwritten, but there are some exceptions. If your handwriting is simply unreadable, you can write a note on your computer, as long as it is very carefully formatted. (And you should probably think seriously about improving your handwriting in the meantime!)

In a few circumstances, e-mail thanks would be acceptable. If your work group routinely uses e-mail, and if a colleague has provided you with information or assistance, a short "e-thanks" would be appropriate. If you are interviewing and the firm has been communicating with you through e-mail, then an e-mail thanks may be necessary, especially if the recruiters have indicated that a decision will be made in the next couple of days (see Chapter 13). For everything else, a handwritten note is best.

The form of a thank you note is as follows:

- Express your thanks for the event.
- Say what you particularly liked.
- Close with something personal.

For example, the following would be an appropriate thank you note for dinner at someone's home:

Dear Raji and Amalia,

Thank you for the wonderful dinner at your house last week. I really liked meeting so many members of the firm who I just knew by name. The Indian food was great, and I enjoyed trying the dozens of different dishes.

With best wishes, Xuanming

11-6 TAKING CARE OF PERSONAL NEEDS

Both in social situations and during recruiting, many young business-people have difficulty in managing basic physiological needs. For example, a job candidate is in the middle of a schedule of back-to-back interviews and is just dying of thirst. Is it impolite to stop and get a drink? Worse, two interviews later, the hastily chugged bottle of water now seeks a place to go—where is the restroom?

We often forget that interviewers and hosts experience the same needs, so we should not be embarrassed about seeking comfort. During an interview schedule, the line "I need to take a short break here" is a way to broach the topic. In social settings, although everyone might realize where you're going and what you're about to do, it's ungracious to announce the specifics of your intentions. The phrase "I need to excuse myself for a moment..." is a sufficient courtesy.

In many countries in the world, toilets are referred to by **euphemisms** (a beautiful sounding word for something less than beautiful). Every culture has its own polite term, and it may be obscure. For example, consider the differences between U.S. and British English. U.S. speakers of English never refer directly to a "toilet" and would be modestly embarrassed if you used the word. Instead, the preferred terms are "restroom" or "men's (women's) room." Some speakers of British English would have no idea what a "restroom" is, but the ever-polite British would offer a guest use of a toilet with the euphemism: "Would you like to use the facilities?" (It's tempting to answer: "Wow! You have Internet here—that's great, I'd love to check my e-mail.")

In U.S. business, if the purpose of your request to take a break is not obvious, and your host does not offer directions ("The restroom is down the hall..."), you'll need to ask. You can do so without embarrassment as long as you use the correct euphemism. You can ask for the location of the nearest men's (or women's) room without further explanation. The room may also be referred to as the "bathroom" or "restroom," although there is no bath in there, and the function of the room is certainly not to "rest"!

In general, men do not accompany one another to the restroom, and you may cause offense if you volunteer: "I'll come with you!" Women don't seem to follow this rule (perhaps because their toilets come with separate stalls), and indeed, in social settings, women may excuse themselves en masse to go to the restroom. However, even for two women, offering to accompany your boss or an interviewer to the restroom might be uncomfortable.

To avoid the social embarrassment of being in the restroom with a superior, most workers plan their restroom breaks when they can see that their boss is clearly occupied. In interview situations, a good trick is to take advantage of the toilets on the floor below your scheduled interview, so there's little chance of running into the person who ends up being your interviewer. If you do run into someone in the bathroom, you are faced with the unpleasant choice of either ignoring him or her or making small talk—either way, it's unlikely to put you at ease. If you enter a bathroom and find yourself "caught" because a superior is using a urinal, a nice pleasantry is to pretend that you just have something to wash off your hands so that you are at the sink and not side by side in uncomfortable closeness with your boss.

The same kinds of euphemisms and bathroom etiquette work if you are invited to a private home, such as to a dinner or party at your boss's home. You may also encounter the additional phrase "powder room." Again, saying "May I use the toilet?" would cause either laughter or offense because it's too direct.

◾ 11-7 PERSONAL ILLNESS

Most Americans are remarkably healthy, and although most U.S. companies have generous policies for **sick leave** (paid time off from work), most executives rarely stay home from work with an illness. Americans treat common colds either as if they are not infectious diseases (although they are, of course) or as if their germs are so endemic (you probably caught the cold from someone else at work) that they are just a hazard of daily life that must be ignored. Minor sports injuries requiring a sling or a cast are considered to be a badge of courage, and no one would expect you to stay home to recuperate.

It's appropriate to stay away from work if you have a fever or if you are actively vomiting. But in that case, you would certainly want to let your supervisor and your coworkers know; phone just after the time when you'd usually arrive at work so your colleagues won't worry about what has happened to you and they can plan to cover your duties. Even when someone has been advised by his or her physician to rest at home, that person is likely to at least stay in touch by e-mail and may indeed work from home for a few days. If illness strikes you while you are in the middle of an important business meeting, it may be foolish to try to ignore your symptoms (see *Business Protocol in Action: "I'm Feeling a Little Queasy..."*).

Your personal health—or illness—is theoretically a private matter outside the workplace domain. However, when an illness requires an absence from work, most American employees would provide a "need to know" explanation to their direct supervisor of the circumstances of an illness, the severity, and likely prognosis. If you have to stay away from work or if you are hospitalized, your company may require a doctor's note (written confirmation that you are under a physician's care and that the severity of your illness prevents you from coming to work). Your doctor's office is set up to provide these notes as a matter of routine, so don't worry about asking for one. Occasionally, at very large firms, you may be required to present documentation to your Human Resources office for sick time. That may involve a rather redundant visit to your doctor's office just to confirm that you have the flu and you need to stay home for a few days.

In interview situations, there may indeed be rare times when you are just too ill to keep an appointment. You wouldn't want to lose the chance of a good job by interviewing when you are not at your best. Discuss your situation with family and friends and take their best advice as to whether this is a time to push through minor discomfort or to call off an interview.

Business Protocol in Action: "I'm Feeling a Little Queasy..."

In January 1992, President George Bush (Senior) was facing a serious reelection challenge, and to show that his administration was getting tough over the issue of a mounting trade deficit between Japan and the United States, he arranged a state visit to Japan. Unfortunately, during a formal dinner he apparently suffered food poisoning (although his press office later referred to it as "stomach flu"), and he collapsed at the table and threw up.

Worse, as he sank into the arms of his host, Japanese prime minister Kiichi Miyazawa, according to some press reports, Bush threw up onto his host's lap. Although Bush gamely went on TV the next day and asked, "Which of us hasn't had an upset stomach from time to time?", the incident hardly helped U.S.-Japan relations. Repeated rebroadcasting of Bush being helped from the scene undoubtedly weakened Bush's presidential image at home and was one small factor in contributing to his defeat in the general election.

The moral of this story is, no matter how important a business function is that you feel you must attend, if you are feeling ill, it is better to make polite excuses and stay home. And if you feel unwell at a function, you should get to a bathroom as quickly as possible.

If you need to cancel and reschedule, call the recruiter as soon as possible and give a clear but not overly detailed description of your situation and ask when you might be able to reschedule. If the recruiter implies that by canceling, you will miss a once-in-a-lifetime opportunity, your line should be, "There has to be some way to work this out." Point out the benefits of you not sharing all your germs with the recruiter's office.

However, you should be careful to never use illness as a false excuse to miss work or resolve a schedule conflict (see *Doing the Right Thing: Never "Call In" When You Are Not Ill*).

■ 11-8 SMOKING IS INVARIABLY DISCOURAGED

Fewer than 20 percent of Americans now smoke cigarettes, and because smoking is more popular among people who have non-office jobs and among people who grew up when smoking was more popular (people over

Doing the Right Thing: Never "Call In" When You Are Not Ill

Beware of claiming illness when you have a schedule conflict, such as when you've committed to one job interview but a better opportunity comes up. In general, Americans show little sympathy for someone who begs off because of a cold (over-the-counter remedies can mitigate the worst symptoms, no matter how bad you feel), and if you lie about illness, the potential for being found out is enormous.

If you falsely claim to be ill to balance a tight interview schedule and your "excuse" is discovered, you'll most likely be ruled out for both jobs. Remember, recruiters in the same industry often get to meet one another at career fairs, and who they've just hired may be the first topic of conversation.

In the workplace, **calling in** (that is, phoning to say that you are sick and must stay home) when you are not sick could lead to instant dismissal. If you miss work to attend a sporting event on sick time, sure enough, when you turn around from picking up your tickets, you bump into your divisional vice president and two important clients. This inappropriate behavior could get you fired immediately.

60, for instance), you are likely to find that fewer than 10 percent of your coworkers smoke. Smoking is universally prohibited on airplanes, in all offices, and in many bars, and restaurants, and even in public places such as parks and beaches in most states. Smoking is also not permitted in cinemas, theaters, and hotel lobbies, as well as in many hotel rooms and rental cars. You will probably find that your firm bans smoking not only in meetings, restrooms, lunchrooms, and cafeterias, but also in your private office, due to the risks attributed to secondhand smoke (exhaled smoke that others, probably nonsmokers, breathe in).

Although some airports may have designated smoking lounges, and some states do permit smoking in bars, the smoker will experience considerable problems in the office environment in the United States. Because your company will probably not allow you to smoke in your own office, you will be required to take your smoking breaks outside the building (see Figure 11-2). In large cities, even in winter, you will see clusters of workers gathered outside the entrance to office buildings, having a smoke. But even this activity is becoming regulated, as many nonsmokers don't want to walk through a gauntlet of smokers on their way into the building, and people complain if smoke drifts in through windows or ventilation.

Figure 11-2   No Smoking in Business
Smoking is prohibited in most office buildings in the United States, and employees who smoke must do so outdoors.
Source: © 2009 Jupiterimages Corporation.

In California, regulations recently adopted have banned smoking within 20 feet of a doorway to a building, so the cluster of smokers outside office buildings has become even more removed. (German visitors have joked that "California is a 'no smoking' state" because of its strict limitations.)

So if you are a smoker, in theory, you manage your habit by planning to take regular smoking breaks throughout the day. In practice, in most businesses, taking these breaks becomes quite difficult. You have to interrupt the flow of meetings, and because most of your colleagues won't be taking these breaks, it is true that they might resent your constantly leaving the work setting. Moreover, if your job requires long-distance travel, you'll be constantly facing long, smokeless plane flights.

You can see that there is tremendous pressure on executives to quit smoking, and quitting is one of your options. If you can't quit, you'll most likely have to cut back your frequency of smoking and work hard to try to take advantage of natural breaks between meetings to grab a few moments to smoke outside. Many young office workers have resorted to nicotine gum or nicotine patches to handle their craving between smoking breaks and while on long flights. Becoming a nonsmoker would probably be a better option to avoid all of the obstacles that smokers face in the business setting.

If you are a smoker, unless you have seen a coworker smoking, you should never offer him or her a cigarette. And you should never ask, "Do you mind if I smoke?" because you would be expected to know that there are strict rules against smoking in most places. Although colleagues might give you permission, they might feel put on the spot and asked to say yes to something they didn't like.

▷ ▷ ▷ PUT THIS CHAPTER INTO PRACTICE

1. Write a formal "thank you" note to acknowledge exceptional service.

2. Ask businesspeople if they've ever received a gift that was excessively generous and ask how they handled the situation.

3. When you are shopping, look for ideas for business gifts that might be appropriate for you to take if you were doing business overseas.

KEY TERMS

calling in	*mitbringsel*
correspondence card	sick leave
Employee Assistance Program (EAP)	*tchotchke*
euphemism	"thank you" note

Multiple Choice Practice Questions: To take the review quiz for this chapter, log on to your Online Edition at www.atomicdog.com.

Chapter 12

Recruiting

No matter how much you love your current job, you should always be looking for your next one.

American business runs in cycles of boom and bust. One year everyone is getting multiple job offers and switching companies after just a few months in a position, and the next year, no firms are hiring. So even when you're satisfied with your current position and your promotion prospects look good, keeping your eyes open for new opportunities makes sense. By keeping your résumé up-to-date, you'll be ready for any opportunities that come your way.

American business is simply not structured for lifetime career opportunities. (If you want to get a picture of this situation, look up which firms were at the top of the Fortune 500 list 10 years ago.) So you should be looking to develop your own career, independent of the success of an individual firm.

Make sure you keep your résumé up-to-date. At the very least, review it twice a year (say, at the beginning of the year and at the Fourth of July). Does it reflect all your skills and interests? Does it include your most recent accomplishments? Does it include details that are now irrelevant?

There's another benefit to this semiannual review: Although it's true that your résumé reflects your life, it's also true that your life reflects your résumé. If you struggle over the "Interests" section and can't find anything new to add, perhaps you're working too hard and you've lost balance in your life. If everything in the "Education" section happened in a previous decade, perhaps it's time to take a new course.

■ 12-1 RECRUITING ON-CAMPUS AND OFF

It's helpful to think about the process of getting a job from the perspective of three different situations. First, there's **on-campus recruiting.** Whether you are completing a bachelor's degree or graduate training, the firms that want to hire will come to you. This is an enviable position to be in, and will be the easiest recruiting experience of your life. You should be sure to take advantage of scheduled on-campus recruiting. Make sure you understand the rules for your university's career center, which may require you to sign up or to "bid" preference points for certain employers. It's likely that you'll be required to submit a résumé in a particular format that is common to all students. Many firms use a process called "résumé drop": You indicate your interest in a firm by submitting a copy of your résumé without a **cover letter**. A cover letter is a short letter in which you express your interest in and suitability for a particular position (see Section 12-16). Once you've submitted your résumé (often by online submission), the firms decide which candidates are to be invited for interviews. Many—but not all—schools permit recent graduates (or any alumni from their school) to participate in on-campus recruiting, sometimes for an additional fee.

The second situation is when you are "between jobs" (a euphemism for "unemployed"). There are many specialized books on job hunting, so this brief summary should not be considered a substitute for further reading if you are in this situation. The main feature of this type of job search is that you should actively seek out job leads from as many sources as possible. Experts say that after the first postcollege job, most people find their jobs through personal contacts, not through applying to posted jobs. If your period of unemployment from your main profession is likely to last for more than a few weeks, it's a good idea to take on temporary or contract work so that you have some income while you are job searching. (You can omit such work from your résumé, and if you are asked at an interview, you should answer honestly but label the work as unimportant in the whole context of your career.) You should make sure that your résumé is available online at the major job-search Web sites and on any site that is specific to your skills.

In some industries, professional recruiters (so-called **headhunter**s) can be helpful intermediaries when you are between jobs. They may know of positions that are vacant but not publicly announced. Sadly, headhunters invariably try to switch people who are employed from one firm to another (they use internal contacts and phone around), while often shunning people who are currently out of work. However, if you get the name of a headhunter, submitting a résumé and attempting to set up a meeting can be worthwhile. If nothing else, a friendly headhunter may give you some pointers on how to improve your résumé or how to direct your job search.

You are much more likely, then, to hear from a headhunter in the third situation—when you are employed. You may be happy with your job and not actively looking. Although headhunters quite often call people at work, it's not a good idea to discuss new jobs from your current office. Headhunters know this and can arrange to talk to you outside business hours. So it's not unusual to have preliminary meetings outside work hours—over breakfast, for example.

When you are already employed and you are contacted by a head-hunter, it pays to be discreet about recruiting. If your current manager learns that you are "looking around," you'll be unlikely to get good projects assigned to you, you won't get promoted, and yours may be the first name that comes to mind if there are layoffs. If your search for a new job gets serious and you need time to go for interviews, you'll have to plan how to take the time off. You can take vacation days, and you don't need to be specific about why you are taking the time off (for example, "I need to take next Tuesday off as a personal day"). But you should never call in sick when, in fact, you are not (see Chapter 11). To your surprise, your interviewer may mention that she is a bridge partner with your current boss. When a rival company from your industry is recruiting you, the new firm will understand your situation and will respect your wanting to keep the overtures confidential.

■ 12-2 NETWORKING

In the 1980s, the term **networking** gained popularity—indeed, it became almost a fad. Young executives would earnestly attend ever-larger "networking events," which sometimes consisted of several thousand people milling around in a hotel ballroom, handing out their business cards to anyone within reach. Then, when they needed some advantage in business, they would call someone whose card they had been given and feign friendship. Of course, such superficial contacts don't really give you much advantage in business ("Who is this again?"). However, you should learn what could be called "smart networking."

If you would like your career to move in a particular direction (for example, away from mere technical work, into general management), you should actively seek out people who can give you advice, both within your firm and elsewhere in the industry. If you want to switch firms, think about whom you know who might know someone at the firms where you would like to work. You're unlikely to be introduced at once to just the right person, but you can ask, "Who should I be talking to?" Most people like talking about themselves and their firms, so they will welcome an opportunity to talk with you. One key is to end every such discussion with: "Is there anyone else I should be talking to?" If you are actively looking for a new position, people who don't have an opening themselves may think of other managers who might be able to hire you.

Active networking can include your regular participation in trade groups, monthly meetings of local alumni groups, and so on. The key to being successful in this endeavor is to understand that networking is a *mutually* beneficial activity. You should work just as hard to help other people at the event and you won't gain a reputation as a *net taker* (someone who expects favors and offers nothing in return).

■ 12-3 RÉSUMÉ BASICS

Each industry has some cultural norms about the format and content of a résumé. Try to collect some good examples from people who've success-fully recruited into your target industry. In some cases, on-campus re-cruiters may hand you a copy of a good example and suggest that you reformat your own résumé similarly. When you talk with recruiters at "firm nights" and career fairs, you can ask specific questions, such as, "What do you think about the bulleted format?" and "I've seen some résumés that run over two pages—is that usual for a professionally certi-fied engineer?"

In most U.S. business contexts, you will be expected to submit a one-page résumé. Prepare a longer document only if you are sure that it's acceptable in your field. There are many different layout styles that are acceptable for résumés, but all formats are expected to contain the same information. Although you can choose any font that is clear and appealing, you should avoid any text smaller than 10-point. To help your résumé stand out, you can choose an unusual (but still readable) font for your name.

In Europe and other parts of the world, it is customary to include some pieces of personal information on a résumé, but that information should not appear with a résumé submitted in the United States.

Do not mention marital status, children, or your citizenship (see *It's Just Different: Getting Personal on the Résumé*). Federal law requires that before someone is hired, he or she must demonstrate the right to work in the United States (in general, a U.S. passport, appropriate visa, or permanent resident status ["green card"]). But employers cannot discriminate against you on the grounds of national origin, so most people do not include such information on their résumés.

Although most résumés for U.S. businesses usually do not include a photo, there are a few industries in which personal appearance is part of the job, including broadcast TV news, acting, and entertainment, and a

It's Just Different: Getting Personal on the Résumé

There are strict limitations as to how much personal information you should put on a U.S. résumé. This is to ensure that a candidate is not discriminated against and doesn't claim a special preference. Contrast this with the systemic discrimination against Catholics in Northern Ireland during the last half of the twentieth century. Even if a recruiter did not guess from the identification section that "McAndrew" was Catholic and "Robinson" was the Protestant candidate, the "Education" section would confirm an applicant's religion because schools were often segregated by religious affiliation.

European résumés include an amount of personal information that would be shocking to an American Human Resources professional. Many have a photo attached and almost all list marital status, and even "excellent health" (the American attitude would be "none of your business, unless my health status would interfere with my ability to do your job"). Consider this example from Finland (clipped from the Internet, with names changed):

> Dr. Marius was born in Helsinki on June 11, 1965. His parents were Tapani Marius (born 1926, deceased 1983) and Inkeri Marius, born Eronen (born 1935, deceased 1995). He has one brother Rico (born 1973).
>
> Dr. Marius is since 1987 happily married to Ritva (born Heikenen) and has three children Teemu (son, born 1989), Tiina (daughter, born 1981), and Lauri (son, born 1996).

It's highly likely that Europe will move toward the American model and limit personal information that has really nothing to do with the position that is being filled. However, after civil disturbances in France, there have been calls that résumés be submitted completely "blind," without a photo or even a name, as a demonstrable bias against candidates with Arab-sounding last names had been shown.

photo might be appropriate. But for business, don't include a photo as part of your layout.

You will encounter two main types of résumés: **chronological résumés**, in which information is presented in the order "most recent first" within specific sections, and **functional résumés**, which list abilities (in any order that seems to make logical sense) and then provide details. People who have had unpaid work experience and those who have been out of the workforce for a long period of time favor the functional résumé. However, there's an overwhelming preference for the chronological résumé, and some firms may require you to rewrite a functional résumé in the other style. In a chronological résumé, the order of information is backward from the way you would tell a story. It's called *reverse chronological order*, and within each section your most recent accomplishments (education or position) come first and then so on back through time. For an example of a chronological résumé, see Figure 12-1.

Almost all firms now require résumés to be submitted online. Indeed, many recruiters who make presentations at on-campus career fairs say: "If you e-mail me your résumé, I'll be happy to have a quick look at it. But nothing is going to happen until you go to our firm's Web site and submit your résumé online." There are various mechanisms for online submission. A firm's recruiting instructions may ask you to send an e-mail with your résumé as an attachment. Unless the instructions say otherwise, you should submit a .pdf (Adobe Portable Document Format) file. That way, the layout and formatting of your résumé will be preserved, just as you wrote it. A similar mechanism is for a firm to direct you to its Web site and require that you "upload" your résumé. Lastly, some firms have a résumé template online and require you to enter your material field by field. Recruiters acknowledge that this reentering process is merely a hurdle to reduce the large number of poorly targeted résumés they receive.

In the rare instances where you hand a paper résumé to a recruiter or submit by postal mail, it's highly likely that the first thing that will happen to your résumé is that it will be scanned and converted to a .pdf file. Why, then, should we bother at all with "on paper" résumés? Well, they are still useful in face-to-face interviews and in casual conversations with recruiters at career fairs and firm nights. In all but the smallest companies, your résumé will be handled electronically.

When you know that the fate of most résumés is to be scanned by machine or processed online, you can readily answer many common questions about résumés:

Benoit LeClaire
bleclaire@hotemail.com

College	Permanent
6933 Martin Luther King, Jr. Way	*282 Blackhawk Drive*
High Point, NC 27260-3930	Danville, CA 94720-1919
(704) 555-6775	(510) 555-1234

EDUCATION

HIGH POINT UNIVERSITY   High Point, NC

Jeremiah School of Accounting and Finance
   BS Finance and Statistics (double major)   *Class of May 2012*

      Trustees Scholar   GPA 3.27 GPA (Finance courses) 4.0

LONDON SCHOOL OF ECONOMICS   London, England

      Study abroad, Fall 2010 Coursework in EU economic policy and corporate finance.

EXPERIENCE
Summer 2011

PRECEDENT CHAIR COMPANY   High Point, NC
Intern, Treasurer's office Responsible for reconciling inventory reports from eight cost centers. Prepared weekly reports. Staff member to internal committee on $0.5 billion pension plan.

Summer 2010

DAN JONES SOCCER CAMP   Danville, CA
Assistant Director Interviewed and hired 12 coaches and 24 counselors for a nationally-known summer sports camp; assigned daily teaching schedules; responsible for briefing parents on students' progress and managing minor sports injuries.

Summer 2009

Coach Developed daily lesson plans for groups of 18 teenage soccer players; counseled students on game strategy and personal training.

Summer 2008

Counselor-in-training Under the direction of Coach, assisted in drill practice and class management for three different groups of 18 students. Provided first aid for minor injuries.

ADDITIONAL EXPERIENCE
Sept 2009-continues

HIGH POINT UNIVERSITY   High Point, NC

Office of the President of the Student Body: Chief of staff Organized calendar for President and Exec. Committee. Supervised disbursement of funds from $35K student government budget to 14 recognized student groups. Resolved space allocation conflicts.

ACTIVITIES

HPU FINANCE CLUB *Active member 2009-continues, Treasurer, 2010-2011* With 5 colleagues, re-founded undergraduate association; raised $600 budget; brought 6 speakers to campus and oversaw development of Website with links to recruiting firms.

MILTON DANIEL HALL, *Security Chair, 2010* Committee member responsible for safety in 120-student residence. Developed new system for handling lockouts and lost keys.

SKILLS

MS-Excel (expert), MS-Word (intermediate), PowerPoint (novice)

French (fluent business written and spoken), German (conversational)

INTERESTS

Traveling, community service (tutoring), skiing, soccer (intramural), and chess

Figure 12-1   Example of a Chronological Résumé
This is the standard one-page format expected by most American businesses. It shows the typical sections and "reverse chronological" order that recruiters expect.

Should I use a special paper?   A scanning machine won't care that you spent a fortune on special linen paper. It just cares that the ink is black and sharp and the paper is white. Using decorative paper may cause problems with readability. However, when you plan to hand your résumé to recruiters at interviews or career fairs, you can certainly use a heavier weight of paper (that is, thicker) to make a good, professional impression. Keep copies of your résumé in a portfolio, nice and flat, rather than folded in your pocket.

Can I submit multiple copies of my résumé?   Absolutely! There are some chance elements to the submission process. For example, if you hand a résumé to a recruiter at a career fair, it might be mislaid and never scanned into the firm's system. Always follow up by making sure that you've also submitted your résumé online.

Can I have different versions of my résumé?   Yes, in fact, most professionals probably have more than one version. For example, someone trained as an engineer probably has one résumé that emphasizes technical skills and another that highlights managerial experience. As long as the two versions are not contradictory, there is no problem. If you interview and are asked about having two versions, you can state the truth: "I have a lot of experience as an engineer, and I've been working for some time in management—the two versions emphasize the two different skill sets."

Should I make a video résumé?   Several new services now allow job candidates to post "video résumés"—short online videos in which applicants explain why they'd be good for a particular job. Although some firms say they find these helpful in choosing people to invite for formal interviews, there are several concerns. Video résumés may encourage the hiring of people who are outgoing and good on camera, even when those characteristics aren't necessarily important to the job under consideration. And firms that encourage video résumés risk being accused of selecting candidates based on ethnicity, which is illegal.

▪ 12-4 RÉSUMÉ CONVENTIONS

Résumés are written in a peculiar shorthand style of sentence fragments that are linked together ("concatenated") in groups of logically related parts. For example:

> GreatCorp. *IT Manager* Expedited customer service requests, developed three new applications, eliminating more than two dozen legacy programs. Maintained 99 percent uptime under strict budget, implemented new off-site backup. Supervised staff of nine graduate engineers, voted manager of the year award.

This form avoids wasting space by endlessly repeating the word "I." In general, résumés leave out the subject of the sentence ("I" is implicit because it's your résumé) and often avoid conjunctions such as "and."

Experts on résumé writing encourage you to use strong, active verbs, and the description of positions that you held should always lead toward a result. The following example:

> *Sales Manager* Responsible for Twin-Cities territory for a leading industrial products manufacturer.

doesn't convey as much information as:

> *Sales Manager* Directly supervised four salespeople with $3 million combined sales; increased active accounts by 20 percent to more than 200 in 18 months.

The standard for what to include in your résumé is this: With the exception of the section labeled "Interests," what is on your résumé should be the result of examination or be capable of verification—or could be. That is, your résumé includes facts, such as employment and degrees and certifications you have achieved (or will complete in the near future). Your résumé can also include skills for which you could pass an exam if given one. For example, you can say: "Expert knowledge of C++" whether or not you've actually taken a course in this programming language, and you can say: "Native-level fluency in Spanish" even if you weren't born in Spain, as long as your Spanish is "as good as" someone who was born there. But you can't say: "Reliable, hard worker." Although this statement may be true, it's not subject to examination, so it belongs in your cover letter (see Section 12-16), not in your résumé.

If you were called to be a witness in a court of law, you would raise your right hand and swear to tell "the truth, the whole truth, and nothing but the truth." On a résumé, you are expected to tell "the truth and nothing but the truth," but you don't have to tell the whole truth (see *Doing the Right Thing: Be Absolutely Honest in Your Résumé*). For example, if one of the main ways you spend your time outside work is in the deeply religious pursuit of spirituality, you might choose not to mention that on your résumé. Similarly, if you worked as one of Santa's elves at

Doing the Right Thing: Be Absolutely Honest in Your Résumé

Studies show that as many as 15 percent of all résumés include what could best be described as "embellishments," if not out-and-out lies. In the wake of the hurricane devastation caused in New Orleans in 2005, the press widely reported that the disgraced Federal Emergency Management Agency director Michael Brown claimed in his résumé to have worked as an "assistant city manager" with substantial responsibility for emergency preparedness. But in fact, he had held the much lower title of "assistant to the city manager," and his previous experience with disaster management was rather limited.

Many of the falsifications on résumés involve people claiming to have degrees when in fact they did not complete their studies. Several executives have hidden behind the excuse that the errors were in a version of their biography released by the company's public relations department and that they merely failed to check. However, these executives had to admit, for example, that although they may have done some "graduate study" or "taken courses toward" a certain degree, they never actually obtained the degree. Some executives have had to resign under pressure, whereas others have simply been fired.

There's only one right thing to do here: Be absolutely honest. For example, if you are writing your résumé in April and you know that you are two courses short of the June graduation requirements, don't put "BA Economics June 2006" on your résumé. If you will actually take courses in summer school but won't receive your degree until a December graduation ceremony, then say honestly: "BA Economics Planned Completion August 2006" to make it clear when you are ready to start work.

Everyone who writes a résumé is entitled to selectively emphasize their best features and make strategic omissions, but there is a clear line that must not be crossed: Don't lie on your résumé.

---

a department store to earn extra money while you were in college, you might choose to omit that job. Selecting what part of "truth" to present is a major part of preparing different specifically targeted versions of your résumé. However, when you have to fill out a firm's own application form, you have to be more complete; this issue is discussed in Chapter 13.

You may well encounter some variations in the order of sections in résumés that are common in your industry. Your industry may use some unique sections (for example, actors might have sections for films, TV, plays, and commercials work). However, the following is a general guide for the sections that are routinely encountered, especially for young college students being hired into their first positions in U.S. business (see the subsequent sections for detailed descriptions of each section):

- Identification
- Objective
- Education
- Experience
- [Additional Experience]
- Activities
- Awards and Honors
- Skills
- Interests

Note that in this case the words "Education" and "Experience" do not take an "s" to make the words plural. Although you may have had many different experiences, the abstract noun "experience" is often treated as a plural (like one sheep, several sheep).

■ 12-5 IDENTIFICATION

Although we talk about the "Identification" section of your résumé, unlike the other sections, it does not have any title (the word "Identification" does not appear).

At the head of the résumé, you place your name and contact information. Most people put their full legal name, such as "Charles Edward Windsor," but you can use a shorter form if you prefer. For example, if you routinely go by a diminutive, such as "Chuck Windsor," you could head your résumé that way. If you have a nickname that's not part of your legal name, you can include that on your résumé, probably as the first name: "Sophia Eun Kee Lim." It's not necessary to set the nickname off with quotation marks, even if it isn't part of your legal name.

Under your name, put one e-mail address that you check regularly. Remove the underline that your word-processing program automatically adds to an e-mail name, as that may make the e-mail address hard to read or scan.

You should have at least one good postal mailing address, although these days it's rare for a recruiter to contact you by mail. (Most recruiters will want to phone you or reach you by e-mail.) Students often have two addresses, with one labeled "College" and the other "Home" or "Permanent." You can use the cover letter to indicate when you'll be where. Clearly indicate one phone number that is best for contacting you, often a cell phone with voice mail. If you need to show two phone numbers that correspond to two locations, home and college, the phone number goes under each address. Otherwise, a good place is directly under your name, just below your e-mail address.

You can include a personal Web page URL if your site is thoroughly professional (no funny pictures of friends), but you should never send a cover letter or e-mail to tell the recruiter, "You can download my resume from..." Asking the recruiter to download your résumé makes the recruiter do extra work, and if he or she is reading your application while traveling, then your application may be passed over. When you are seeking recruitment, you should be especially careful about any postings that mention you by name on social networking sites (see *Business Protocol in Action: The Friend of My Friend's Friend*).

■ 12-6 OBJECTIVE

There are two schools of thought on whether you should use an objective on your résumé. You'll hear some people say that a résumé without an objective is unlikely to succeed. On the other hand, many people believe

---

Business Protocol in Action: The Friend of My Friend's Friend

Most college students have an online presence on a social networking site such as Facebook or MySpace. Many personal pages contain information that is silly, unprofessional, or even worse! This is especially true of comments that friends write back and forth about each other.

When you are seeking recruitment, make sure your privacy settings are restrictive so that only your real friends can see your material. Recruiters are increasingly doing broad searches to check on candidates' online presence. The new "friend of a friend" whom you don't recognize could be working as a researcher for a potential employer, seeing how you present yourself when you are "off duty."

that an objective is likely to limit your opportunities. For example, you have good spreadsheet and analytic skills and you announce your objective as "Financial Analyst." Then your résumé is passed over for an analyst job in the Marketing group of a major retailer that you would have really enjoyed.

An additional reservation about the "Objective" section is that it takes up a lot of space on the page that could be used for giving more information about yourself. You can make the case that the same information could be conveyed in a cover letter. However, thinking about an objective could be helpful if you are writing two versions of your résumé—say, one technical and one managerial. You could begin drafts of the two versions by including an "Objective" section such as: "Objective: Line management position with P&L responsibility," and then write your résumé, selecting facts that match that objective. Then, repeat the same process for the technical résumé. At the end, you would delete both "Objective" sections, as they should serve only to guide your writing and are not needed in the final résumé.

A clearly stated objective is useful when you would accept only a certain type of job. For example, if you were trained in several different computer operating systems but, for career development reasons, want to work in only one environment, then using an objective such as "Network systems developer for Windows Server" makes sense. This is particularly true in computer programming, where résumés are often circulated by e-mail without cover letters.

■ 12-7 EDUCATION

The "Education" section begins with your most recent degree, and if you are currently enrolled, you include the degree that you hope to obtain. You can use the phrase "candidate for BA in History, May 2010" or simply append a date that's in the future: "BA History, May 2010." For a U.S. résumé, you don't need to spell out the specific years that you attended college—except if you have completed your studies in an exceptionally short time, such as just three years for a U.S. bachelor's degree.

If you have a double-major, or an **academic major** (specialty of your degree) or a **minor** (second specialty), you would mention that fact here, along with any honors you achieved at graduation, such as *cum laude* (with honors). However, don't be too impressed by status, as it means more in college than in the real world. In recent years, more than 90 percent of Harvard bachelor's degree candidates have graduated "with honors," so the distinction has lost some of its meaning (see Section 12-11).

You'll find cultural norms with respect to reporting your **GPA (grade point average)** and your SAT (Scholastic Aptitude Test) scores. Almost all U.S. universities calculate a GPA as part of students' transcripts: Awarding four points for each "A," three points for each "B," and so on, multiplying by the number of units for each course, and then dividing the total number of points by the total number of units completed. Some industries (such as financial services) expect to see both the GPA and SAT scores, but in other industries, reporting your GPA on your résumé is seen as tasteless bragging. Ask among friends and colleagues, and particularly try to look at copies of résumés of people who've been successfully hired in the industry that you want to join. If reporting a GPA is typical, you can include more than one GPA, such as your GPA in your major or your GPA in science classes. You calculate the *subsidiary GPA* (science classes) yourself, so it's up to you to decide which courses to include in your calculation. If you are showing more than one GPA number, put the best one to the right, especially if you're trying to "bury" a less impressive overall GPA (sometimes called "cumulative GPA") in the middle of a line. However, you must follow this rule: If you calculate a subsidiary GPA, you must also state your cumulative GPA, exactly as it shows on your college transcript. If you don't report it, recruiters might presume that your cumulative GPA is exceptionally poor. Don't worry too much if your GPA has been diminished by a couple of rough courses or one really bad semester. In the words of one recruiter: "Big deal. Everyone gets *one* C."

In the "Education" section, you can give details of coursework that you've taken (often with the subheading "Relevant Coursework"). This information is useful if your degree is in one subject but you've actually taken a lot of relevant coursework in another field. If you've studied abroad as part of your education, you would place this information immediately after the institution that will grant your degree (even if the study abroad is "most recent"). Be sure to say specifically what courses you took to show the benefit of your experience.

People who have worked hard at odd jobs to support themselves through school will sometimes make a notation in this section to that effect, such as:

50 percent self-supported through on-campus employment.

Most U.S. résumés do not mention high school or earlier education. If you have special distinctions, such as being a national champion athlete in your pre-college years, you may consider including that information farther down the résumé. The reason for ignoring high school is that one presumes that anyone at a competitive university did indeed graduate from high school, so mentioning this fact doesn't add much value.

■ 12-8 EXPERIENCE

The key to the "Experience" section is remembering the rule of telling "not necessarily the whole truth." Both in your selection of jobs and in the description of jobs held, you will be making strategic omissions. For example, many summer jobs include chores such as photocopying and getting supplies. These tasks aren't really relevant to career positions. On the other hand, whatever you do put on your résumé does have to be truthful. A 19-year-old who had a summer job with a stock brokerage firm describing his duties as "Planned multi-million dollar portfolio allocation for high net worth individuals" just isn't credible.

For jobs that you've held, begin with the most recent and work backward. You will show the dates of each employment using the form "2005—present" or "2005—continues" for a job that you still hold. If you've held more than one position at the same firm, try to group the positions under a single statement of the firm's name and location. You can use a similar form for positions that you held concurrently:

> Investment Firm, Inc. Tiburon, CA *Retail broker* (2005–continues) and *chairman of the investment committee* (2006–2008).

Firms will be concerned about any gaps in your employment. You shouldn't lie (starting and ending dates can easily be confirmed by talking with your old employers), but you should attempt to have a good "cover story" for interviews, even if you were unemployed and looking for work. For example, "Well, I'd planned to go back to graduate school, but then I heard about a great job opportunity, and I decided to begin work there instead."

Because the title "Experience" doesn't specifically say "employment," some people include volunteer experience and unpaid internships in this section. With the continuing warning that your résumé must be truthful, it's fair to note that the word "intern" is routinely inflated. Your paycheck may have shown you as "Temporary Clerk 3B," but if your boss thought you were her intern and you thought you were an intern, go ahead and use that title. It's not essential to indicate which experiences were unpaid, but you should know that many people do put the words "unpaid" or "volunteer" immediately after job titles to be sure that they are not accused of misstatement on their résumés. If you have a mixture of paid and unpaid experience, you may choose to add the next section, "Additional Experience."

■ 12-9 ADDITIONAL EXPERIENCE

You may have heard this old adage: "You need to have experience to get a job. To get experience, you need to get a job." It's circular! Many young people find themselves crafting a résumé in the face of very limited work experience. In this situation, you can either use a single "Experience" section for paid and unpaid work or have a second section titled "Additional Experience" that will allow you to describe work-related activities and demonstrate what you've learned. For example:

> St. Joseph's Hospital, *Volunteer* In more than 240 hours of community service, assisted ward clerk and triage nurse in an urban emergency room with more than 1,200 nightly visits. Responsible for checking insurance eligibility and explaining covered benefits to family members.

Some elected college positions, such as student body president, amount to a full-time job, so you could make entries in this section to describe them.

Instead of "Additional Experience," you may wish to add a section that organizes and presents information about yourself that goes beyond the usual student and community "activities." For example, if you have been involved in campus governance, a section entitled "Student Government" may be useful. Similarly, if much of your time has been spent on university sports teams, you could consider adding a section "Student Athlete," whereas theater majors could add a section "Performance Art," and so on.

Many ex-military personnel who return to college after service have been encouraged to contort their armed forces duties to civilian terms. Although it's true that most military acronyms are meaningless to civilian recruiters (NCOIC attaché to CINCSEURCOM, for example), forcing enlistment and progressive promotions into generic categories such as "Leadership" may make the résumé too difficult to read and understand.

Most recruiters will honor service to your country and it makes sense to have a separate "Military Service" section and then organize the progression of duties and promotions in reverse chronological order. Avoid acronyms and explain in civilian terms what you did: "Responsible for the training and discipline of eight enlisted soldiers," for example.

■ 12-10 ACTIVITIES

In the "Activities" section, you should describe clubs and associations to which you belong, and your role in them. Many college students are daunted by this task of résumé writing because they can't truthfully say much more than "active member" in describing their roles. Recruiters don't expect everyone to be the president of every club he or she belongs to—but they do hope to see some significant contribution and a reasonable progression year to year. They are more impressed by results in one or two groups than in membership in dozens of different organizations. So if you work hard for a club, be sure to take responsibility for a specific function while keeping your résumé in mind:

> *Young Business Club* Active member responsible for managing parking for annual career fair with more than 200 professionals attending.

■ 12-11 AWARDS AND HONORS

No section means more to résumé writers and less to recruiters than "Awards and Honors." If you are a good student at a competitive university, it goes without saying that you won the prize for best reader in your kindergarten class. Honors that merely "pile on" (you have a good GPA, so that means you are on the dean's list) don't convey information to employers. Almost all applicants can point to local high school prizes which they won—but such a listing doesn't set any of them apart, and a long listing merely looks self-congratulatory. Many scholarships are awarded as a routine part of financial aid and do not require much personal effort. So the standard for inclusion is this: How comfortable would you be discussing this information at an interview? If the best that you can say about the "HJM Alumnus Scholarship" is that it's a part of your financial aid package this year (and you don't know who HJM was), leave it out.

On the other hand, if you've been selected for a highly competitive scholarship or have won a regional or national championship, then that information belongs here:

Morehead Scholar One of 12 scholars selected from 2,000 applicants for a full tuition scholarship in a statewide competition.

National Collegiate Debate Champion, 2006 Won individual forensics title in field of 200 contestants from all 50 states.

■ 12-12 SKILLS

In the "Skills" section, you will list specific lab, computer, and foreign language skills that you possess. Remember, the standard is that you have taken an exam in a skill, or could pass one. So, for example, if you know how to operate an electron microscope, although there probably isn't a corresponding course with a final exam, there could be an exam for this skill. It's a skill that few people have and is worth mentioning. There's an old line from newspaper advertising copywriting: "The more you tell, the more you sell." So list all skills that you think might possibly be of use in the workplace. However, for professional positions (managerial work), most people don't list skills such as typing and "current driver's license," which are presumed for all Americans. Listing these basic skills detracts from other, more special skills that you have.

You should list all the computer programs that you know, and you can consider adding qualifiers such as "basic," "intermediate," "proficient," or "expert." The same applies to foreign language skills—try to accurately describe your level of proficiency. There are many levels to explain your competence of a certain language, from "basic" to "reading knowledge" or "traveling knowledge" through "fluent" to "native speaker." Try to elaborate on languages that are useful to an employer, such as "fluent written and spoken Spanish." Unless you know that an employer has a particular need for your skills in a dialect that isn't used much in business, you should be thoughtful about how much you emphasize this point. For example, suppose you grew up in Wales in the United Kingdom and you were fluent in written but not spoken Welsh (a type of Celtic language). Unless you are applying to be the rare books librarian in a university language department, this is an interesting personal characteristic that doesn't mean a great deal to a potential employer.

In this section and in the next, the order of your ideas is not reverse chronological, so you don't have to put your most recent skill first. Instead, the most important idea should come at the beginning, and the second most important idea at the end. "Bury" incidental, or less important, information in the middle.

■ 12-13 INTERESTS

The "Interests" section is the great exception to the rule of having taken an examination or being able to pass one. For that reason, some résumé experts advise against including this section. However, a very good case can be made for including your interests. First, the "Interests" section may convey something about your personality. For example, listing intramural indoor soccer and basketball as your activities signals that you are a team player. If you list mountain climbing, an employer can see that you are not afraid of hardships and situations that require great endurance.

Second, there's a small chance that an interviewer will be interested in the same activities as you, and that's always a good starting point for a congenial interview. But even when there is no good match, an interviewer can often refer to interests as a way to get you talking about yourself: "So, tell me about your figure skating hobby…"

It follows that you should not list anything that wouldn't be a good lead-in to a pleasant discussion at an interview. You can be selective about the interests you list and avoid any that you feel might sidetrack an interview. Be thoughtful about stating activities and interests with a strong political or religious element. In general, it's best to say "Active in volunteer work with church group" rather than "Elected twice as lay member of Lutheran Social Services" unless you accept that some interviewers might not relate to this particular denomination. Worse, overemphasizing a group identity could imply that you are seeking preferential treatment as a member of that group.

■ 12-14 REFERENCES

In the conventional modern form of a U.S. business résumé, there is no standard ending phrase. Because it's assumed that a résumé will be one page, there's no need to indicate that you are at the end. The phrase "References available on request" once possibly served as an ending statement, but this phrase is invariably omitted now because it's assumed that any credible candidate will have some references.

You should arrange to have three or four people who will give you a reference, if asked. Technically, the person who gives the reference is a "referee"; a written letter about you is a "reference" (although in practice, people refer to the person who will say good things about you as the "reference"); and you are the "referent." However, few firms will ask for references (see Chapter 13), and they are used mainly in academic circles, such as for applicants to graduate school. But you should be prepared just in case.

Try to choose a group of people who know you from different backgrounds. For example, you should make an effort to have a group of referees who are not all professors or not all work supervisors. There will likely be some overlap in what they see as your best qualities. For example, two or three people could describe you as hardworking and conscientious. However, you should suggest to each referee the area that you would like him or her to be responsible for covering. Make sure to talk with the referee in person if possible, or at least by phone, and if it's been a long time since you worked together, remind her or him of the key facts of your association. Never ask referees to comment on something they don't know from their own experience. For example, don't ask a college professor to comment on your community service work, unless you worked together in the same association or club.

You can use a well-prepared reference list as a way to move the hiring process along. If you've been talking back and forth with a company, and you are not getting to the point of an offer, you can ask, "Would you like me to provide you with references?" Presenting a neatly formatted list, as shown in Figure 12-2, can signal your seriousness about a position.

In the United States, almost all references are taken up on a case-by-case basis for each opportunity of employment. A general letter of reference that is written in advance is not considered to be very useful to employers (see *Business Protocol in Action: To Whom It May Concern* in Chapter 7).

■ 12-15 FORMAT FOR A FUNCTIONAL RÉSUMÉ

Career coaches recommend functional résumés for people who have been out of the workforce for a long time or who have had many different jobs

Reference List for Benoit LeClaire
bleclaire@hotemail.com
(704) 555-6775

Referees, contact information	How they know me	What they can say
Thomas Efrem (o) (510) 111-1234 tefrem@sportsecamp.org	My supervisor for three summers at sports camp	General employee reliability, work habits, good team member.
Sheila Patel, Ph.D. (o) (704) 222-1234 (h) (704) 333-1234 finguru@hpu.edu	Professor for my Finance 21 class	I ranked 2/132 in this class and prof. offered me the TA's job next semester. Can talk about my study habits, math abilities and computer skills.
Father Maurice Bonilla (cell) (415) 555-1234 padremau@heaven.net	Family friend, has known me for 20 years	Can confirm I'm honest and trustworthy.

Give the contact information (office, home, cell phone) that the referee prefers

Give the context

Discuss the "what they can say" with your referees

Figure 12-2   Sample Reference List
Develop a reference list that is more useful than just a list of former supervisors—put together a team of people who can verify your skills and abilities—and list the best way to reach each person.

without a really coherent pattern. A functional résumé begins with the same "Identification" section, and most experts who prefer this form encourage the use of an "Objective" section.

The sections that follow can be anything you choose, based on groups of skills such as "Office Procedures," "Team Management," or "Supervision and Training." You could even imagine a section such as "Cooking for Large Groups" for someone who had raised a family and done a lot of volunteer work. Of course, the subheadings should relate to the specific skills that you imagine are needed in a particular job.

Some functional résumés have jobs grouped under each category or have separate sections for employment and education, although these usually come toward the end of the résumé rather than at the beginning, as they do in a chronological résumé. Figure 12-3 is an example of a functional résumé format.

It's worth saying that many employers don't like this format and will demand that an applicant resubmit a chronological résumé or fill out a chronological employment application. However, the functional résumé might be a "foot in the door"—and it may create an invitation to interview.

12-16 COVER LETTERS

Professional recruiters will offer all kinds of opinions about cover letters. Some recruiters believe they are more revealing than the résumés themselves; some feel they are useful at the margin, to choose between two similar candidates; and still others rate them as irrelevant. If you can, try to find out from a firm's presentations and background information how much weight it gives to a cover letter. But given the number of applications that firms process, if a résumé receives only a minute or two of consideration, you should know that most cover letters are looked at for less than a minute in many instances.

Very occasionally, a job announcement will ask for specific material to be included in a cover letter, such as detailing why you want to work for the firm, or whether you would be prepared to relocate. To weed out thoughtless online submissions, many firms set a hurdle of asking you to describe in your cover letter (e-mail) how you would approach a specific business problem or to state what you understand about current industry trends.

In the absence of specific instructions, keep your cover letter short, and organize it in these four sections: identification; how your personal qualities match the job; the "ask"; and, finally, contact information. Each section should be about a paragraph long, but in some circumstances, such as when you want to explain a unique experience, you might use two paragraphs in a section.

Benoit LeClaire
bleclaire@hotemail.com

College
6933 Martin Luther King, Jr. Way
High Point, NC 27260-3930
(704) 555-6775

Permanent
282 Blackhawk Drive
Danville, CA 94720-1919
(510) 555-1234

OBJECTIVE

Position in junior management that will permit me opportunities to apply my analytical and organizational skills.

PROFILE

Highly motivated recent college graduate with excellent computer skills and substantial experience leading teams of co-workers to achieve superior results.

SKILLS

Analysis Consolidating and summarizing operating and accounting results, data verification, graphing of quantitative information, mastery of multiple computer systems. Proficient in MS-Excel and MS-Word. Expert chess player.

Organization Schedule management for work group, recruiting and hiring, implementing training programs, staffing committees, preparing timely written reports.

Team Leadership Clarify team objectives, motivate team members, respect deadlines. Captain of intramural soccer team.

EMPLOYMENT

Textbooks Direct (Territory High Point and Winston-Salem, NC) Campus representative. July 2009 – present

Precedent Chair Company, High Point, NC. Intern, Treasurer's Office. July – August 2011

Dan Jones Soccer Camps, Danville, CA. Assistant Director, June – August 2010, Coach, July & August, 2009, Counselor-in-training, May – July 2008

EDUCATION

University of Western North Carolina, Cullowee, NC. Certificate in Entrepreneurial Management, December, 2009

High Point University, High Point, NC. BS in Business Administration, May, 2012

Wake Technical College, Raleigh, NC. Associate in Arts degree, General Studies, June 2010

Figure 12-3   Example of a Functional Résumé
The functional résumé layout deliberately de-emphasizes education and experience in favor of highlighting skills. The writer selects the groups of skills that show her or his best advantages.

First, you identify who you are, where you are in your career or training, and the exact job that you are applying for, such as "Summer Intern in Corporate Finance in the Houston Office." This information should help your résumé to be sorted into the correct pile. You should clearly state any geographic preferences and limitations in this first section. On the other hand, if you are willing to relocate, this can be mentioned here. Although one usually doesn't mention family matters while seeking recruitment, if there is a specific reason why you want to move to one city, it's appropriate to mention that point here: "My fiancée has been accepted as an intern at the M. D. Anderson Cancer Institute for medical school, so I am enthusiastic about moving to Houston."

The middle section is the most important part of a cover letter. You should use it to get across the personal characteristics that can't be included on a résumé. You use the facts of your résumé and tie them in to what you believe to be the demands of the job:

> In my work on the U.S. Census, I had responsibility for checking numeric data and submitting material according to strict deadlines. I demonstrated that I'm able to work hard with great accuracy under pressure.

In the third section, you should ask for the interview. You don't need to thank people for their consideration—they're being paid to read your résumé, and your application should be welcome. Try not to be vague: "Feel free to contact me for additional information" is very weak. At the least, end with: "I look forward to an opportunity to meet with members of the firm to discuss this position." At best, you should announce your intention to phone and ask for an interview. Many job applicants feel this approach is too pushy, but most firms would take it as a declaration of serious interest.

The final part of a cover letter should include information about how you can be reached, especially if your résumé has two addresses: "I will be traveling in Europe until the end of May, but after June 1, I will be at the Atlanta address." It's also sometimes helpful to signal availability for an interview: "We have planned a house hunting trip to Houston during Spring Break, the last week of March, and I would be available to interview all week."

▶ ▷ ▷ PUT THIS CHAPTER INTO PRACTICE

1. Visit the Web sites for three firms you would be interested in joining and see if they accept résumé submissions by uploaded files or require you to reenter material into their template.

2. Collect three or more résumés from successful professionals in the industry you want to enter. Analyze them and try to generate rules for the cultural norms for résumés in that industry as compared with other fields.

3. Take a friend's résumé and critically edit it to conform to the general rules discussed in this chapter.

KEY TERMS

academic major

academic minor

chronological résumé

cover letter

functional résumé

grade point average (GPA)

headhunter

networking

on-campus recruiting

Multiple Choice Practice Questions: To take the review quiz for this chapter, log on to your Online Edition at www.atomicdog.com.

Chapter 13
Interviewing and the Hiring Process

Interviewers are often as nervous as the candidates—help them do their job well.

Managers will tell you that they rely heavily on interviewing to choose the candidate who is the best "fit" for their organization from among the many people who have the same paper qualifications. However, research on interviewing shows that interviews are not a very good personnel selection technique—all candidates are on their very best behavior during an interview and even the worst candidate can sound motivated and charming for half an hour.

In spite of the importance that executives attach to interviewing, many interviewers are poorly prepared. Some firms mistakenly view on-campus first-round interviews as an opportunity for on-the-job training for their staff. When interviewers have had no formal training in interviewing, they are left to invent an interview style based on all interviews that they've experienced themselves, anything from a social chat to a "stress interview." They usually haven't even thought through the specific purpose of the interview and its place in a series of interviews.

Sometimes poorly trained interviewers can move into inappropriate areas. Although it's not technically illegal to ask someone, "Oh, will your boyfriend be moving to Boston with you?", a female candidate who did not get a job offer might wonder if gender discrimination underlaid the rejection. Here's how to handle inappropriate questions: If the interviewer's slip appears innocent, you can ignore the question and carry on ("Tell me more about the internship training program that you offer in Boston"). If the question is direct and improper—for example, "Aren't you kind of old to be going for this kind of job?" (potential age discrimination)—laugh good-naturedly and say: "Wow! I don't think we're allowed to discuss those sorts of things in a formal interview." If the violation of good protocol is more severe (such as a recruiter repeatedly asking, "So, which bars do you like to go to?"), terminate the interview and report the misconduct to your school career service or to the firm's Human Resources Department.

■ 13-1 GENERAL INTERVIEW PROTOCOL

You can avoid the problems of poorly trained interviewers by preparing well and having an action plan. To prepare, at the minimum you need to research the firm and the specific unit that is hiring. An Internet search on the company can yield a lot of factual information, and discussions with industry insiders at other firms can tell you about the target firm's corporate culture and perhaps some details about the decision makers. Make sure you've clearly understood the **job description,** and be prepared for questions about areas in which you don't quite meet the company's needs. Remember that a job description is an "ideal," but all firms operate in the real world. So if the firm ideally wants someone with five years of experience and you've had only three but you've had increasing responsibility, approach this issue with confidence in the interview.

Although you may see an interview as a passive process, or at least one over which you have no control, plan ahead concerning what points you want to get across. Write down three points you want people to be sure to know about you—for example, that your enthusiasm and willingness to learn make up for modest experience, that you have fluency in three languages relevant to the firm's business, and that you are willing to relocate. There's a good probability that these issues will come up naturally in the conversation, but if not, you should work them in, especially if the interviewer appears unprepared and is just asking generic questions. If one interview doesn't cover some of the points you think are important, the firm may have a strategy in which someone later in the process will be asking you about that issue (for example, whether you are willing to work in certain geographic locations). However, there's no harm in slipping in these points at the end of an interview, during your closing:

> "Well, thank you for meeting with me. I just wanted to mention—one area we didn't cover—I know that most of your operations are in Hawaii, and I wanted to be clear that I'm prepared to move if that's where the job is located."

Whatever the setup a company has chosen for your interview, you'll want to be well dressed and neatly groomed, as described in Chapter 14. You should aim to arrive about 5 to 10 minutes before the time of your appointment (see Figure 13-1). However, you should always allow for delays in travel, so in practice you may arrive much earlier than that (for example, if you've set out 1 hour early to allow for a canceled train or bus).

Figure 13-1   Interviewing
When you're interviewing, dress appropriately, arrive early, and be sure to have extra copies of your résumé in a professional-looking portfolio.
Source: © 2009 Jupiterimages Corporation.

If you know that a firm is interviewing several candidates, you should check in with the receptionist and, because you're early, volunteer to go and get coffee and return, or some such pleasantry. If another candidate is running late, you'll be asked to start early; you'll be a hero, and you'll have an advantage over the competition.

If the interview is in an unfamiliar location, if at all possible check out the route and destination the day before. There's nothing worse than arriving with 10 minutes to spare before an interview and finding that the building you always thought was MegaPlaza is in fact MondoPlaza and that you are in the wrong place. A scouting trip like this is also a good opportunity to learn about the firm's dress code.

Try to travel light. You don't want to arrive with a suitcase, briefcase, computer case, and overcoat over your arm, looking like a traveling merchant on the way to a bazaar. If you are interviewing out of town and you

must bring your belongings with you from a hotel, ask the firm's receptionist if you may store your bag:

> "I wonder, is there somewhere I could store this? I don't want to be carrying
> these bags around all day."

The same advice applies to overcoats—don't carry them with you
from one interview to the next. The key is that you want to look like
someone who works at the firm, not like someone who is a visitor.

The most you should carry with you is a **portfolio** (a leather or imita-
tion-leather folder) in which you have copies of your résumé. You should
always arrive with as many copies as there are people you expect to meet,
plus one extra for yourself (you can easily forget details of how you
worded things and be caught off-guard by questions). Quite frequently,
interviewers will have seen your résumé before but may be unable to lay
hands on it at once. You'll help your interview go much better if you are
prepared and can hand over a copy.

Whether you have one interview or several during a day, never fail
to introduce yourself with your full name and context ("Hello, I'm
Alexander Grace, one of the candidates for the summer internship").
Shake hands confidently with each new person that you meet, as described
in Chapter 2. If you are going to have a full day of interviewing, make sure
to take care of physiological needs such as stopping for a drink of water or
taking a bathroom break (see Chapter 11).

You should try to learn as much as possible about the format for the
interview and the type of interview before you start. If there is a whole day
of interviewing, the firm will have a typed schedule—ask for a copy if it's
not offered to you, and ask polite questions about who the various people
are on the list. The people in the firm will know who is the vice president
and who is the junior assistant, but you may not have a clue. The approach
you take to each interview and the questions you ask will depend on
whom you are talking with. The most important point to understand
about interviewing is that it has many different formats, and there are
many different types of interviews within each format.

■ 13-2 FORMAT FOR INTERVIEWS

Most companies' recruiting process involves several "rounds." Many
people are invited in for a first-round interview, and then selected candidates are advanced to a second round. There can be many subsequent

rounds, and for interviewing that begins on college campuses, there is invariably at least a final round at the firm's offices. There are very few industries in which formal, written tests are part of the assessment, although these tests are common for certain types of civil service jobs. The first interview may be a short one-to-one meeting in an on-campus interview suite or at a hotel or by phone.

It's important to treat a **phone interview** with the same formality and importance as a face-to-face interview. First, determine whether the phone call is a brief scheduling call ("Can you come in next Tuesday at 10 o'clock?") or an actual interview. If you are surprised by a phone call while you are working on something else, or if you feel unprepared, make a polite excuse ("I'm afraid I was just on my way out...") and ask to reschedule. Of course, if an interviewer says that rescheduling is difficult ("I'm at the airport on my way to Hong Kong, and we either talk now or..."), you must go ahead with the interview. Make sure you are in a quiet place (turn off the TV, music, and any other distractions). If you are speaking from home, you should have forewarned your roommates to respect your interview time. Nothing sounds worse to a recruiter than a candidate having to shout: "Hey, guys! Can you just shut up? I'm trying to interview here!"

Begin a phone interview by sitting at a desk with a copy of your résumé in front of you. Imagine that you and the interviewer are face to face. If you have been able to schedule the interview, you should dress in your best interview outfit. This may sound silly, but it works. Sit up straight and respond formally with your best professionalism. If you are in your own home when the recruiter calls, there's a great temptation to lapse into informal chatting instead of properly presenting yourself.

Some in-person interviews may have two or more people firing questions at you. This type of interview can have several purposes: It may be an expedient so that two people hear what you have to say at the same time; one interviewer may just be acting as an observer; or there could be a conscious effort for the two interviewers to take different roles (good cop/bad cop). While you should try to diagnose the format as quickly as possible so that you can respond appropriately, the main action step in this situation is to include all of the interviewers in your eye contact and gestures, even if only one is asking the questions.

Most candidates dread a **group interview** in which several candidates are brought in at the same time to interact with one or more people from the firm. The hiring firm may want to see how candidates act in group situations or may simply be trying to save time in the early rounds of a selection process. The group interview may include a problem-solving exercise in which all candidates must cooperate. This is a difficult situation—there is pressure on all candidates to speak up, and they may try to out-do each other in taking a leadership role. Many quiet, thoughtful candidates have been passed over in favor of less intelligent extroverts in this situation.

When you are faced with a group interview, you won't have any group norms from which to work and the group of people thrown together will not have developed a comfortable working style. As a result, the interactions are likely to be stilted, unnatural, and full of false cheeriness toward the other candidates: "That's a wonderful idea, Jonathan!" At best, this type of situation is a measure of how you perform under pressure with strangers. The most you can do is to anticipate the situation and act calmly and pleasantly, perhaps by reminding yourself that this is just a preliminary round and you'll be able to demonstrate your personal qualities better in a later round of interviews. Beware that sometimes the person who is evaluating you may look like one of the other candidates (see *Business Protocol in Action: "He Was So Friendly"*).

Business Protocol in Action: "He Was So Friendly"

Many firms build in a deliberate test of how much you are on your best behavior during formal interviews. They can ask for input from receptionists and other support staff about the candidate's behavior outside of the interview setting or they can ask for a report from the person who shepherds people from one meeting to the next.

One firm actually assigns a "ringer"—someone who looks like another candidate but is actually a junior employee at the firm. This friendly person chats informally with candidates while they are waiting and makes notes on their "off camera" demeanor. Be warned that sometimes the most important part of the selection process does not take place in the interview room!

■ 13-3 INTERVIEW STYLES

When junior members of a firm are assigned to conduct interviews, they may have no thought about what type of interview they are planning to conduct. The result is likely to be that the interview dissolves into a pleasant chat—as you might say, a "noninterview." If the firm is strategic and plans well, the interview could be one of the following specific types:

- Fact check
- Getting to know you
- Technical skills
- Case interview
- Job sample
- Behavioral
- Stress

Many first-round interviews and phone interviews are simple **fact check** conversations. They serve the purpose of checking the facts of your résumé and cover letter. For example, a résumé may state, "Senior standing" (that is, the third year of a U.S. university), but a student may have been on campus for only two years, having arrived with additional credits (advanced placement units) from high school. The firm wants to be sure when the student is planning to graduate. In the fact check interview, the recruiter may press for more details about gaps in your résumé. For example, if you had summer jobs two years in a row and nothing was shown in the third year, you could expect to be asked about how you spent the time. You should have a good answer prepared: "I wanted to graduate early—so I enrolled in summer school."

If you have special circumstances, such as dropping out of school or having been dismissed from a job from which you know you won't get a good reference, you should carefully plan your strategy. The rule "not necessarily the whole truth" should still guide you—you don't need to tell people more than they need to know. But you definitely cannot lie in an interview. Suppose you took time off from school to help your family with a medical crisis. When the interviewer presses for the gap in your education, you'll want to tell a limited amount of the truth: "I had to leave school to help my family. However, I'm happy to say, those problems have all been solved, so I'm now back on track." You want to convey that the problems are behind you and will not interfere with your future employment.

In the **getting to know you** type of interview, the interviewer wants to get a sense of your personality, beliefs, and attitudes and will be trying to assess whether you fit with the firm's culture. This style of interview is sometimes conducted early in the interview process, in which case it may be colloquially referred to as "the smell test" (an unflattering reference to an imagined simple check to make sure you don't smell too bad to work with). The questions are likely to be easy, and it is your style of responding, rather than any specific information, that the interviewer is looking for. So you should plan to relax and be yourself. You can anticipate that later rounds will give you a more strenuous interview.

The getting to know you interview may also appear late in the recruiting sequence. If you have already been through several rounds of interviews, in the next stage you may be introduced to senior management (your future boss's boss) for a brief interview. Again, this is likely to be pleasant and low key and is just to get the manager's final approval of you as a candidate. Another late-in-the-process version of this style of interview is called the **airport test.** The test is that after deciding that you are technically qualified for a position, the members of a work group have to decide this: If they were stuck in an airport with you for three hours due to a flight delay, could they stand your company? It is quite likely that you will have to meet *all* members of the team during this process. If you determine that this type of test is happening (or a friendly insider tells you, "It's just the airport test"), you should be relaxed and friendly, open, and cheerful, but not too pushy or "bubbly."

Surprisingly few interviews focus on **technical skills.** Recruiters may decide that they know enough from your previous work history or schooling and can assume that you can do the work. However, when the interview is designed to test your knowledge and problem-solving abilities, you'll likely be given some advanced warning. Financial services firms assess mathematical abilities with mental arithmetic puzzles. It is your line of reasoning rather than the correct answer that the recruiter is most interested in. So make sure you talk through your thinking and don't sit in silence for several minutes before blurting out what you hope is the correct answer. Most firms have given up using the element of surprise as a diagnostic tool—it only demonstrates that even the best candidates can be unnerved if treated badly enough. So you should pay attention to information that the firm gives in presentations, brochures, or Web sites beforehand so that you can practice and prepare for the interview.

A variant of the technical skills interview is the **case interview.** This is popular with firms such as consultancies that want to test the candidate's ability to sort through complex fact situations. Candidates are presented with brief background information on a business situation and asked what their advice would be to the firm. If you are planning on seeking recruitment in strategy, you will need to spend a lot of time preparing for this type of interview (often including your work in several university courses). In general, before rushing into what you hope is a brilliant answer to the case problem, you should carefully assess the facts presented to you. What conclusions can you reasonably draw? What additional information would you need before you make a recommendation? Often in case interviews, the recruiter is looking more for your questions and your logic flow than for a specific "right answer."

The **job sample interview** has recently become popular in business (and has been used in public safety promotions, such as police and fire departments, for many years). In this type of interview, candidates are presented with a real-world situation and asked to demonstrate how they would handle it. For example, a candidate for a sales manager position might be asked to review a set of quarterly sales figures and then counsel someone playing the role of an underperforming worker. Of course, extensive job sample interviewing is expensive and time-consuming, so you are more likely to see it in interviews for mid- and senior-management promotions than for your first job.

Behavioral interviewing has become very popular in a wide range of industries and positions. It consists of a series of general business situations; each question begins with "Tell me about a time when…" For example, "Tell me about a time when you made a mistake at work." The appropriate structure for your response is to begin by briefly outlining the situation:

> "Well, on my first warehouse job, I was responsible for making sure that the forklift trucks were plugged in so that they could recharge over night."

Then concisely state the problem you faced:

> "One day, I got home and realized that I'd forgotten to do this."

Next describe the action you took:

> "So I called the night security guard and asked him to do it for me."

(At this point, you've demonstrated your responsibility and a little bit of creative problem solving.) Finally, you should end with "What I learned from this..." For example:

> "So I decided each day I'd leave my car keys in my locker and that was my little reminder—I couldn't start my car to go home until I'd taken care of the forklifts."

You should collect a list of potential behavioral interview questions by talking with friends and business associates, but here are some examples. "Tell me about a time when":

- You had a disagreement with someone at work.
- You were working as a member of a team and other people weren't pulling their weight.
- You had conflicting deadlines.
- You had to deal with an irate customer.
- You discovered an error in a colleague's work.
- You became aware of an ethical problem.

In a behavioral interview, expect some follow-up questions, such as, "How did other people react?" or even, "Have you encountered a similar situation where you were not successful in resolving the problem?"

Few firms routinely subject candidates to a **stress interview**—one in which there are endless challenges and arguments to see whether you get nervous under pressure and whether you can still think clearly. However, you are quite likely to experience a challenge to your thinking if an interview is well planned. If you make a logic error, it will be brought to your attention. Are you defensive? Do you continue to stick to your position even when it has been shown you're wrong? Do you immediately give in, even if it involves agreeing with a false proposition? If you don't make any errors, you'll find yourself challenged on every assertion of fact ("Well, Japanese cars are inexpensive." "Really? What about the Lexus and Infinity?") or opinion ("Nixon was a great president." "Really? Most people don't think so"). The trick is to defend your thinking without being defensive. If this is difficult for you, try to get a lot of practice with friends and colleagues before you start interviewing. Remember, it's not about winning a point in an argument—this game is about winning a job.

▪ 13-4 HAVE A FLEXIBLE NARRATIVE STYLE

People learn best from stories. For example, relating how you found alternative accommodations for your sorority sisters after a flood made your house uninhabitable makes a compelling memory for the recruiter. The simple statement: "Yes, I was president of my sorority for two semesters" is not so memorable. In an interview, you will communicate your skills and abilities by a series of stories about your life that give examples of what you have done and how you approach business situations.

Nothing is worse than having to listen to someone go on and on at length in excruciating detail about a story that could be simply summarized. You should plan to have three versions of each story. First, a *standard version* is the three- to five-minute story that you will tell in most circumstances. Second, you may have to make a *condensed version,* especially if the story covers a matter of fact that you want to make sure doesn't take up all of the interview time. This is similar to a business term when long documents are referred to "by title only" rather than read completely. For example, "Well, yes. I missed a year of school. There was an accident and I was hospitalized—but I'm fine now, thank you." You may also have to summarize stories if the interview schedule is disrupted and you have less time with a key decision maker than was originally planned (better that the key executive hear the highlights of five stories than the detail of one). Finally, you should prepare an *extended version* of a story to fill time if, for example, you and your host arrive for lunch and other people will be joining you but they are much delayed. You don't want to be sitting in stony silence.

The conventional wisdom that you should avoid discussing religion and politics holds true for interviews. No matter how funny the latest joke you've heard, you should probably avoid that, too. Although you don't want to be bland, you don't want to cause offense with people whom you don't know well.

▪ 13-5 GENERIC INTERVIEW QUESTIONS

You may encounter some standard interview prompts and questions that, even though expected, are nonetheless stressful for most people.

The first of these is, "Tell me about yourself." You should approach this prompt in much the same way as your cover letter. First, provide a brief summary of where you are in life ("just graduated" or "learned a lot on my first job") and what you're looking for ("I'm planning to move from technical sales into district sales management"). Then permit yourself some nonboastful recitation of your accomplishments, and end with the reason you are approaching this particular firm or position.

Nearly as bad as "tell me about yourself" is the question "What's your biggest weakness?" You may find yourself tempted to wallow in self-deprecation: "I'm never as good a friend as I plan to be." But you should try to avoid the urge to be self-revealing—an interview is not a group therapy session, and no one wants to hire a loser. Also, resist the urge to be facetious: "My biggest weakness? Donuts!" And don't be self-serving: "Sometimes I just care too much! Every Saturday last month, I came into the office to check the invoices. I should really just let it go sometimes!" The conventional wisdom is that you should acknowledge some small imperfection and note what you are doing to overcome it. For example, "I'm getting better at public speaking, but I realize that it needs work—I'm still a bit nervous, so I'm always looking for opportunities to practice."

Many interviewers end with: "So, do you have any questions?" This question is difficult for many candidates—they may have researched the firm well and have no questions except for: "Will I get the job?" In general, recruiters don't like it when a candidate has no questions. You should make sure to have a few questions that show your enthusiasm for the position: "I was interested in your expansion into Eastern Europe. Which countries do you think you'll be going into next?" Avoid intrusive questions such as, "How much of a bonus did you make last year?" and generic weak questions such as, "So, what's a typical day like?" (You should know the responses already from your research.)

If you really can't think of any questions to ask, say that all of your questions have been answered and reflect on some detail: "I was really interested to hear about your new product line." Unless you know what the next stage of the recruiting process is going to be, you should end every interview with an enthusiastic inquiry: "What's the next step?" Shake hands with the interviewer again and be businesslike about moving to the next part of the process or returning to a waiting area.

■ 13-6 TAKING UP REFERENCES

References from current or previous employers aren't as useful these days as they were in the past. America is a litigious country, and firms have been sued for what they've said and not said. Some large American corporations instruct their executives not to write letters of recommendation, and the company will only confirm dates of employment and whether an ex-employee is "eligible for rehire" (if the person is not eligible, that implies that he or she was terminated for some misdeed). As a result, many employers no longer ask for references, and of those that do, fewer than 1 in 10 firms actually goes through the process of **taking up references** with the names they've been given. One exception is the background checks made by firms in financial services (see Section 13-10).

Just to be on the safe side, have a reference list ready, as described in Chapter 12. Be sure to contact "referees" (the people who'll be speaking for you) in advance to alert them to the possibility of a call so that they are not surprised.

■ 13-7 INTERVIEW FOLLOW-UP

After an interview, you should send a written "thank you" note to the firm (see Chapter 11). The purpose of the note is to indicate your continued interest in the job opening. If your interview has consisted of talking with a series of people, it is not a good idea to write to all of them (it signals you have nothing better to do). Select two people—the hiring manager and the lower-level staffer who was most helpful to you—and address them. Make the letter specific, for example, by mentioning your particular interest in some of the firm's current projects or new initiatives. Timing is important in sending these notes. Of course, if you wait two weeks, the decision may already have been made and your note would be pointless. On the other hand, be careful about appearing *too* eager. *The Wall Street Journal* recently quoted a hiring manager who received a cliché-filled thank you e-mail as saying, "It came so soon, it must have been written before the interview and sent from his BlackBerry® as he was walking down the stairs." Sending a note too early robs it of signaling that you've considered the job carefully and are really interested.

Even when an interviewer has told you, "We'll be in touch next week," quite often a candidate won't hear back from the firm within the designated time span. Many candidates assume they've been passed over or that the offer has gone to another candidate and the firm is just waiting to have a signed contract before dismissing all other candidates. Although this may be true, it is not always the case. Indeed, when a company's management staff has agreed to hire someone, the interviewers often go back to their primary duties and assume that someone else is working on the offer—when in reality, no one actually is. At other times, there may be debate about which candidate is the top choice. Of course, you don't want to be a pest, phoning repeatedly and pushing people for a decision. But you may well improve your chances by following up politely. Identify one person as the decision maker (manager) or your contact person (someone in Human Resources), and when the deadline for calling you has been reached, give a little slack out of politeness (one or two days at most) and then phone him or her. If your contact person tells you there still hasn't been a decision, be sure to ask when you should call back and check again. Some gentle persistence may work in your favor.

If you get bad news—that the firm has chosen another candidate—try to position yourself as the person the firm would call if there is a new, similar opening or if its first choice backs out. "Oh, that's too bad! I really enjoyed meeting members of the team. Well, let me just say, I'm still interested in working for Bigco—do call me if anything else comes up." Many successful executives have earned their first lucky break by responding well to a rejection.

■ 13-8 THE JOB OFFER

Congratulations! You are the top candidate and a firm wants to hire you. You are likely to get an informal notification first—either a phone call or an e-mail message. Surprisingly, you should not respond with excessive enthusiasm at this point. Although you're excited, many candidates have regretted making an oral commitment to a job, when a better offer was on its way. The phone notification isn't really an offer. The offer can be made only in writing. So the correct response is to thank the person who's contacting you and say, "I look forward to receiving the offer."

The **offer letter** is formal and contractual. It will specify the job title, work location, and salary and is likely to refer to company documents for benefits, vacation, and so on. Most often, there will be two copies of the letter, and you'll be asked to sign and return one as your indication of acceptance. Be careful—this letter amounts to a legal contract, so do not sign it if your mind is not made up completely. Most offers will have an expiration date: If you do not sign and return it by a specific date, the firm will conclude that you have rejected the offer. (For this reason, you should either hand-deliver an acceptance or send it by overnight delivery.) An offer with a due date is called an "exploding offer" in colloquial speech.

Before you sign the letter, you should be sure that you understand all of the terms of your offer and get them in writing. For example, if you are joining a small firm, and during the interview the manager said, "Oh, everyone takes about four weeks of vacation," you should politely ask for that point to be put in writing, even if it means sending you a second, revised offer letter.

■ 13-9 NEGOTIATING THE OFFER

You may just receive a letter that announces the terms of your offer in a one-sided manner without any negotiation, or you may have been talking with a firm's representatives for weeks about the details of an offer. No matter: Just because an offer is written, it doesn't mean that you can't negotiate terms. Most recruits concentrate on salary alone—there isn't anyone who has ever been hired who doesn't think that he or she is worth at least 20 percent more! However, it's shortsighted to focus only on a single number, especially when you're comparing offers from two or more firms. Table 13-1 outlines some of the parameters of employment that differ from firm to firm. Understanding the details may be important in evaluating one offer or comparing offers from different firms.

In a large corporation, many of the benefits, such as health insurance and whether the firm offers a **401(k) plan,** are fixed and not subject to negotiation. A 401(k) is a supplemental pension plan in which employees contribute part of their paychecks tax-free for retirement benefits. The firm may or may not match their contributions (put in an equal amount).

However, other terms of your employment can often be discussed. For example, a firm may have a general rule that employees don't become eligible for participation in a pension plan during the first year of employment. But many senior managers negotiate this point, saying that they will change firms only if they are offered immediate **vesting** (enrollment in the

Table 13-1 Points to Consider When Negotiating a Job Offer

Negotiating Point	Details
Salary 	Everyone wants more. Be prepared to provide evidence (from surveys, your previous employment, or other offers) if you think the offer is out of line.
Bonus–signing 	Many firms offer recent college graduates a small signing bonus to pay for relocation or new work clothes, so find out what's typical in your industry and geographic area.
Bonus–annual 	Discuss whether a bonus is based on the firm's performance, the work of your group, or your own efforts. In some industries where bonuses are common, if you are leaving midyear (and giving up rights to a bonus), you can negotiate a "guaranteed" similar sum from your new employer.
Moving allowance 	For senior executives, this can include the actual expenses of moving, plus hotels and airfare to search for housing, and some of the expenses of buying a new home. For recent college graduates, a firm may offer a lump sum that you can spend on moving or anything else you choose.

(Continued)

Negotiating Point	Details
Start date 	You may be able to negotiate a delayed starting date that allows you to take some extra time to move or to take an extended vacation before you begin your new job.
Vacation 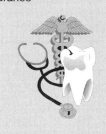	A firm is likely to have rigid policies for which holidays are observed and for how many days a year of paid vacation you are awarded; however, you might be able to get an agreement to take additional times as "leave without pay." Find out whether vacation time you don't use in one year can be carried over to the next (accrued) or whether you can be paid cash for days you don't use.
Insurance	Almost all firms should offer health insurance, and there is usually at least one option that costs nothing to the employee. Additionally, your firm may offer life insurance and disability insurance, and these may be free or require that you pay at least part of the premium.
Pensions 	Because U.S. employees often switch firms, many companies are moving away from the type of pension awarded as a monthly payment after years of service. The firm will have a rule on when you are considered "vested"; that is, after a certain number of years of service, you will be able to receive benefits from the plan, even if you leave the company.

(Continued)

Negotiating Point	Details
Education 	In some industries, part of the hiring process is for firms to agree to reimburse new employees for costs associated with getting a graduate degree. Some firms will pay for any course taken during employment, others only for courses approved by the company.
Commuting expenses 	The firm may provide parking, or this could be a substantial daily expense. The offer may include free or reduced-cost mass-transit tickets.
Clubs 	Your offer may include a free or reduced-cost membership to an athletic or dining club.
Entertaining and travel 	If the job is likely to involve client entertainment or travel, many people agree on the level and terms in advance. For example, in some companies, employees are expected to always fly on the cheapest ticket, but other companies will pay for business-class travel.

plan) or even credit for several years of contributions to the plan on their first day of employment. There's nothing worse than starting work and finding that everyone else in your training class received a signing bonus except you—just because you didn't ask about it.

■ 13-10 FORMAL HIRING PROCEDURES

At some point in the recruiting process (either at the beginning or, in some firms, right before you are to be given an offer of employment), a large firm is likely to ask you to complete an **employment application** on a form that the company has designed or online. When you fill this out, there are two important differences from your résumé. First, when the form or Web site asks for "Name," this must be the full legal form of your name (the form that's on your passport and on your university transcripts). If you've been recruited under an informal name ("Buddy") or a diminutive ("Rick"), you can indicate that form of your name in a space labeled "Former Name." If that option doesn't exist, e-mail your recruiter: "Just to let you know, my formal legal name is Iakov Bartholomew, the Russian form of my name; however, I go by 'Yakov,' as it's easier for people to spell and pronounce."

The second change from your résumé is that it's likely that the firm will ask you to "List all employment," and you should carefully fill out every detail of every job you've had. If you are asked later, "Why doesn't your work as an elf in Santa's Workshop appear on your résumé?" you should give an answer such as, "I didn't feel it had much relevance for my work as an audit accountant." Firms that have fiduciary responsibility for their customers (that is, they look after valuables such as cash or stock) may fire you at once if they later discover that you've omitted something from their employment application. The reason for asking you to list every single employer is that a firm may need to know not to put you on certain accounts and transactions where you've worked for a direct competitor in the same industry (even if your employment was just a summer job).

If there is something you need to report that is embarrassing or awkward (such as a long period of unemployment or dismissal from a previous job), fill out the form truthfully and ask to discuss the matter with the person who's hiring you before you hand it in (or before you submit online). "I wanted to tell you personally about something you are going to read on page 3…" would be a good way to introduce the topic. As long as the bad news is not a felony conviction or being fired for something related to the new job, most people will be forgiving. But be warned: Just as many criminals are eventually convicted on perjury, rather than on the underlying crime, a firm can use any false statement on an application to fire you at once.

At the time of the offer, the firm may ask you to undergo a physical (medical) exam and will quite likely conduct a drug test on a urine sample. If you use recreational drugs that are illegal in the United States, the firm has a right not to hire you. Other than that, under most circumstances, a firm cannot refuse to hire you if you have a medical condition, such as high blood pressure, that is not directly related to the performance of your duties.

It's quite likely that a large firm—or a firm working with sensitive data—will ask to conduct additional background checks. The firm can ask your permission to check with local police to see if you have any warrants out for your arrest. If you have a problem, such as a family situation in which the police have been called, or multiple traffic arrests, you'll have to get advice from an attorney on how to handle this situation. You may be instructed to say nothing and let the firm find out whatever it can (which may not be much), or you may be advised to tell your side of the story in person first.

Many firms also ask to perform a credit check. Although your company will not be providing you with loans (in fact, you'll be providing them with credit by waiting until the end of the month for your first paycheck!), your credit records have a lot of information about where you've lived and how you run your affairs. A company could make a reasonable case that someone who's head over heels in debt might be more of a risk to sell industrial secrets and so on. In most jurisdictions, this type of background checking is legal. If you are uncomfortable with these checks or the information the company might uncover, your only choice is to refuse to undergo the check and give up the job offer.

If you have a disability that is covered under the **Americans with Disabilities Act (ADA),** the law requires that firms make a reasonable effort to accommodate your desire to work. So, if you could do a job but you need a special type of computer keyboard, the firm is required to find out what you need and to spend the money to provide you with the equipment. Of course, the standard of "reasonable" is open to interpretation. Almost all large U.S. firms have done a very good job of complying with the act. It is permissible for a firm to ask, "Would you need any special accommodations to do this job?" at an interview, but it's not permissible for a firm to choose one candidate over another based on the ease of providing accommodations. So most firms won't ask this question until later in the hiring process, after the offer has been made. If you feel that the ADA applies to you, you should seek some counseling as to how to work with your firm to get the equipment you need and any appropriate modifications to your work schedule or duties.

■ 13-11 HANDLING MULTIPLE OFFERS

With good luck, there will be a few times in your life when you have job offers from more than one firm. Many people try to solve this "problem" by a simple calculation of which firm is offering the highest starting salary. Of course, you should take many other factors into account, such as future prospects for promotion, the type of work, how convenient the firm's location is, and so on. Remember, two offers that are the same on paper may be worth more or less than each other, depending on the cost of living in the city where each job is located.

When you're experiencing difficulty choosing between two offers, you can talk with friends and business associates to get their opinions on the two firms' reputations and outlook. But at the end of the day, the decision will be yours. You should seriously consider which group of colleagues you will find most congenial for long days and demanding projects. A good way to evaluate your choice is to ask for one more visit to the firm you think you will prefer (or even two or more firms if you really are having difficulty deciding). Ask to **shadow an employee** in the group where you'll be working. ("Shadowing" means following someone around while that person goes about his or her routines.) A whole day would be nice, but at least visit from mid-morning to mid-afternoon and go to lunch with your future colleagues. Ask yourself, "Is this the group I'd like to be part of?" Listen carefully for how group members talk about one another and their work. Ask them over lunch, "So what's a really bad day like around here?" If they say, "Well, at the end of the quarter, we never get out until 10 P.M. putting the numbers together, but we usually celebrate the next week by going skiing," you know that's a good place to work. However, if there's a problem in the work group, such as a boss who's a "screamer," an informal lunch with potential colleagues is where the truth will come out.

You should not turn down one good offer until you are sure of the other offer. A job offer should be made in writing. After you've signed and returned the offer, you can let other firms know that you will be working elsewhere. Many people get anxious about this part of the process, but they shouldn't. As one recruiter said, "I'm a recruiter—I've been turned down before. It's part of my job." So begin by understanding that an offer is only an offer, and as such, it can be rejected without offense. You should contact the person you've been negotiating with (recruiter or manager) by the same medium that he or she has been using to reach you—most likely by phone. Most people feel that it isn't appropriate to leave a voice mail for such information. When you reach the recruiter, choose your words carefully. You don't need to give a reason for turning down the offer or to say explicitly what you are doing instead. If the recruiter asks, you can briefly summarize your decision and reasoning if you choose.

When you turn down an offer, your word choice is important. Bear in mind that there might be a time when you want to talk with this firm again—perhaps the firm's prospects improve, or perhaps your first-choice job doesn't turn out to be as good as you've hoped. If you have exaggerated a reason, it may cut you off from future consideration by that firm. Suppose, for example, you say to a recruiter, "I just decided to stay here in St. Louis. I really don't want to move to New York." Although this statement may be true, you won't look credible if you reapply to the New York firm in the future—the recruiter will decide not to waste time with you. If the job offer that you accept is for substantially more money and you feel the offer you are turning down was underestimating your worth (or the market rate for such jobs), you can politely communicate this information.

The process of reigniting interest in your candidacy with a firm you previously turned down isn't completely unheard of. If you ended the process on good terms and handled your rejection of the firm with courtesy, you can certainly see whether positions are still open. In this circumstance, there's nothing that can beat a little honesty: "As you know, I had accepted at Bigco, but they just announced they're filing for bankruptcy," or "I really did have a plan to move west, but my wife has just been promoted, so we're staying here." If a firm liked you well enough to have made you a job offer in the past, most will have some interest in your reapproach.

Even when a job offer is made in writing, you don't have to decline it in writing. It's certainly good etiquette to make contact with the firm so that it knows that the offer wasn't misplaced, but you don't have to send a formal letter rejecting the offer—nonacceptance by a cut-off date has the same legal effect.

You may find yourself in the awkward situation of having a definite written offer from your second-choice firm, while you've interviewed and not yet heard back from your first-choice firm. In this circumstance, you can phone your first-choice company and state the facts: "I need to let you know that I have an offer from Second-Choice-Co on my desk, but I really enjoyed my interviews with your firm. I'm up against a deadline—when will you be able to make a decision?" Once again, recruiters encounter this situation frequently (they understand that top candidates will get multiple offers), so you shouldn't feel embarrassed about this call.

A more difficult situation exists when you have one offer but haven't yet begun the interview process with a firm that you think might be more to your liking. You can certainly call your preferred firm, explain your situation, and try to advance the interview schedule. You may be able to get the first firm to extend its deadline—but that's unlikely. At worst, if the interviews can't be moved up and the offering firm won't give you more time to decide, you face the tough choice of having to turn down a certain offer and hope for a better one or having to go with a firm that wasn't your top choice. This is a difficult personal decision, for which there is no easy solution. You'll have to talk with friends and family and then make a choice. In any job search, offers are likely to come in at different times. The one thing you cannot do, however, is accept one job and then later back out when you get a better offer, which is a very unprofessional process called "reneging" (see *Doing the Right Thing: Reneging Is Never Costless*).

■ 13-12 HANDLING NO OFFERS

If you have been actively seeking recruitment and you've received lots of interviews and call-backs but no offers, after awhile you'll need to diagnose the reason for this situation. Are you really overqualified for the

Doing the Right Thing:
Reneging Is Never Costless

In the recruiting business, there's no uglier word than **reneging**. This is the situation in which a candidate has accepted an offer in writing but then decides not to start the job. In theory, the company could sue the reneging candidate for monetary damages. After the candidate accepted, the firm dismissed other applicants and then had to bear the expenses of restarting the search. Although few legal actions are taken in practice, the damage to your reputation could potentially be extreme if you renege. The recruiter from the spurned firm could phone the firm you've accepted and say, "I just want you to know what's going on here..." Even if you don't lose the second job on the spot, you'll begin your new job with a reputation for being untrustworthy. Even if you think that turning down Firm A is costless and you take an "it's all fair in love and war" approach, you may find to your dismay that the recruiter from Firm A is actually married to your new boss at Firm B! Managers from competitive firms in one industry often talk, and the chance that reneging will have zero effect on your career is, well, zero.

The social costs of reneging may be even larger. Even if you graduated from college a few years ago, word may get around that people from your school can't be relied upon. For this reason, most university career service offices take reneging very seriously.

The only possible reasons to renege are when you have extraordinary changes in your family circumstance ("My mother is terminally ill, and I've decided I can't move now") or when your plans to enter the workforce have changed. For example, if, to your surprise, you receive a graduate fellowship that you hadn't expected and you decide to go to school instead, you could withdraw from a previously accepted offer (under the doctrine of "employment at will," which is discussed in Chapter 15). You should definitely make a phone call as soon as you know, and you should speak directly to the person with whom you've been negotiating. Explain the circumstances and your decision as clearly as possible. Because this is not good news for the company and will cause extra work for the recruiter, you should anticipate that this phone call will not be pleasant. Because you have accepted an offer in writing and it is contractual, you must now withdraw your acceptance in writing (in addition to making the phone call).

positions you're seeking? Do you lack a critical skill or certification? Are you holding out for too much money? As you go through cycles of interviewing, whenever you receive notification that you've not advanced to the next round or have not been selected for an offer, it is very professional to ask, "Is there anything I can learn from this? Do you have any feedback for me?" Many recruiters will recede behind a wall of platitudes ("It was a tough decision...everyone liked you...there were so many good candidates"), but once in awhile you'll find someone who can give you good advice—for example: "Well, we thought you were qualified, but a couple of people said you came off as just too desperate for a job," or "You knew the answers to the questions, but some of the interviewers commented that you didn't really show much enthusiasm for our firm."

If you are finding it hard to get feedback, try to take a practice interview with someone in the same industry—an alumnus from your university who's not currently hiring, or a friend of a family member whom you've not met before. Many people will be willing to do this and to give you some pointers for improvement. If you are recruiting through an on-campus career center, there should be a routine for practice interviews, and the university staff may collect and summarize feedback from several recruiters. If you lack certain technical skills or knowledge, you know what you have to do to become a more attractive candidate. If you have the right qualifications but are interviewing badly, you'll need some good coaching.

Treating a scheduled interview with a firm (on-campus or at the firm's office) as a practice interview is something that career center staff may advise you not to do. And other candidates won't appreciate your taking up an interview slot if you have no intention of working for a firm. However, all successful applicants who've talked to numerous firms will acknowledge that their interviewing improved from one interview to the next. For this reason, many experts recommend that you make a deliberate effort to schedule interviews at your first-choice company later in the sequence. Make sure you're an experienced interviewee before you go off to meet people at the firm where you most want to work.

There can be few life circumstances that are more depressing than looking for work and not finding it. The truism "Everyone eventually finds a job somewhere" is probably of little comfort to you, but it is true! If your industry is in a slowdown, either it will pick up and you'll find a new position or you'll realize that your skills can be applied in a different field. You can remind yourself that there are some advantages to the American system of hiring and firing (see *It's Just Different: The Advantages of No Security*). The most important determinant for success is to keep a cheerful mood—if you become dispirited, it will be impossible for you to interview well. You should think about the activities and friends

It's Just Different: The Advantages of No Security

To a European, American firms are positively heartless in their treatment of employees. They fire people without hesitation when business takes a downturn. Many people outside the United States can't imagine working under such a harsh regime. In Germany and France, it is very difficult to lay off workers, and throughout Europe it is not uncommon for a low-performing worker to be offered as much as six months' salary just to agree to resign from a firm.

However, this apparent high job security environment isn't nearly as good as it seems. Because it is difficult to fire workers, firms are very reluctant to take on new workers. This is especially true for young adults. In France and Germany, the overall unemployment rate has often been much higher than the rate in the United States and at times has been over 20 percent for people under age 25.

So although the rough and tumble of the U.S. job market may seem to completely lack security, most American workers aren't particularly anxious. True, their current job may go away in a heartbeat, but there are likely to be more new opportunities waiting that may even involve a promotion and more money!

that keep you energized and avoid those that depress you. If you have been laid off during a recession or industry slowdown, you'll have to make a decision about what to do until the market comes back. Some people make use of the opportunity to take additional schooling, and others travel. If you are facing a long period of unemployment, you should consider getting a simple job (such as working for a temporary agency or in a retail store or warehouse) to make money for basic living expenses while you're searching for a permanent position.

13-13 TERMINATION—BEING "UNHIRED"

There may come a time when you decide to no longer work for a firm; Chapter 15 discusses the process for making a graceful exit. But you may face a circumstance in which your firm has decided that your services aren't needed anymore, and you will be **fired**. In many countries, the only reason someone would be fired is that he or she has done something terribly wrong. In America, that's not true. Firms constantly make estimates of their future workload and add and subtract people very quickly.

The colloquial term for being fired is to be **let go.** (It's a silly term that implies that employees are constantly straining to be released from their work.) If you encounter this situation, you might hear that the company is "downsizing," that your department or project is being eliminated, or at least that the industry is undergoing a slowdown. You should begin the process of discreetly looking around for opportunities with other firms.

When the end does come, it will be ugly and ungracious. You may look up from your desk to see a Human Resources person, or your boss, probably accompanied by a security guard. You may be asked to gather your personal belongings and leave at once. This process is very hard on people who are terminated and is unnerving indeed for those employees who are left behind—they wonder, "Who's next?" U.S. companies do this very sudden firing to protect computer systems and proprietary knowledge. You'll be asked to surrender your corporate ID badge and may be searched to make sure you are not taking anything with you that belongs to the firm. The process is alarming, upsetting, and humiliating. The best you can do is to keep your dignity by maintaining a professional demeanor.

An alternative form of dismissal is that all employees in a group or division are brought into an "all-hands meeting." At this point, most people have an idea that bad news is about to hit. After a general announcement of the situation, employees are taken in small groups to be told whether they are retained or will be dismissed.

When a firm fires employees in a **reduction in force** (RIF, hence the phrase, "I've been **riffed**"), they will usually be asked to sign one or more documents in return for some severance pay. There is little requirement in law to provide much, if any, severance pay under most circumstances. About as much as you can hope for is payment for time worked, payment for vacation days owed, and as little as two weeks' additional pay. However, firms that are trying to reduce head-count will usually offer some additional compensation to encourage employees to leave quickly and quietly. A typical offer is one month of salary for each year of employment, but there's a wide range of what may be offered, depending on the firm's financial situation.

You should be careful about what you are asked to sign. The form might be a simple receipt for money paid to you, or it might contain "non-compete" clauses, saying that you won't go to work for a competitor. Because working for a competitor is precisely what you have in mind, signing such a document may not be in your best interests. You should take the document and ask that you have time to read it and perhaps consult with a lawyer. Arrange for a time when you can trade the signed document for your severance check.

You may be offered the opportunity to sign a letter of resignation. The advantage for the firm is that you then pretty much give up your right to sue for wrongful termination. This is not much of an offer—if you don't sign, you'll be fired anyway. And if you resign, you may be ineligible for unemployment benefits. In many countries, and perhaps in the United States in an earlier age, being fired was considered a terrible thing. But so many people (you could almost say "most people") have been riffed at one time or another that there's no great stigma to being fired. It is not unusual for employees who have been terminated due to a reduction in force to trade signing a resignation letter for getting something they want, such as continuation of health care benefits for a few months.

Many firms arrange for a type of counseling called **outplacement.** This service is run by a specialized employment counseling firm to help you identify your transferable skills, to decide whether you need additional training, and to make a realistic appraisal of the type of job you can find next. You should definitely take advantage of this counseling if it is offered to you, and if it's not, try to negotiate that the firm will pay for outplacement.

Firms have a great deal of latitude in whom they hire and fire (see Chapter 15). You may be the most recent hire or the most long-standing employee or you may be the person with the best performance reviews. You have grounds for suing your now ex-employer only if there was discrimination on the basis of age (firing only older workers), gender, or race. You'll need to hire a lawyer, and any settlement will likely be many years away. So as a practical matter, although you may hope to recover compensation from a firm for wrongful dismissal in the far distant future, you'll need to get on with your life in the short term.

▶ > > PUT THIS CHAPTER INTO PRACTICE

1. With a friend, take turns practicing a response to a phone call in which you are told you've not been selected for a job you wanted. Work to position yourself as a good backup candidate or a candidate for future openings at the firm.

2. Practice telling the same story in three versions: standard (about 3 to 5 minutes), extended (20 minutes), and condensed (summary and conclusion only).

3. Arrange for a practice phone interview. This should be with someone you don't know well, such as an alumnus from your school or business associate of one of your parents.

4. Make a list of up-to-date behavioral interview questions by talking to people who have recently been through the interview process.

▌ KEY TERMS

401(k) plan

airport test

Americans with Disabilities Act (ADA)

behavioral interview

case interview

employment application

fact check interview

fired, "let go"

getting to know you interview

group interview

job description

job sample interview

offer letter

outplacement

phone interview

portfolio

reduction in force, "riffed"

reneging

shadow an employee

stress interview

taking up references

technical skills interview

vesting

Multiple Choice Practice Questions: To take the review quiz for this chapter, log on to your Online Edition at www.atomicdog.com.

Chapter 14
Looking the Part: What to Wear

Say farewell to the necktie.

Just as visitors to the United States joke that it's a country where no one has last names (all introductions are on casual, first-name terms), they'll soon be going home saying that it's a country without neckties. Although fashion shifts in business attire are slow, there are some gradual developments. A look back at corporate photos from the 1960s, for example, will show men all wearing hats and women wearing white gloves as they arrive for work—which is no longer the trend.

In the last few years, it has become acceptable to wear full business attire, including a business suit, but with no necktie. There are several reasons for this change. First, it is a leakage from "casual Fridays" to the rest of the week. Second, a necktie serves no function, unlike other parts of clothing that keep the wearer warm. Third, neckties have become a symbol of old-fashioned attitudes. Most importantly, however, the vast majority of wearers would say they are just plain uncomfortable.

Many politicians are now forgoing a necktie during much of their campaigning. They want to signal that they are in touch with ordinary voters. Although fashion trends come in waves, with both ebb and flow, it's likely that in a few years, neckties will become as extinct as top hats.

14-1 DIFFERENT FIRMS, DIFFERENT "UNIFORMS"

To be successful in contemporary American business, you should be aware of the possible options of dress and then make some effort to diagnose the preferred style in the firm in which you'll be working. Although few U.S. employers want office workers to wear a company-issued uniform, in practice, every firm has a dress code. In a large company, the expectations will be written down (quite often in terms of what is *not* acceptable), but in a smaller company, the code may be unwritten, but nonetheless should be taken seriously. If you don't understand or follow the code, you may look as if you don't fit in, and that may limit your effectiveness in projects in which you need to engage the cooperation of your peers. You may be overlooked when it comes to prestigious assignments that involve presentations to clients or to senior management. It's possible to be both underdressed (you look shabby compared with other people) or overdressed (you look too stiff and formal, as if you are play-acting your role rather than being an effective professional).

Somewhat paradoxically, **business attire** is not necessarily the everyday "uniform" in all U.S. businesses. Traditionally, office workers were expected to wear conservative clothing that consisted of a dark suit, white blouse or white shirt with a sober tie (that is, one without a distinctive color or pattern), brightly polished shoes, and a matching belt. There are subtle variations to this outfit, depending on cultural norms. For example, in the entertainment industry and for Capitol Hill lobbyists, slip-on leather shoes (loafers) were acceptable, but in banking, they signaled "I don't really belong here." These days, on an invitation you might see the notation "Business attire" to indicate strict formality of dress at a client presentation or an important business social function. The implication here is that the rest of the time, most workers would be in something less formal.

Many firms encourage **business casual** dress on some days (for example, "casual Friday") or in certain circumstances (for example, if you have a day when you come into the office but are not expecting to meet with clients). Some firms have adopted "casual summers" (allowing casual dress every day for four months of the year), whereas others have adopted a relaxed dress code year-round: "We have a *business casual* work environment here." Diagnosing exactly what a specific firm and its culture mean by "business casual" will take some careful observation. A typical interpretation of business casual would be as follows. For men: Dockers-style pants (everyday pants in khaki, gray, or blue that are not jeans) and dress shirts without a necktie; for women: tailored slacks and a nice blouse with at least a quarter sleeve.

However, there are variations: In some firms, jeans *are* acceptable if they are clean and not ripped. In some firms, T-shirts are acceptable, as long as they are plain, without any printing, slogan, or logo design. At a few firms (for example, California computer games design shops), even senior executives wear shorts and loud, graphic T-shirts. Keep this range in mind, try to observe what your firm means if it says "business casual," and ask: "So, is there anything that would *not* be acceptable here?" (see *Doing the Right Thing: Don't Strut Your Stuff at Work*).

Doing the Right Thing: Don't Strut Your Stuff at Work

If you have an interest in fashion, you may take some pride in choosing different outfits and accessories for every day at the office. But remember to be practical and avoid dressing in a manner that might be seen as deliberately sexually provocative. This applies to both genders: Men should not wear super-tight T-shirts or muscle shirts no matter how casual the "casual Friday" seems to be at the office. For women, tube tops, halter tops, and micro-miniskirts should never make an appearance at the office.

If you are in any doubt about what's appropriate, imagine how you'd feel if someone from your firm whom you don't really like came up to you at a coffee break and said: "Wow, you are looking so fine today!"

■ 14-2 DRESSING FOR INTERVIEWS

The old standard was that you should always wear your best suit for job interviews. But these days there are many firms at which you'd be uncomfortable in a suit, and you'd feel as if you were signaling: "I don't really belong here!" The trick is to carefully diagnose the firm's dress standards and then wear one level above what you would actually wear on the job. For example, in the case of the California technology company in which even the boss wears shorts and a loudly printed T-shirt, you might wear very stylish jeans and a nice golf shirt (knit shirt with collar) to an interview. As a second example, suppose you were interviewing to be an assistant buyer with a Midwest department store and the manager sets up the appointment by phone, saying, "Oh, and since it's Friday, remember we'll all be in jeans." In that case, you'd be "one level up" by wearing slacks and a nice, colorful blouse.

Because the interpretation of both "business attire" and "business casual" are subject to subtle variations, you can understand why it's a good idea for job candidates to make a scouting trip to the company before the interview and visit the lobby of the firm's headquarters building to get an idea of the dress code.

Remember that what you wear to look your best in a social setting with peers isn't going to be the same as what is expected in business (see *Business Protocol in Action: Where's the Funeral?*).

Business Protocol in Action:
Where's the Funeral?

Although most business suits for both men and women are dark gray or navy blue, many college age and recent graduate job candidates consider a plain black suit to be the height of fashion. Paired with a plain white shirt or blouse, this looks remarkably somber in the interview situation. Add a plain black necktie to complete the stylish look and the result looks positively funereal to interviewers from an older generation. They might be tempted to begin the interview with, "I'm sorry for your loss."

Although there's no doubt that a plain black shirt can look smart on many young adults, the combination of black shirt with a black suit and tie is best saved for clubbing. If your one best suit is plain black, soften it with a pastel shirt or blouse and an interesting coordinating tie (men) or scarf (women).

In an interview situation, you need to pay attention to the details of your clothing: Your shirt or blouse should be professionally laundered, starched, and ironed, and your shoes should be properly polished. Pay attention to the discussion of perfume and cologne in Section 14-5—in general, you should carefully avoid any strong scent. There are several negative cultural associations to sunglasses: They prevent eye contact, and people wearing sunglasses may subconsciously remind a recruiter of dictators of third-world countries or "bad cops" (corrupt police officers) from movies. So although many people wear sunglasses, especially to drive or to appear fashionable, you should always remove them when you're interviewing. Indeed, many people feel that the same rule applies to photochromic lenses (lenses that automatically darken in sunlight) on eyeglasses. Because they darken moderately under the fluorescent lights used in most offices, you should avoid them if at all possible.

If you have several rounds of interviews on different days with the same firm, it's a good idea to keep track of what you wore on each day so that you can rotate your choice of shirt and tie or blouse and jewelry. You want to give the impression that you know how to dress professionally all the time, not that you just have a single nice outfit. If your interviews are for a whole day and into the evening, planning for a change of clothes before dinner can freshen your appearance and your outlook.

14-3 WHAT TO WEAR AT BUSINESS SOCIAL FUNCTIONS

In Chapters 10 and 11, we covered the different types of social functions associated with business. There are many styles of clothing that are appropriate for business events, and for that reason, the invitation often signals the dress code. You might receive an invitation that dictates, "Please come to a reception to meet the new treasurer. Attire: Sports jackets." What would you be expected to wear? Table 14-1 summarizes the dress codes that might be expected at ceremonies and other social situations, organized from most formal to informal.

14-4 DEVELOPING A PERSONAL STYLE

As soon as you are comfortable with the implicit dress code in your firm and work group, you can choose clothing that is a variation within the cultural norm and that becomes your personal trademark. For example, you

Table 14-1   Types of Attire for Business Situations

How It Might Be Referred to...	What It Consists of...	When to Wear It...
"Tails" or "white tie"	*Men:* Black tailed coat, black pants, waistcoat, black polished shoes (or shiny "patent leather"), stiff white shirt, white bow tie. *Ladies:* Ball gown (ankle length), heavy jewelry.	The highest level of formality. Used on rare "state occasions," such as an invitation to a White House dinner.
Morning dress	*Men:* Dark or gray jacket usually with long tails, striped gray pants, waistcoat, stiff shirt, bow tie in any color or "four in hand" tie (looks like a folded silk scarf). *Ladies:* Day dress or very chic suit; typically not pants. Modest jewelry.	Quite common for members of a wedding party; for instance, if you are the best man. Men's outfits are invariably rented—no one owns or regularly wears them. *(Continued)*

How It Might Be Referred to...	What It Consists of...	When to Wear It...
Tuxedo, or "black tie" (called "dinner jackets" in British English). Also called "formal" when the invitation is to an evening event.	*Men:* Black (or off-white in summer) suit-coat-length jacket, black pants with a silk stripe on the side, stiff white shirt, cummerbund or waistcoat. Bow tie of any color (even if it says "black tie"), often in a fancy pattern matching the cummerbund. Most tuxedos are rented but some people whose business requires them to attend many formal functions might own such a suit. *Ladies:* "Cocktail dress"—probably knee length, and very elegant; often plain fabric but possibly with embroidery or beaded decoration. Jewelry can be flashy.	Standard for formal evening events such as charity balls, galas, and banquets. Still expected in some cities for the most expensive seating areas of the opera or theater.
Business suit, business attire, or business formal ("lounge suits" in British English) 	*Men:* Business suit, most often dark gray or navy blue, possibly with a faint stripe. Plain shirt, probably white or pale blue. Nice necktie, subtle pattern OK. Dark socks—even in summer. Shoes and belt match, often black but dark brown is acceptable (although a little less formal). *Ladies:* Women's business suit—pants suit or skirt and jacket with a formal blouse or twin set (popular where outside temperatures are hot but buildings are highly air-conditioned, such as in Hong Kong or Miami). Modest jewelry.	This is the "default" wardrobe for U.S. business. That is, if you are not sure what dress code is expected, choose this.

(Continued)

How It Might Be Referred to...	What It Consists of...	When to Wear It...
Blazers 	*Men:* Navy blue blazer (brass buttons are considered flashy—most people avoid them) and gray pants (most of the year). Khaki, off-white, or plaid pants are acceptable in summer. Shirt can be any color, patterned or plaid. Necktie optional. Shoes are usually slip-ons (loafers) or "deck shoes" (leather shoes in a moccasin style with leather laces and flat soles); dark socks except in summer. *Ladies:* Stylish tailored pants or "designer" jeans and short-sleeve or sleeveless top (but not "spaghetti straps") with a cardigan sweater. Costume jewelry is acceptable.	Very popular in Europe for everything from the opera to casual poolside barbecues. Slightly casual for "serious" U.S. business (for example, when first meeting a client, or when negotiating a contract), but could be considered "dress up" at a convention or off-site conference meeting.
Sport jacket	*Men:* Jacket that looks like that of a business suit, but in a different fabric and pattern than the pants. Pants are tailored slacks in a complementary color. Shirt can be colored or patterned, necktie usually optional but may be required in some restaurants and clubs. Golf shirt (without tie) also usually acceptable. Leather shoes, usually brown, and any color of socks except white. *Ladies:* Tailored pants with blouse or finely knit sweater, or day dress. Costume jewelry.	Not frequently designated on invitations in the United States, although used typically for dining out or attending routine religious services on the weekends.

(Continued)

How It Might Be Referred to...	What It Consists of...	When to Wear It...
Business casual (see text for more discussion); might be called "dressing down" 	*Men:* Khaki pants or "Dockers" (pressed cotton pants of any color), shirt with collar in any plain color. No necktie. Leather shoes that match belt. White or light-colored socks possible. Sweaters are acceptable if they don't have lettering or logos. *Ladies:* Slacks with blouse or simple top with at least short sleeves. Cardigan sweater. Any leather shoes. Very little jewelry.	Becoming the routine for West Coast and East Coast businesses, but still used only occasionally in the Midwest and South.
Athletic attire (might vary for specific sports such as tennis or swimming)	*Men and Ladies:* Sweatsuit or jogging suit over T-shirt and shorts. White socks and sneakers ("trainers" in British English). "Logo" sweatshirts from college or favorite teams are acceptable.	Might be mentioned on the invitation for some active social event; you might also see "outdoor gear" for something that involves camping or hiking.
"Come as you are" or "Dress: casual." The phrase **"cas-nice"** (pronounced "cazsh" as in "casual-nice") is one level up from "casual," close to "blazer" or "sports jacket"	*Men and Ladies:* A range, from business casual down to T-shirt and smart shorts. Clothes should be clean and carefully chosen (for example, avoid T-shirt slogans that might offend).	Frequently used for invitations to neighborhood functions (e.g., potluck suppers). Despite the wording, "come as you are" does not really mean to come over as you are—if you have just been cleaning out the garage or gardening.

might be the only person in your group who wears suspenders rather than a belt. When everyone else is wearing golf shirts, you might be the one who wears Hawaiian shirts. You might be the only woman in your group who wears heels with jeans. Even just adding a small unique piece to an outfit can express your personality. If it's your personal style, you look good, and you are comfortable, go for it! If you do this right, you can signal conformance to group norms, but with a little bit of individuality. The advantage of having a consistent but personal "look" is that it becomes easy for people in your firm who interact with you intermittently to recognize you. However, you might also need to adapt to your office environment. If your office is particularly hot or cold, you'll have to adjust your wardrobe to be able to work effectively (see *It's Just Different: Freezing in the Tropics*).

When you are building your professional wardrobe and defining your personal style, there will come a moment when someone at work walks in with the outfit you just have to have. Although "Your dress is lovely!" is a nice thing to say, "Where did you get it?" usually crosses over a social line.

Your colleague with the fabulous fashion sense is undoubtedly flattered that you've noticed her good taste. But the last thing she wants is to know that at the next quarterly sales meeting, she'll walk in to find you

It's Just Different: Freezing in the Tropics

Hong Kong is Asia's business hub—in the Central district, innumerable skyscrapers and building projects jostle to be the tallest building. The weather in Hong Kong is euphemistically described as "subtropical." In reality, except for a couple of pleasant months in winter, it's invariably hot and sticky. But to workers in many Hong Kong offices, their days feel "subfreezing," not subtropical.

Owners of tall buildings are eager to signal that they have adequate air-conditioning to handle the heat, so buildings are often air-conditioned down to 70 degrees or even as low as 64 degrees in some studies. The result is that many office workers in the Special Administrative Region spend their days shivering at their desks. Receptionists keep sweaters and lap-blankets at their desks, and many executives have wool jackets that they put on when they arrive at work!

The good news is that Hong Kong residents are beginning to address the excessive use of energy that this "killer air-con" requires. This problem may be corrected in the future as people become increasingly sensitive to the wasteful use of energy that this excessive air-conditioning requires.

wearing the exact same dress. For this reason, a recent column in *The Wall Street Journal* suggests that you'll have to forgo trying to get the exact same dress yourself. Wearing the same dress to the same function at work would be embarrassing for you and your fashion mentor.

If you are friendly with the colleague and really can't live without buying the same dress yourself, you'll have to approach the fashion leader very tactfully and promise that you'll never wear your version of the same dress to work or any business function.

■ 14-5 GROOMING

No matter how casual the workplace, you should always be impeccably groomed. For example, you can have your hair long or short (or even choose to shave your skull—it's fashionable in some circles), but your hair should always be neatly trimmed and not unkempt. The same applies to shaving: In almost all industries, it's permissible to wear a beard or mustache, but if you choose to do so, keep it neatly trimmed.

All U.S. office workers take at least one shower a day, and many bathe even more often. For example, someone who goes jogging at lunchtime or goes to the gym at the end of the workday will often take two or more showers a day. Americans are highly sensitive to body odors and are likely to be offended by smells that would be considered natural in other parts of the world. So you should always use a deodorant after showering.

On the other hand, avoid strong-smelling perfume, cologne, or aftershave. Although it's true that many people enjoy and admire a subtle fragrance, unfortunately not everyone has the same taste, and your coworkers may find your favorite to be overwhelming and annoying. Most businesspeople don't wear a fragrance at work; if you really want to do this, you had better plan on checking with a trusted colleague to see if your choice is acceptable and not too strong. Because some people have allergies to certain scents, some firms have resorted to banning the use of any fragrances.

For women, whether to wear makeup at all (hospital nurses often wear none, for example) and how much to wear (some department store sales clerks are heavily made up) will depend on your firm and the culture within your industry, together with your personal preference. If, for example, you are working in an accounting firm where everyone seems to "put on a face" every morning but you hate makeup, you will feel under some pressure to at least use lipstick if you want to fit in at work. On the other hand, if you enjoy makeup but it seems against the norm, try to come up with a simplified "look" using only light makeup for the workplace, and save your most glamorous efforts for evenings and weekends.

■ 14-6 JEWELRY AND PIERCINGS

In Table 14-1, there are notations on how much jewelry is acceptable. For ladies, this is definitely an area for personal style, and you may wear a little more or less than your coworkers. However, don't try to show off wealth with excessive amounts of gold jewelry, and don't wear pieces that would be distracting in the workplace. Women often wear what is called **costume jewelry,** which is acceptable jewelry that looks as if it's real but is actually made of plastic and cheap metal. For men in very conservative firms, any jewelry beyond a wristwatch might be considered strange. But in some industries (such as the West Coast entertainment industry), men routinely wear not only gold necklaces, but metal bracelets too.

Pierced earlobes for earrings are now more common than not for women in the workplace, and many men have one or both ears pierced too. However, men don't generally wear earrings in the most conservative settings. In conservative businesses, any piercings other than women's ears may not be accepted at all. Although there are differences by region and generation in the acceptance of piercings (such as eyebrow rings), most middle-aged people are not accustomed to seeing—and are not comfortable looking at—lip or tongue piercings (see Figure 14-1). Be warned that if this type of self-expression is important to you, it may limit your choice of employment. Although some piercings are permanent, many can be temporarily removed and replaced with "keepers," which make the piercing unnoticeable during work hours.

■ 14-7 BUILDING A WARDROBE

When you first start into the workforce, you may be overwhelmed at the thought of all the clothes you have to buy. Don't despair—you don't have to buy them all at once, and you should be able to buy most of them on

Figure 14-1   Body Piercing
Body piercing is a form of self-expression that may make some colleagues uncomfortable. Consider temporarily removing piercing rings in the workplace.
SOURCE: © 2009 Jupiterimages Corporation.

sale. Let's begin by considering the circumstances in which you need business attire—for example, if you were beginning work as an accounting auditor, where it is expected that most of your time will be spent in clients' offices. Whether man or woman, if you are required to wear a suit, the minimum number you'll need is two. Conventionally, one of them should be a dark, charcoal gray, and the other a navy blue. To add some variety to your wardrobe, choose one of them to be completely plain and the other with a subtle stripe (pinstripe). Stay away from broad stripes (chalk stripes) that look like clothes from a 1930s gangster movie. They are a fashion statement that can look dated very quickly.

If you have just a couple of suits, try to avoid plain black, perhaps unless you work in New York City, where plain black clothing seems to have dominated business attire for the last 30 years. Although black is fashionable in some circles, it doesn't suit everyone's complexion and coloring and is a look that is better for after-hours entertainment. Don't be afraid to choose another suitable dark color for your business suits, even if everyone else seems to be wearing black.

Men can choose a suit with either a single-breasted or double-breasted style. A double-breasted coat (where one side of the jacket overlaps the other) looks good when you are standing up (so it makes a good first impression), but it should be unbuttoned when you are sitting. This makes for some awkward "stage business" (unbuttoning and rebuttoning) if you have multiple seated meetings, so it's not the best suit for interviewing. A double-breasted suit looks good on people who are large (it can break up the bulk of a large torso), and the formal padded shoulders can help to bulk up someone who is very slender. However, it is harder to tailor one well for someone with a very athletic shape (broad shoulders and narrow waist). At present, almost no one wears a vest—"waistcoat" in British English—(a so-called three-piece suit) even in winter, although this is subject to fashion, and three-piece suits might return.

Most of the time that you are required to wear a suit, you'll soon remove the jacket. Make sure you put it on a hanger to keep its shape. One trick is to buy two pairs of pants (or a skirt and pants) with one jacket. Although you shouldn't dry clean a suit too often, you'll be able to send one pair of pants out to be cleaned while using the second pair or skirt.

Women must make a big decision about skirt length. Whether fashions are short (micro-mini skirts) or long ("peasant" length to the ankle), it's best to be conservative and choose a length close to the knee. A skirt that's too short will require very careful sitting and movement if you are not to embarrass yourself, and one that is too long will be an inconvenience when you're commuting to work.

Don't be afraid to buy good-quality brand-name clothes on sale or from discount stores. Department store sales of business suits are frequent (at least twice a year), and many designers have stores in outlet malls, where you can pick up a bargain. Don't hesitate to get something that is a little big or a little too long. For a small amount of money you can have

a tailor make alterations so that the suit fits you perfectly. Careful altera-
tion is probably more important than the price you pay in achieving a
strong professional image. A skilled tailor can accommodate any body
type and make your clothes enhance your appearance.

When you have your two basic suits, you can begin to branch out. A
suit with a faint check about two inches square ("windowpane check")
might be next, followed by a more casual type of suit with a subtle plaid
(usually called "Prince of Wales check" if black on gray, or a "Glen Plaid"
if brown). These suits can be used only on semiformal occasions, but they
can be a nice change from the gray/blue routine. Most suits will be suitable
for three seasons (fall, winter, and spring), and you might then move on to
some lightweight suits for summer, depending on the climate where you
live. Women might expand their wardrobes with a beige or olive-green suit,
depending on color preference. Once you've built up a collection of five to
seven suits, you should have enough for even the most formal work environment. You can wear your suits in rotation and buy two or three new suits
each year, while retiring some that you've owned longest. That way, you
can keep a substantial business wardrobe without bankrupting yourself.

After establishing the basic formal business wardrobe, men should
add a blazer and a sport coat. These items of apparel are useful for a semiformal look. Women should shop for nice **twin sets** to pair with skirts for
the same semiformal look. A twin set is a chic, tailored sweater or T-shirt
with a matching cardigan.

If your firm embraces business casual dress at least part of the time,
you'll need an inventory of skirts and blouses or pants and dress shirts.
In some climates, you'll also add a sport jacket or a plain sweater,
depending on the norm you observe in your firm. In business, most
people have their shirts or blouses professionally laundered. This gives a
very crisp appearance because the laundry uses starch (stiffening), high
temperatures, and special ironing machines. Of course, this pounding is
stressful for shirts, and they tend to shrink substantially over the first two
or three launderings. To counteract this problem, buy shirts that are one
full size larger than you would normally buy. Dress shirts for business can
probably withstand only about 15 to 20 launderings and still look sharp.
This suggests that you should aim to quickly have at least a dozen shirts
in your wardrobe. Half will be at the laundry at any one time. Once you've
established the base wardrobe, plan to purchase 12 to 14 new shirts or
blouses at least each year.

Most blouses and shirts are made of cotton **broadcloth,** but some people prefer a fabric in which the strands of thread are doubled in the weaving, called **Oxford cloth.** Oxford cloth shirts usually have button-down collars, which is a slightly less than formal look. Most broadcloth shirts for business have plastic collar stays to keep the points sharp and uncurled (you remove these stays before sending shirts to the laundry and put them in again before wearing). Cuffs can be "barrel cuffs" (what you would expect on a collared shirt for leisure wear) or "French cuffs," that is, with an extra length of material that is folded back and secured with cuff links. This particular style is highly favored in some firms (such as in certain investment banks) but might be considered old-fashioned in many industries and cities.

You can build up a collection of nice shoes, again, often by shopping on sale. A glance at your colleagues will give you an idea of what middle-of-the-road styles are acceptable, and your own common sense will tell you which fashion-forward styles should be reserved for after-work entertainment. You can choose black or dark brown (which may be called "chestnut" or "cordovan" if it has a deep red tone) for most business purposes, although black is always more formal. Light brown or tan shoes go only with casual attire. For men, shoes and belt should match in color, and for women, shoes and purse should match. Women may have more color options than men for their leather goods.

The convention for socks is that they should match the pants, or at least not detract from them. So navy-colored socks with navy pants and dark gray or black socks with a gray suit would be typical. However, in all but the most formal or fashion-conscious industries, you can simplify this convention by choosing to always wear black or very dark navy socks. Light-colored socks (for example, beige) may be acceptable with casual dress, as can be some subtle patterns. However, no matter how hot and humid the weather, businesspeople in the United States never wear white socks with pants or suits. The only exception would be when boat shoes or sneakers are worn with jeans, and even then, many people might still wear dark socks. Women are expected to wear pantyhose in almost all circumstances with business attire, even when it's hot. Because hose tend to snag and run, it's prudent to keep a spare set in your desk drawer or purse. Unless you're aiming for a particular fashion statement (for example, black hose with a black suit), you should choose one flattering color that matches your skin tone (it may be called something like "nude" or "tan").

If you commute by car, you won't need much in the way of outer garments such as overcoats, scarves, and hats. However, if you commute by public transportation, your purchases should include one very good quality heavy overcoat in black, dark gray, or navy, and one nice raincoat, which can be in almost any color. If you live in a very cold city such as Minneapolis or Chicago, you'll need a hat, too, although in practice, when the weather is really cold, even professional people resort to ski clothing such as anoraks with attached hoods. If you're wearing a hat, remember that men are expected to remove their hats at once upon entering a building, whereas ladies can keep their hats on. There's no justification for this behavior; it's just an etiquette rule.

■ 14-8 CARING FOR YOUR BUSINESS CLOTHES

As you begin to build your business wardrobe, invest in some systems to keep your clothes properly. Leather shoes will last much longer if you put in "shoe trees" (shoe keepers that return shoes to their natural shape) when you're not wearing them. Good-quality wooden hangers will keep suits in the proper shape, and hanging pants upside down with the correct hangers allows them to naturally shed wrinkles.

Business clothes are expensive, and maintaining a professional wardrobe can be a big hit to your budget. However, the good news is that most people dry clean their clothes way too often. Yes, if you have a spill or sweat profusely, you'll have to send your clothes to the cleaners. But if you have arranged a wardrobe with a wide selection, you just need to carefully rotate your suits and shoes so that you are not wearing the same ones day to day. Hang them carefully in your closet and allow them to "rest." If you decide that cleaning is necessary, perhaps only the pants of a suit need to be cleaned (see the two-pairs-of-pants tip in Section 14-7). If you send your suits to the dry cleaners too often, the fabric will become shiny as the outer fibers get lost and only strong thin fibers are left. Sending your suits to the cleaners no more than four times a year should be enough if you are careful with sweat and spills, and you could achieve just twice a year if you have a large collection of suits. If you can minimize the number of trips to the cleaners, your suits should last for more than two years, and of course, that will help you build up a good-sized wardrobe with lots of different choices.

▶ ❯ ❯ PUT THIS CHAPTER INTO PRACTICE

1. Conduct an online survey of news photos of politicians and count how many of them have given up neckties, even in semiformal situations.

2. Make an inventory of your current business clothes and then make a list of what you'd like to have in an ideal wardrobe. Comparing the two lists, develop a plan for buying fundamental business wardrobe items that you'll look for at the next department store sale.

3. See how "business casual" is put into practice at various firms by carefully observing what employees are wearing. You can conduct this survey informally and unobtrusively by hanging out in a nearby coffee shop.

▌ KEY TERMS

broadcloth

business attire

business casual

cas-nice (casual-nice)

costume jewelry

Oxford cloth

twin sets

Multiple Choice Practice Questions: To take the review quiz for this chapter, log on to your Online Edition at www.atomicdog.com.

Chapter 15

On the Job

With good business protocol you can define your success.

Congratulations! You got the job! Now comes the moment of your first day at a new firm. You may feel as if you don't have much control over your schedule and activities, but this chapter will show you what you can expect and how you can advance your career.

First impressions are important, so when you begin a new position, make every effort to introduce yourself often, as discussed in Chapter 2. Make sure you give people the context to get to know you, such as saying, "I'm the new accountant in Plant Operations." Make an attempt to learn the names of the people you are working with and know how to look up names, phone numbers, job titles, and reporting relationships on your firm's internal Web site.

As soon as you can—as early as the interview process—determine who works for whom and how reporting relationships are structured. If you are an engineer, for example, do you report to the chief engineer at the firm's headquarters, or is your ultimate boss the plant manager where you are located? If the relationship is not clear, you can ask politely, "So at the end of the day, is my ultimate supervisor Vice President Engineer or Mrs. Plant Manager?" Then, within your work group, learn the work routines. For example, do all of your peers (people at the same level and job title as you) give work to a team assistant to perform, or is the boss the only person who can assign tasks to the assistant? Again, if the routines are confusing, you can reasonably ask.

Because most U.S. businesses have an aura of informality, you may feel that the relationships within your group are as unstructured as a primary school pick-up game of soccer. If everyone jokes around and calls the boss by his nickname, "Buddy," it may be hard to discern power relationships. However, there are always subtle cues that will help you diagnose the hierarchy. In meetings, note who sits where and who is expected to sit at the head of a table—that's the person who is "in charge." In meetings, you'll notice that the moment one person walks into the room, the meeting starts—that person is important. If other people rush in afterward, they are lower in the hierarchy. During discussions, pay attention to who can interrupt whom. The person who can cut someone else off has more power.

Next, try to get a sense for relationships between groups. Your coworkers may tell you openly: "Accounting always gets things mixed up," or "Remember, people in Accounting control your life—and they can be very helpful." Again, if the information isn't given to you explicitly, try to learn whose advice is welcome and whose comments are ignored. Who seems to get the attention of people in your group? You'll learn where to make alliances within the firm and where you may have to brace for conflict, or at least a cool reception.

15-1 DEFINING YOUR DUTIES AND ROUTINES

During your first few days at a new firm, try to clearly define the duties of your position. What are you expected to do, and what must you not do? You may be given a formal job description, but it will likely be phrased in very broad language, such as: "Prepares budgets at the direction of senior staff," and it may not give you the details. A common problem that occurs is when reporting relationships have not been clarified. You may think that you work for the department manager, but in reality, you find that duties are being assigned to you by a coworker who is at the same level as you but has longer tenure at the firm. Seek to clarify the situation at once. With a pleasant tone, check with the boss: "I was working on editing the report, but Rosalie asked me to switch to reconciling last month's trades. Should I take direction from her on what my job priorities are?"

During your first few days and weeks on the job, you'll be given a lot of credit if you ask well-thought-out questions: "I wanted to check with you...In general, is this the sort of document you'd like to review before I send it out?" By asking specific questions, you'll convey an appropriate professional image—after all, no one expects you to know everything about a firm at once. On the other hand, you'll want to avoid acting "dazed and confused." So avoid making statements such as, "I really don't know what I'm doing yet!" (Even if it's how you feel!) You will also need to learn what incidental activities you are supposed to do yourself and which tasks to assign to support personnel (see *It's Just Different: You Want Me to Do What?*).

Early in your employment, ask your supervisor to define specific priorities and goals for your success with the firm. Try not to trivialize this by saying: "So what three things do you want me to work on?" A good boss should answer: "Well, there are one hundred and three things that I want you to work on!" However, most jobs involve competing priorities, and it's a good idea to get your manager to set those out for you in the most concrete terms.

It's Just Different: You Want Me to Do What?

In most U.S. companies, if you approached an assistant with a document in your hand and said, "Make me a copy of this right now," your coworkers would laugh hysterically. Then someone would kindly explain and say, "Look, let me show you where the copy machine is and how you can do that yourself." American executives largely do their own typing, make their own copies (except for very large orders), and fetch their own coffee. For incidental tasks, such as faxing a one-page document, most managers feel that by the time they've explained what needs to be done, they might as well just go ahead and do it themselves.

However, protocol rules and etiquette differ considerably in the rest of the world. In Hong Kong, for example, getting a cup of coffee for yourself may be a huge violation of protocol. Every firm employs a "tea lady," and serving yourself would imply that the tea lady doesn't know how to do her job. In Mumbai, India, a modestly middle-class family employs not just a chauffeur but three chauffeurs: One for each parent, and one to take the children to school. It's also expected that part of the job of "driver" includes not just driving the car but also being its security guard during the day. So an expatriate who insisted on driving herself would be considered strange indeed!

Most people who come to America soon realize that the "do it yourself" culture comes from our high wage economy. It's just too expensive to hire people to wait around and operate a fax machine or copier when a manager can do these functions just as easily himself. There may be assistants and copy departments for major projects, but the number of chores you are expected to handle without delegation may surprise you. You don't need to worry too much about the particular routine at your firm, but if you are in doubt, just ask a colleague: "Is this the sort of thing I should do myself, or do I assign it to someone else?"

■ 15-2 THE WORKDAY

Workdays are long in the United States. It's a paradox of the great wealth of the country that instead of taking increasing leisure time (as is common in Germany), Americans seem to work harder and harder the higher they move up the corporate ladder.

Most firms will expect you to be at your desk by 8 A.M., although you may find 9 A.M. is the norm in a city in which everyone commutes by mass transit, such as New York. If you are in an environment in which other people are working in shifts (such as a hospital or factory), the implicit start time for office staff may be 7 A.M. (because shifts are often 7 A.M. to 3 P.M., 3 P.M. to 11 P.M., and then 11 P.M. to 7 A.M. if there's an overnight shift).

As a new employee, you'll certainly want to be one of the first people into the office. Indeed, in financial services, it's considered essential that juniors be at their desks early. For example, on the West Coast (three hours time difference from the East Coast) because the New York exchanges open at 9:30 A.M. EST, most people are in the office working way before 6:30 A.M. PST. You'll have to make a difficult decision as to whether to be at your desk before your boss arrives. In most instances, the junior staff members are expected to arrive ahead of the supervisor, who may come in quite late after meetings with colleagues or associates outside the firm. On the other hand, in some businesses, the boss likes to be in first, to assign work to people as they come in. If you try to beat your boss into the office, you might violate an unspoken rule and upset her or his work routine. You can diagnose this situation as follows: On your first day, you are likely to be asked to come in quite late (you won't have keys in any case). Don't interpret that late time as your expected routine start time. Ask your peers, "So, when do people usually get here?" You'll want to be one of the first ones in the office (no matter what your commute) to make a good impression as the newest employee. So gradually advance your start time by coming in earlier and earlier. You'll soon find out whether it's the group of ambitious juniors who are in first, or whether it's just you and the boss.

At the end of the day, you may find that people routinely work very late. In investment banking and at law firms, for example, many people work as late as 9 or 10 P.M., at least Monday through Thursday, and may also come in on the weekends too. This schedule can be very hard if you are not used to it. You may also find a cultural norm that everyone stays until, say, 6 P.M., whether they have productive work to do or not. Ideally, you'll be aware of the work routine before you accept a position. But in any case, you'll have to adapt to the firm's style, and this may mean changing family meal times or giving up some hobbies.

Handling long workdays requires flexibility, professionalism, and a little bit of leadership. First, if it seems that people are staying at their desks late, busy or not, just to create an impression, you should not follow their lead. Make sure that your important tasks are finished, that you are prepared for the next day, and that your desk is cleared. Then choose one or two days to leave promptly at, say, 5 P.M. With luck, people who are just staying around to create an impression of hard work will realize your initiative and no longer stay late just to look good.

Secondly, the long hours of the American workday cause special problems for executives with young children. Although they can make childcare arrangements, very few people have a "nanny" taking care of their children at home. More likely, their children are in a commercial childcare arrangement with other children from many other families. In that situation, there will probably be a strict time limit when the center closes and when parents must pick up their children. Six o'clock is typical. Working parents learn to drop everything at work to make the deadline, or they'll face stiff fines from the caregiver.

In some firms, childless workers have found that they take on a disproportionate share of the after-work projects. When something just has to be done, the manager declares, "Dolan has to leave and get his kids… Can you stay and do this?" If this situation occurs, you will find yourself in a very delicate position. If you complain about the extra workload, it will look to your manager as if you are complaining that Dolan is a slacker. However, if you say nothing, you may end up doing more work for the same salary. Keep a note of these extra impositions. If they happen just once in awhile, you can hope that the workload will eventually even out. But if they are a substantial, continuing burden, you'll have to speak privately to your boss. With your notes as evidence, make an "appeal to equity." You can't expect to change Dolan's childcare situation or the firm's need to have urgent projects completed, but with documented overtime, you can reasonably ask for a **comp day** (a day off in compensation for extra hours worked) from time to time. If you schedule your requests for comp time in a way that respects the workflow of your team, your request is likely to be granted. If the uneven work demands continue and your boss refuses to see your side of the problem, you might have to look for a different job.

If the norm for your group is to work very long hours, you can maintain your energy and balance your day by breaking it up. For example, in investment banking, there is a big rush of work early in the day and then it slows down. Then late in the afternoon, mid-level managers come out of meetings and assign new tasks to the juniors, who are expected to stay late until the work is done in preparation for the next day. You'll find that many of your peers may waste time in the middle of the day during that lull, gossiping or chatting with friends on Instant Messenger. With luck you might also find one or two people who are amazingly productive and make use of the downtime in the middle of the day to go to the gym, go walking, or go shopping for daily necessities. You are likely to be much more efficient in your work if you split up a long workday by taking a break.

Similarly, you'll see many people eat lunch or dinner at their desks and work—very inefficiently—for hours and hours. Perhaps it would be better to take a short meal break away from your desk and then feel reenergized to finish your work efficiently. Don't hesitate to take "miniature rewards" in a very long workday, such as saying to yourself, "OK, I'm going to put in 45 minutes of solid work on this spreadsheet, and then I'm going to take a break and walk downstairs to get a cup of coffee and a snack."

Even if everyone seems to come into the office on both days of every weekend, they are quite possibly being inefficient—doing some work, yes, but also e-mailing friends or taking personal phone calls. It's much better for your mental health and to avoid **burnout** (loss of motivation after working too long at one job or task) to declare that on at least one day each weekend you won't go into the office. You should find that this will make you more productive on the days that you are at your desk. You'll find some people who seem to put in hours and hours but don't get a lot accomplished, and other people who do indeed get their work done in fewer hours. Look for good role models and follow their style. People will be more impressed if you meet deadlines and get your work accomplished than if they see you laboring long into the night, seven days a week. If you feel yourself being burned out, make a reasonable plan such as, "After the new product launch, I'm going to take one day of vacation so I can have a complete three-day weekend with no work," and discuss it with your supervisor, who may be more sympathetic than you imagine. Certainly, though, you'll want to avoid the temptation to play "get back" (to take revenge on a firm that you feel is not appreciative of your exceptional efforts) by taking unearned benefits from the firm (see *Doing the Right Thing: Don't Play "Get Back" for Long Hours*).

■ 15-3 LIFE IN A "CUBE"

One of the most difficult adjustments that many people face in an office environment is working in a **cubicle** (a work space set between partitions), also known informally as a "cube." Firms have adopted this style of office layout for its many advantages. First, there are substantial cost savings when compared with providing all office workers with their own private office. Second, the firm gains some flexibility in being able to expand and contract various departments and work groups. Last, there is a genuine

---

Doing the Right Thing: Don't Play "Get Back" for Long Hours

To compensate employees for their long hours, most large firms have several benefits to make it easier for people to do their work. Those who stay in the office past 6 P.M. are allowed to charge dinner to the firm; if they work past 9 P.M., they get to take a taxi home at the firm's expense rather than commuting by subway.

If your firm requires long hours and offers these types of compensation, you'll soon find that there's a group of people who enjoy gaming the system. They order in dinner, but it's not just take-out Chinese, it's $80 sushi. Every day they seem to work until 9:05 P.M., and then ride home in a cab. It doesn't stop there. Once they learn that firms will routinely pay for laundry expenses during business travel, they pack their dirty laundry and charge it to the firm even on a two-day trip!

You'll often hear the supposed justification for their behavior: "Hey, they ruined my Saturday, I figure they can pay for my dinners this week." But that conduct is unprofessional and extremely poor business protocol. You might be the only person in your group who doesn't play this game, and you probably won't be rewarded for your ethical behavior. Indeed, your supervisors may not even notice and compliment you on your good cost control. But you'll have the satisfaction of knowing you're doing the right thing, and you'll avoid the temptations that come from the slippery slope of taking advantage of your firm's extra benefits.

hope that the open environment will promote collaboration—people working on the same team will be able to quickly get information from one another, and in general, everyone on the team will be highly involved.

Of course, this openness comes at a price. You may feel a huge loss of privacy—lots of people can overhear your phone conversations and you'll never know when someone will pop their head around your door. When you first start to work in a cubicle, you will likely feel that you have no privacy for your personal phone calls. You'll hear coworkers scheduling dentist appointments and so on, but there are other ways to handle the lack of privacy. Most people who work in cubicles have a cell phone with them in addition to the company desk phone. If you need to place a personal call, you can take your cell phone to a conference room or step outside. Although you can't spend the whole workday away from your desk attending to personal matters, stepping out with the words, "I'll be back in 10 minutes" to your coworkers is acceptable and as much explanation as is required in most firms.

As a student, if you've been used to retreating to your own room to work with a door you can close, working in a cubicle will take some adjustment. You should be aware that there are some unwritten rules for respecting your colleagues' "virtual offices." Treat other peoples' cubes as if they were actual offices and don't just walk in uninvited (see Figure 15-1). If a colleague is on the phone or clearly engaged in a complex project, pausing at the entrance to the colleague's work space and saying, "May I interrupt you?" or actually saying, "Knock, knock" would be a polite way to indicate that you are seeking permission to enter. Some firms have unwritten codes for when someone is absolutely unavailable: People hang paper signs on the wall, put on headphones, or, in one particular firm, wear red baseball caps to signal: "Don't bother me unless it is a life-and-death matter. I'm working on a deadline."

You will show courtesy and consideration for your colleagues by paying attention to how your behavior in your own space affects them indirectly. The chief friction points among cubicle inhabitants are noises and smells. In a cubicle environment, people learn to ignore the sound of others in their work group making and answering routine phone calls, but talking on cell phones is more distracting to others. You often have to talk louder than normal on a cell phone (recall the "cell yell" from Chapter 6), so be very aware of how loud you are speaking. In the working environment, every little sound can become more and more annoying, so

Figure 15-1   Cubicle Etiquette
When you work in a cubicle, you have to learn how to control interruptions.
SOURCE: © 2009 Jupiterimages Corporation.

considerate cubicle dwellers will keep their noises to a minimum. Be careful to set your computer so that it does not announce each new e-mail with a loud "DING DONG!", and choose the quietest possible setting for phone ring tones. If you have a scheduled long phone call (particularly one where you may have to speak loudly, such as on an international call), you may want to arrange to take it in a conference room where you can close the door.

Smells, especially of spicy food, can be particularly annoying. So if your lunch is a revisiting of last night's fish stew, it's a good idea to take it out to the park or eat in a lunchroom. Your use of cologne or perfume should also be very light to avoid bothering your colleagues who must share the open workspace (see Chapter 14, Section 14-5).

Because other people can see the interior of your cubicle, your firm may have some strict limits on what pictures you can display. Posters for one particular political party or social cause are in general a bad idea. If your firm does not have rules on artwork, just make sure that what you choose to put up is not likely to be offensive.

When you first see your new work environment, you may notice that there are two types of cubicles—those with high walls and those with low walls. High-walled cubes are about as high as a person walking by and therefore fairly private, and low cubes have shorter walls where it's likely that your work will be interrupted by each passerby. The latter type is really suitable only for people whose job it is to greet visitors. If you are offered a low-walled cubicle and your duties include programming, financial analysis, or confidential work, you can reasonably object to that desk space. Of course, as the new member of the team, you won't get a prestigious cubicle. You'll soon see that there's a hierarchy of preferred cubicles (away from the noise of the copy machine, close to the window, away from the air-conditioner, and so on), and as soon as someone with a great cube location is transferred out of a group, the others will begin jockeying to grab the best cubicle!

Because your cubicle is your own office space, how you handle intrusions into your privacy is particularly important. If the social norms about interruption have not been established in your group, you can set your own personal limits. If a colleague asks, "Can I interrupt you?" and you are too busy, you can reasonably answer, "Not right now, I'll lose track of what I'm doing here." If someone wants to hang and chat too long in your cubicle, you can make an excuse to leave your own space: "OK, walk with me while I go and copy this," then retreat with: "Now, I do have to go back to work." Just as, in college, you probably developed a secret place to study (the stacks of the law library are often favored by undergraduates), you may adapt to intrusions by taking your laptop to an unused conference room or break room if your surroundings are too noisy for serious work. In some firms, you can arrange to work from home for a few days or for part of each workweek if you have a technical project that requires sustained attention.

◼ 15-4 ORIENTATION

Your firm may well offer a formal **orientation** (an overview of the firm, its history, and policies) or even a training program that lasts for several weeks. However, many firms don't offer such orientations, and even when they do, they invariably present too much information at one time. While you are still trying to figure out where the bathrooms are, you get stuck in a two-hour lecture from Human Resources about options for your pension plan at age 65. Ideally, firms should practice "continuous orienta-tion" with information spread over several days or weeks that gives you just the information you need to know at the time you need it. However, that does not often happen, so the most you can hope for from the usual "overload orientation" is to develop a personal index to the information (for example, "My company has both long-term and short-term disability insurance—that's not something I need to know right now"). Then try to map the topics to either the person who can give you more information or the place where you can look it up (a brochure or online through an intranet), when you need it.

Table 15-1 outlines some topics that should be covered in an orienta-tion. If you are not offered a formal orientation, you should use this table as a checklist to make sure that you understand company policy.

Table 15-1	Topics Typically Covered in New-Employee Orientation
Topic	**Notes and Details**
Security and access	Company ID badge—must it be worn at all times? What keys and card-keys do you need? Do you have the right to be in the building after normal work hours?
Time and record keeping	Do you have to keep track of how you spend your time ("billable hours")? How do you report sick days and schedule vacation days? Which public holidays does the firm observe?

(Continued)

Topic	Notes and Details
Sexual harassment training 	Your firm will carefully explain its rules on socializing with other staff members and will remind you of the rules on avoiding harassment.
Parking and transportation 	Does the firm pay part of your commuting expenses? What are the rules for parking, and where do you get a pass?
Business dining 	Are some meals with clients and associate firms reimbursable? What are the rules, and what are the limits?
Business travel 	Must travel be approved in advance? Does the firm make arrangements, or do you seek reimbursement after the fact?

(Continued)

Topic	Notes and Details
Using company resources 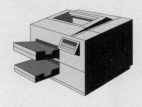	Is it acceptable to use company resources for occasional personal needs such as photocopying a few pages or e-mailing a friend during your lunch hour? Is this discouraged or forbidden?
Document policies 	How long must documents be retained? What is the timetable for destruction of old records, and what is the procedure for destroying records that are no longer needed?
Confidentiality 	Is it permissible to mention the names of your firm's clients in discussions with other clients or with people outside the firm, or does your firm insist on very strict confidentiality, including forbidding you to even mention the names of clients?
Insurance benefits 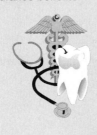	What decisions do you have to make to be enrolled in company-paid health or life insurance? Are there additional benefits you need to know about? What do you have to do to enroll family members?

(Continued)

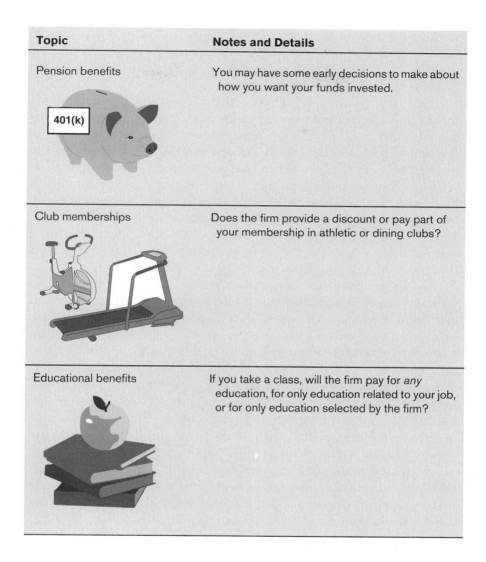

Topic	Notes and Details
Pension benefits	You may have some early decisions to make about how you want your funds invested.
Club memberships	Does the firm provide a discount or pay part of your membership in athletic or dining clubs?
Educational benefits	If you take a class, will the firm pay for *any* education, for only education related to your job, or for only education selected by the firm?

■ 15-5 TIME MANAGEMENT

You may start out your new job with a few days when you wonder why you were hired, because there doesn't seem to be enough work for you to do. Treasure these moments. There's not a person working in America who doesn't have more to do than can possibly be accomplished in the workweek. So one of the most important skills to develop is time management. A great deal has been written about this topic, and your firm may send you to a two- or three-day seminar about time management, but here is a brief outline of the important issues.

First, don't waste time. Many activities look value-added but nonetheless distract you from finishing projects on time. Opening mail is at the top of most people's list of time-wasters. Mail is interesting and distracting. Put it aside and go through it while you are waiting for a meeting to begin or if you are on hold on the phone. Just chatting to colleagues is probably the next biggest time-waster. You can manage this by engaging in pleasant social chitchat away from your work area. You can bring conversations to a natural and polite close by honestly saying, "Well, better be getting back to work." If you routinely hang around colleagues' desks chatting and allow them to do the same at your desk, you'll find time slipping away from you.

In Chapter 6, we met the next most common thief of productive time: difficulty terminating phone calls. Develop a personal style of short, efficient calls. If you have an associate who loves to chat, call him or her right before another event on your calendar; begin by announcing, "I have only a few moments before I have to leave to go to a meeting, but I did want to call you and…" If someone calls you at your desk and seems to want to chat, you can say, "Well, I can answer a quick question, but I'm really in the middle of a project here." If your caller doesn't get the hint that you need to go, you can interrupt and take control of the conversation—if necessary with the words, "I hate to interrupt, but I need to complete a presentation for later today. Can I just summarize where we are?"

At the beginning of each workday, take a moment to review your schedule and make a realistic assessment of the tasks you plan to complete this day. If you do this well and have a system to make commitments to do some tasks in the future, each day will be more productive. Your PDA (personal digital assistant), contact manager software, or e-mail program should have a "Tasks" or **"to do" list.** This tool can be helpful for making a record of a task that you can put off for awhile. If you find yourself overwhelmed, remember to make a difference in your mind between what is *urgent* and what is *important.* There are many important tasks in business that need to be done but that don't have to be done right now. You should begin each day with a manageable list of at least three action items that you want to get accomplished. Then scan your e-mail for recent urgent messages and check your voice mail. Decide whether you have any action items that need urgent attention.

Successful time management depends on making a careful balance between short tasks that might as well be done at once (such as refilling an empty stapler on your desk) versus finding that the whole morning has slipped away in little tasks with no major projects accomplished. Experts in time management suggest that activities that can be done in less than two minutes can be treated as **"do it now" tasks.** In just 20 minutes, you can accomplish a dozen "do it now" tasks and have the rest of the morning for your planned meetings and major tasks.

If you are facing a large project, you can make it more manageable by breaking it down into stages and developing a timeline. If you complete small, preparatory steps, you won't feel overwhelmed, and you can see that not all the work needs to be done at once. One way to sustain your motivation is to tie little personal rewards to completion of tasks. For example, you may plan to stop and have a coffee break at mid-morning. But make it a miniature celebration and refuse to take the break until you have accomplished one of the tasks on your "to do" list.

At the end of your workday, a moment or two spent in tidying up and planning can make the next day more efficient. For example, sticking little notes on documents on your desk—"Copy and discuss with Finance" or "Ready to go, just needs signature from Steve"—can make your work get off to a fast start the next day.

Of course, you'll be punctual for meetings. In general, even if other people in your work group are less structured ("Oh, he always runs late!"), earn a reputation for being on time, and your leadership will help other people work efficiently with you. If you join a work group in which meetings always start late, you'll see that the team may waste as much as half an hour just gathering people together. Address this issue head on. Although you may be reluctant to take the lead in bringing this issue up for discussion as the new member of the team, it's most likely that this has been a long-standing nagging problem, and people will appreciate your bringing an end to it.

If you have seemingly impossible conflicts between several tasks at once, begin negotiations early with people who are expecting your work from you by a specific date. Some due dates are nominal. As an example of a nominal deadline, your boss may say: "Get it in by the first of the month," knowing that other people are going to use your work product at some point during that month, but the specific date when the work is needed may be somewhat later. If you discuss the conflict with coworkers, you may find that someone needs only part of a larger project ("If you could just give me the personnel costs—I can wait for the rest of the figures"). Friendly forewarning is much more professional than begging for an extension after you've missed a deadline. Recall from Chapter 1 that an important part of professionalism is to manage your own commitments realistically. When you accept projects, try to set sensible expectations: "I'd be happy to work on that, but I won't be able to start on it until next week, after I've finished the supplier reviews."

If you are faced with schedule conflicts that you cannot resolve, you'll have to engage your supervisor. The science of management is all about allocating resources in the face of competing demands, and your boss is being paid to make the tough decisions.

■ 15-6 MANAGING YOUR BOSS

Many books have been written on the subject of "how to manage your boss." The idea is that in addition to your supervisor's direction of your work as such, you must adapt also to his or her style of leadership. It's important to start by understanding that there are many different management styles, and no single best approach. You should be prepared to diagnose your boss's style and work with it as best you can.

Work groups and their leaders have preferred channels of communication. In some teams, nothing is discussed unless it's face-to-face, but in other firms, everyone may communicate by e-mail, even if two workers are just a few feet apart. The same is true for managers/supervisors: Some may prefer that every issue be presented as a formal memo on paper, whereas others may prefer phone calls and actually try to avoid in-person meetings. Observe how your coworkers interact with the boss and follow the same style.

When you are assigned work, it's good to paraphrase the instructions and repeat them back so you can be sure that you are not setting off in the wrong direction. Here's an example:

> "So, you'd like me to develop this year's capital budget, but you feel that last year's should not serve as a guide. And it's OK with you if I talk directly with people in the other departments?"

Your manager may also prefer regular, semiformal meetings (for example, once a week) or may encourage you to interrupt and drop into his or her office at any time (see Figure 15-2).

It's probably true for every boss in the world that no one likes surprises. So if you have bad news to deliver, get it communicated as soon as possible. Begin by foreshadowing the problem with your manager. For example, you might say, "I'd like to talk with you about the cost estimates on the new project—we're having a lot of difficulty in meeting the targets." In general, you should keep your direct supervisor up-to-date on the status of projects that you've been assigned, without "grandstanding" (boasting of your accomplishments). If you are having difficulty with a project, it's usually best to seek help early to reasonably avoid panicking about every last detail. You don't want to get the reputation of being unable to do anything without extra help.

Figure 15-2   Meetings with the Boss
Some bosses may encourage you to drop in, while others prefer regular, more structured meetings.
Source: © 2009 Jupiterimages Corporation.

Part of managing your boss depends on learning the style that your supervisor prefers when problems arise. Some managers want only a statement of the situation. Others may want a problem definition and a range of options (for example, "So we can spend money from reserves now or delay implementation until the next fiscal year"). Still other managers will want a problem definition, range of options, and your proposal for one specific solution. You may find that your manager has a style of debating and challenging your ideas to test your reasoning or to refine her or his own thinking on the matter. You shouldn't take offense at this friendly sparring.

Try to learn how your manager handles success. Some managers will give you immediate, detailed feedback, telling what they liked—and didn't like—about your work. Other managers may accept projects and reports with a mere "thank you"; and some other managers may never say a word unless things are going wrong. It's ideal if you can work for a manager who takes the role of being your coach—always encouraging improvement but continually acknowledging your efforts. Such managers are rare.

In business, there is always something that doesn't go according to plan. You'll learn your boss's personal style for dealing with adversity. Some managers have a tendency to panic and exaggerate difficulties. Others can accept imperfections with grace. When a team member makes a mistake, the manager's response can vary along a scale from suffering in silence, through annoyance and a mild rebuke, all the way to a screaming tantrum. There are quite a few bosses who would be described as follows: "He blows up pretty wild, but don't take it to heart—he's never personal about it. He's a bit of a screamer when things don't go right, but it's soon over." If you have a volcanic boss, it's helpful if your peers can warn you. Try not to take the outburst as personal criticism and never respond in kind. Your professionalism and calm demeanor will model appropriate behavior.

A very bad situation occurs if you find that you are working for what has been called a "toxic boss"—someone who seems to get joy from belittling people and who constantly criticizes those around him. If you haven't been able to develop a good working relationship with your boss, in the long run it may be best for both of you if you found another position. However, looking for a new position in the same firm is a risky proposition. You should be aware that if you begin to mention that you are considering other situations, the news is likely to get back to your boss sooner than you intend, and you should be prepared for a confrontation. You should plan a euphemistic explanation:

> "Well, it's true. I do feel that I'd be better suited to a position that makes more use of my background in computers, so I had mentioned my interest to other people."

The problem with bosses who shout and scream is that employees with healthy egos soon move on to better work environments. The people who are left are shell-shocked survivors. Because all new employees make mistakes on simple procedures, it's easy for the toxic boss to start ranting and raving and showing how incompetent the newcomer is. If you find yourself in this situation, discuss the matter with people outside your firm. Older family friends with experience in business can give you feedback as to whether you are being unnecessarily sensitive about a minor blow-up or if you've stumbled into a truly bad situation that you need to leave as soon as possible.

■ 15-7 ATTENDING BUSINESS CONFERENCES, TRADE SHOWS, AND CONVENTIONS

As part of your duties, you may be required to represent your firm at industry events. The number of business conferences you will have to attend will depend on the exact job you hold and the line of business your firm is in. Some people in sales may attend as many as 10 out-of-town conferences a year, whereas other executives may rarely attend even one trade show or convention a year.

Although you may be excited at the thought of an out-of-town trip on someone else's budget, remember that the firm is paying you to work. Before you go, be clear about what the firm wants to achieve. Although it's possible that the firm may want to reward you for six months of hard work by giving you a few days of recreation in Las Vegas, it's more likely that the firm has a specific agenda, possibly some of the following items:

- Attract new customers
- Show off new technology

- Maintain contacts with existing customers
- Understand industry trends
- Assess the capabilities and strategies of key competitors

You need to be aware of a few potential pitfalls of attending conventions and trade shows. First, you should be very clear what new products and technologies you can talk about and at what level. For example, your firm might have a specific plan to scare off a potential competitor from entering a line of business in which your firm is successful, and you might have a strategy of announcing publicly, "We've found a new way to make a product that is twice as fast, at half the cost." On the other hand, your cost structure might be considered to be top secret. Make sure you understand the details before you go.

Second, any discussion of pricing with competitors leads your firm open to a charge of antitrust violation. You should check on your firm's rules. Some firms have adopted a rule that there are to be no meetings (either open in hotel bars or private in hotel suites) with competitors' staff. Even innocently remarking in casual conversation, "Well, we're certainly hoping to keep our prices high for quite a bit longer" could be construed as attempting to set up an implicit agreement in a competitive industry that everyone will "stay high" and not compete on price. A firm can avoid the accusation of collusion by making a public (press conference style) announcement: "We plan to defend pricing by adding features and avoiding discounting." But it's a dangerous area, and you should make sure you are well briefed before you go.

Finally, be warned that conventions come with some personal temptations: Conferences are often held at hotels, and everyone indeed has a bedroom just upstairs. You are away from familiar constraints (such as having to explain to your roommates or family members why you didn't come home last night). The atmosphere is convivial, and alcohol may be freely flowing. In short, romance is in the air. No one can dictate affairs of the heart, and no doubt many happily married spouses have met one another at trade shows and conventions. But some common sense and restraint are good ideas.

You should anticipate that a few people specifically go to conferences looking for short-term liaisons. You don't want to come home heartbroken and the star of a new round of office gossip, with your colleagues snickering about your adventures.

■ 15-8 DATING AND BUSINESS

In Victorian society, many spouses met one another through family connections or through church or temple. But in the last half of the twentieth century, *most* husbands and wives met each other either at college or through work. Dating between people in the same firm runs up against a desire by many large companies to limit workplace romances. The reason for this is a great fear that the firm will become the target of a complaint alleging sexual harassment.

Dating someone from work is not illegal. What is illegal is either offering a *quid pro quo* (for example, "Come out with me on Friday, and I'll put in a good word about your promotion") or creating a **hostile work environment.** A hostile environment is one in which unwanted sexual comments or materials (for example, "girlie" calendars) are routinely displayed, or in which an employee is subject to repeated sexual innuendos or comments. Merely saying, "You look nice today, Carol" probably won't get you into trouble, but: "Ow! I just go crazy when you wear that red dress!" almost certainly will. For that reason, many U.S. managers avoid any comment—complimentary or not—on other people's appearance (see Section 15-9).

Inviting a coworker on a date definitely does not constitute sexual harassment, and you should be relieved to know that many romances are formed in large American companies. However, repeatedly asking out someone who keeps telling you "no" could be considered badgering and unwelcome attention. However, because the conventional form for a polite refusal is to claim to have a competing engagement, it's hard to know if you are being turned down or if there is a genuine conflict. "Oh, I'd love to, but my Italian class meets on Tuesdays" isn't a clear "no." So it's probably reasonable to ask someone out two or three times for different sorts of activities, and if you are still getting "regrets," you should hear the message that your attentions are not welcome.

If a colleague appears to be pursuing you romantically but you are not interested, you should work to make sure that your polite refusal is quite clear. In the previous example, being "busy on Tuesday" implies that other days might be possible. So you should practice an unambiguous turndown:

"Oh, that's kind of you to ask. But I'm really so busy with my work and other responsibilities, I just don't have time to take on anything new."

Most firms will have policies about office romances, some stricter than others. However, in all firms, you can't even think about dating when there is a direct supervisory relationship. You can't ask your boss out, and you should never ask a subordinate to see you after work in any setting that could remotely constitute a date (that is, when the two of you are socializing without other people present).

A very sensitive issue occurs when there is a supervisory relationship between two people who are romantically involved. If the junior is promoted, the other members of the work group suspect favoritism; if the junior is held back, the firm can be accused of discrimination, with the allegation that romantic disappointments spilled over into the workplace. So if you find yourself attracted to someone you supervise, you should seek advice quickly so that one or the other of you can be transferred. Of course, this is not as easy as it sounds, as both of you may have a strong commitment to your current projects.

Fortunately, the United States is not a totalitarian state, and your firm cannot control whom you fall in love with—and you can become seriously romantically involved with someone at work. However, the firm may have a rule that the two of you may not be on the same work team. If romance blooms, see your supervisor together and ask for a reassignment, according to the firm's policy. Both of you will probably appreciate being able to focus on work while at the office.

Whenever you take a new job, if you are single and looking for a life partner, it makes sense to carefully learn the firm's rules about dating coworkers during your orientation. Smaller firms tend not to have official policies on dating at the office, but there will likely be some unwritten rules or strong opinions that you can uncover by some discreet questioning.

15-9 BEING "POLITICALLY CORRECT"

Many international visitors are anxious about doing business in the United States because they are afraid of running into trouble if they are not **politically correct.** On the other side, U.S. managers who are hosting colleagues from other countries may cringe when a visitor starts a joke that makes fun of people of one ethnic group or gender.

However, a newcomer to the United States shouldn't be anxious. Being politically correct ("PC") doesn't mean anything more than using common sense and good manners. Here's some history on where the PC movement originated. Social interaction in the workplace often involves the expression of personal opinion and sharing jokes (Americans tell a lot of jokes). During the civil rights movement of the 1960s, liberal Americans (of all ethnicities) realized that jokes that demeaned all members of a race as being slow or stupid or the like were really just a covert way to express deeply held hostile feelings. The excuse "Aw, c'mon! It was just a joke!" didn't take away the real damage that these jokes caused, and indicated that the joke teller might have held serious underlying prejudices.

This period was followed by the women's movement of the 1970s, when educated women began to point out to their male university contemporaries that jokes that portrayed all women in a certain way (for example, as poor drivers or mechanically inept) were neither factually accurate nor very funny. Later social movements drew attention to similar prejudicial attitudes toward issues of sexual orientation and disability.

Jokes about the imagined characteristics of an entire group of people present a hostile environment for work or study for members of that group. Under various federal laws, workers can sue for discrimination if they can point to attempts to restrict their admission to, or advancement in, certain types of jobs or education. Evidence of a hostile work environment would support a claim, and the financial damages assessed against large companies can be huge.

If you are working for a large U.S. corporation, you'll undoubtedly be offered diversity training (which will explain political correctness) as part of your orientation. But if you are working for a smaller company, or are just visiting a U.S. firm, the rules for politically correct speech can be summarized as follows.

Remember that politically correct speech is no more than common courtesy and good taste. You should never make a comment or joke that implies that everyone knows that all people of a certain group behave in a certain way, suffer from the same character defect or limitation, and so on. For example, you'll be in trouble for saying, "Well, that person probably does that because..." based on one of the following:

- Race, ethnicity, or national origin
- Gender or sexual orientation

- Religion
- Disability

If you realize that you've made a mistake and have offended a business associate, you should apologize quickly and completely, and perhaps explain that you are working to adapt to U.S. culture. Then move on with the business at hand. You won't help the situation by allowing it to grow out of proportion, so make sure that your behavior toward other people shows that you are not prejudiced and that the verbal slip was an isolated incident.

In addition to forging a good working relationship with your boss, one implicit task when you are new to a team is to get along with your coworkers. Although "valuing diversity" can be used as a thoughtless label for nondiscriminatory behavior, there are always things that we can learn by understanding value systems that are different from our own (see *Business Protocol in Action: Truly Valuing Diversity*).

■ 15-10 GETTING AHEAD

No matter how much you like your colleagues and how pleasantly you get along with your boss, you should keep an eye on your own career and not stagnate. No one expects you to work for 15 years at the same position (even if it makes your manager's life easier to have one function covered with a solid, reliable worker). It's perfectly appropriate to talk about your career path and to discuss new challenges with your supervisor. You don't want to take on ever-increasing responsibilities at the same salary, but you are more likely to be promoted if you can master new skills, functions, or areas of business.

Most large U.S. firms have a formal review process—typically an **annual review** (a once-a-year formal evaluation of your work and consideration for promotion or a bonus). This review may be done in a number of ways. You may be asked to begin by writing a self-review, which your supervisor then critiques. You should define accomplishments and things that are different about this year compared with the past. Alternatively, your manager may complete a written evaluation without your input and present it to you for comment. Finally, you may be subject to an extensive review, called a **360-degree review,** in which your firm seeks input from your colleagues and subordinates, people in

Business Protocol in Action:
Truly Valuing Diversity

As part of your orientation at any large American firm, you will most likely have a session labeled "Valuing Diversity." You will be reminded that it is illegal to discriminate against anyone in employment, housing, granting credit, and many other business transactions based on ethnicity, national origin, gender, religion, or sexual preference. This may sound like a whole list of "don'ts." However, the American values of pluralism and tolerance have very positive aspects.

Think about the people who graduated with you. Now, imagine you lived in a country in which half the people in the class were told that they could not have jobs. Imagine that the "no job" people were picked at random. You'd agree that that is unfair. But then something worse happens to the country—without the contribution of those workers to the economy, the rate of economic growth slows dramatically. If you ever wonder why the United States has by far the world's largest economy, it's because business functions as a *meritocracy* (the brightest people get ahead) and no one is excluded based on irrelevant criteria. As you look around the globe, you see other countries whose economies are held back because they treat one gender or class or ethnic group as "unsuitable."

Beyond merely giving everyone equal opportunity, good companies understand that there is much to be learned from understanding differences in culture. Consider this scenario: You are working for a high-technology company and you learn that a highly regarded computer engineer is being assigned to your group. When you are first introduced to Engineer Ryani, you are a bit surprised—you had assumed the engineer would be a man, but you see that the engineer is a Ms. Ryani. You worry that your workdays will be filled with lectures from your new coworker on your behavior and how insensitive you are being.

However, as your working relationship develops, you soon get to know that the new engineer is one of the most cheerful and cooperative colleagues you've ever had. As a professional engineer, she is remarkably perceptive—she seems to know what to do next, without being asked, and routinely finishes tasks ahead of time. After several months of working on the same team, you learn that Ms. Ryani uses part of each lunch hour to pray privately. Your first reaction is that you couldn't imagine doing that yourself. Later you reflect that your new engineer seems to have renewed energy after her lunch break, and that she is able to handle problems much more calmly than other coworkers. You then decide that, although you are not going to change your religious habits, you are going to commit to taking a real break away from work problems each lunchtime, just like Ms. Ryani does in her own way.

Truly valuing diversity is more than just being politically correct. It means being open to differences and willing to learn from them.

other departments, and even customers. For many people, criticism is hard to take. When you are presented with your review, you should correct errors of fact but try not to be defensive by engaging in argument. Strive to hear negative comments in the context of an overall evaluation (which may be quite positive) and convert them into positive action steps for the future. When there has been a problem situation, address it in terms of what you have learned from it and what you will do differently next time.

As a new hire, you may also have a provisional review after three or six months. Although this may occasionally be an opportunity for your first raise, it is typically just a procedure where the firm can quickly terminate someone who is really not working out. Assuming that this doesn't apply to you, try to learn as much as you can from the review. If your boss passes you off with platitudes, "Everyone thinks you're doing just fine," ask what more you can do, where you can improve, what additional skills you can learn, and so on. Then you'll have plenty of positive things to report at the time of your first annual review.

One problem that comes up quite often is the delay in annual reviews. You know that your chances to move to the next salary level depend on your review, but your boss hasn't gotten around to doing it yet. You are reluctant to push the issue because you don't want to provoke a negative review. Here's how to approach this: Deep down, your boss knows that the review is overdue and needs to get done. Use your good judgment and don't insist that a review be completed at the same time as next year's marketing plan or this quarter's financial report. But do address the issue directly and with a neutral tone: "I know it's a busy couple of weeks, but it is past time for my annual review. Could we do this? Could we schedule it for the first week of next month? I could start to work on my objectives and accomplishments now." If all else fails, in a big firm in which your evaluation is being endlessly delayed, you'll have to discreetly enlist help from the Human Resources Department.

■ 15-11 TIME TO SAY "GOODBYE"

Even when you feel you have a great job, there will come a time when you want to move on. Perhaps you want to go to graduate school, move to another geographic location, or simply experience a different firm or industry. The general legal principle underlying your employment is called **employment at will.** That is, just as your employer can fire you at any time and for any reason, your employer cannot demand that you continue to work at the same job (that would be indentured servitude) and, in general, cannot require long periods of notice. (To "give notice" means to communicate to your employer that you plan to quit.) Unless you have signed an employment contract to stay with a firm for a specific time period (and very few firms ask for such a contract), even high-level executives usually give quite short notice, often as little as two weeks.

Once you've given your notice, you will want to maintain your professionalism right until the last moment. Don't gossip and boast about your new opportunity. Make an orderly transition for projects you are working on and agree to the appropriate wording to use when talking with customers to let them know that you won't be continuing with the firm. Keep your good work habits of promptness and consideration for others. If you are leaving because you really don't like the situation, it's best to leave on good terms. You never know when your old company will buy your new company and you'll be working with the same team, or when the one person whom you detested will be hired at your new firm as your coworker.

You may be asked to take part in an **exit interview** with your manager or with people from the Human Resources Department of your firm. This is a formal interview to review your reasons for leaving and to make sure you understand when your benefits, such as health care, end.

There's a great temptation to use an exit interview to unload every frustration and to vent about every shortcoming of your experience with the firm. Unless you feel compelled to leave because of fraud or sexual harassment, it's best to leave as much as possible unsaid. As we often say in business, "It's nice to be nice."

▶ ❯ ❯ PUT THIS CHAPTER INTO PRACTICE

1. Conduct an informal survey of young alumni who have recently entered the workforce on the topic of workplace dating. What were they told during orientation?

2. Analyze your time management today. Since you woke up, how much time has been spent on nonproductive activities (e-mailing friends, looking at social networking sites) and how much "time on

task" did you give to major projects? Make an action plan for improving your personal efficiency and time management skills by limiting nonproductive time.

3. Think about a supervisor you've had in the past. How would you diagnose her or his style according to the dimensions in Section 15-6, "Managing Your Boss"?

KEY TERMS

360-degree review	employment at will
annual review	exit interview
burnout	hostile work environment
comp day	orientation
cubicle ("cube")	politically correct
"do it now" tasks	"to do" list

Multiple Choice Practice Questions: To take the review quiz for this chapter, log on to your Online Edition at www.atomicdog.com.

GLOSSARY

360-degree review A periodic review of work performance (for example, an annual review conducted once a year) in which input is solicited not just from a worker's supervisor but also from the worker's subordinates, peers, and sometimes, customers.

401(k) plan A federal government program that allows employees to save money in tax-deferred accounts for retirement. A firm may or may not offer a 401(k), and if the employer doesn't offer it, an employee cannot participate in this program on his or her own.

A

academic major In American universities, a major is the chief subject of specialization, which corresponds to "honours in [subject]" in universities based on the British model. See also *academic minor.*

academic minor In American universities, a minor is the second specialization, less important than the academic major, and with fewer courses taken. See also *academic major.*

active voice The active voice is the form of speech or writing that puts emphasis on the subject rather than the object of a sentence. "The boy hit the ball" is active voice. "The ball was hit by the boy" is passive. It is the preferred voice in *Plain English.* See also *passive voice.*

airport test Refers to whether a job candidate would be pleasant company during a three-hour or longer layover at an airport. A euphemism for "personality" in recruiting circumstances.

alias Literally, an alias is an alternative name, such as a pen name or stage name. In e-mail, it can refer to a nonpersonal name, such as room-reservations@bigco.com, or to a distribution list of several people, such as teamA@bigco.com.

alternate greeting In a voice-mail system, a temporary message to callers—for example, when someone is out of the office on business travel.

Americans with Disabilities Act (ADA) U.S. federal law enacted in 1990 that prohibits discrimination based on disability in public accommo-dations, including the workplace. An important feature of the act is that employers must be prepared to provide "reasonable accommodations" to disabled applicants who are selected for a job. Because employers can face fines for discriminating in hiring (choosing a nondisabled less quali-fied candidate), most firms have adopted the practice of not discussing disability and accommodations until after the selection process has been completed.

annual review A routine but formal review of an employee's work, usually conducted once a year by the worker's direct supervisor.

attachment Something sent with a letter or e-mail. When postal mail is used, the attachment usually isn't physically attached but is just enclosed. For e-mail, it's a way to send a file along with a message.

audience heterogeneity The concept that audiences are made up of individual members who may have greater or lesser expertise and famil-iarity with the subject matter of a presentation and greater or lesser interest in the topic at hand.

autodelete Colloquial term for a coworker whose e-mail messages are often sent to too many people so that most recipients automatically delete messages from that person without reading them.

B

behavioral interview A popular interviewing format that consists of questions about a series of general business situations. Each question begins with, "Tell me about a time when…"

blue screen A plain blue physical background used in some videocon-ferencing setups that allows a technician to superimpose a different back-ground by electronic editing.

boilerplate Routine recitals (that is, wording that is always the same); usually inserted for legal reasons to cover all possibilities.

bounce-back Message from an e-mail system that a message could not be delivered as intended. Not all systems will generate a bounce-back message, so a mistyped e-mail address can lead to a message that is never delivered.

broadcloth Ordinary fabric for shirts that is not *Oxford cloth.*

burnout Exhaustion that comes from performing a demanding job over a long period of time without relief. Often seen in high-stress jobs such as dealing with customer complaints or handling death and injury.

business attire Formal clothes to wear to an office, such as a dark business suit, shirt and tie, and polished leather shoes.

business casual Clothes worn to the office, but not the same as "formal." Typically, shirt with collar (but no tie) and slacks but not jeans. There are many variations in acceptable "casual" attire.

business protocol Aspects of business communication and the parts of etiquette that relate to professional life.

C

calling in In U.S. business terminology, a general term that implies that a staff member is ill and unavailable for work. "He's not here—he called in" means: "This employee is on sick leave. He telephoned to say that he would not be in to work today."

case interview An interviewing format in which candidates are presented with brief background information on a business situation and are asked what their advice to the firm would be. This format is popular with consulting firms.

cas-nice (casual-nice) A style of clothing requested for certain social gatherings; it implies clothes that differ from business attire but are still appropriate for a special event.

catastrophizing A tendency to treat small mistakes (especially during public speaking) as if they were great problems or catastrophes.

channel of communication The medium that a person chooses to communicate with another. For example, a message could be written in an e-mail or delivered by a phone call. In this case, "e-mail" and "phone" are two different channels of communication.

chronological résumé   The most usual format for the summary of a person's education and experience. Within each section, the most recent work is presented first.

cliché   Generalization that, although true, is so overused as to be meaningless, such as: "This is not the time to play the blame game."

closing   The set form of the end of a business letter. Historically, it was a profuse expression of fealty, but today it has been shortened to the most common "Sincerely."

colloquialisms, colloquial   Use of speech that is understood by some speakers of a language but not others. For example, in Australia, "I'm going to stop in for a quick one" means: "I am going to make a short visit to this bar for a drink."

comp day   "Compensatory day," a day off in place of a day worked. For example, if employees are required to work on a Saturday, a supervisor might promise: "If you can help us meet the deadline, I'll let you take Monday as a comp day."

conference call   A phone call with more than two people able to hear at the same time.

context, business context   Each communication falls on a continuum from social or everyday purpose to nonroutine, or contractual. The context of a communication determines the appropriate level of formality.

contraction   Shortening one or more words; for example, "don't" is the contraction of "do not."

copying up   The practice of sending a copy of an e-mail to a person's supervisor.

correspondence card   A card approximately 5 × 7 inches, preprinted with the sender's name and with matching envelopes.

costume jewelry   Jewelry that is not made of precious metals.

cover letter   Part of the formal process of applying to a firm for employment. The letter that goes on top of (covers) your résumé.

cubicle ("cube") A partly enclosed work space, without a door or windows; a subdivision of a larger office where several workers share the same space.

cultural norms Patterns of behavior that are shared by members of one country, society, social class, or group. Cultural norms determine what is considered appropriate behavior and what is considered rude or unsophisticated.'

D

dangling participle Beginning a sentence with part of a sentence and a subordinate clause instead of the simpler structure in which the main clause comes first.

distribution list Within an e-mail system, the ability to make a short name for a group of people so that typing the name (example, "LegalAff") will send a message to all the people in a work group (in this example, the members of the Legal Affairs staff).

"do it now" tasks A part of time management. The approach involves completing tasks at once, immediately, rather than setting them aside and going back to them later.

document As a verb, a term meaning to make a written record.

dominant culture A culture that has overwhelming influence in how international affairs and commerce are conducted.

E

e-mail name The part of an e-mail address that goes before the "@" symbol (e.g., "johnsmith" in "johnsmith@bigco.com").

emotional impact The feelings a recipient has about receiving a message.

Employee Assistance Program (EAP) A scheme at most large firms to provide counseling about personal difficulties for staff members. EAPs will refer people who are in trouble to appropriate community resources. Such programs save managers from getting involved in the personal problems of their colleagues.

employment application   A form asking for specific information in a specific order, unique to each firm, for job candidates. Firms are restricted from asking about certain topics, but applicants must answer all questions truthfully and fully. Lying on an employment application can be grounds for instant dismissal.

employment at will   A principle of common law that all employment is temporary and that both employers and employees continue the relationship only as long as both wish to do so. This means that except where an employee has a specific employment contract for a particular term, such as one year, an employer can fire a worker without reason or a worker can quit at any time without reason.

endnote   A comment or citation (note on the source of data) placed at the end of a chapter or report.

ethnic food   Also called "international cuisine." At a restaurant, food from a country other than the United States. Most American food is derived from the cuisine of other countries (French fries are from France), but many styles such as Italian food and steaks have become mainstream. "Ethnic dining" implies somewhat exotic food that will be interesting— but might not be to everyone's taste.

etiquette   Rules of social behavior governing courtesy and politeness.

euphemism   Literally, "beautiful speech." A way to talk about something unpleasant without resorting to unpleasant, graphic terms. For example, "Harold passed away last year" is a euphemism for "Harold died last year."

exit interview   When an employee leaves a firm, he or she may be interviewed either by a supervisor or by someone from Human Resources, most often to find out the reasons for his or her departure so that organizational problems can be identified and addressed.

F

fact check interview   A preliminary interview that serves the purpose of checking the facts of a candidate's résumé and cover letter.

fired, "let go"   Typical turns of phrase for ending employment other than when the employee chooses to resign. "Fired" often implies that the employee was terminated "for cause," that is, that he or she did something wrong. "Let go" implies that all employees are straining to leave their companies all the time, which is silly, but it saves the embarrassment of using the word "fired." See also *reduction in force.*

flame A colloquial term that means an e-mail of hostile tone. Don't send or forward flames.

footnote A comment or citation (note on the source of data) placed at the foot (bottom) of the page it refers to. Most word processing programs manage footnotes automatically.

formal, formality A style of communication that signifies seriousness and importance.

functional résumé A type of summary of a person's abilities that emphasizes skills rather than positions held.

G

gender-neutral Writing or speaking in a way that is inclusive of both men and women. It avoids using "he" when the person referred to could be male or female.

getting to know you interview An interview style that helps get a sense of a candidate's personality, beliefs, attitudes, and fit with the company. Can occur early in the process (a "smell test") or late in the process to help decide between candidates.

grade point average (GPA) A numeric representation of a student's academic ability calculated by multiplying the number of semester (or quarter) units for each course by a point system relating to the grade earned in the course, and then dividing the total of all such sums by the total number of units a student has completed. It is also possible to calculate a *subsidiary GPA*, for example, "GPA in Finance classes."

group interview A style of interview in which several candidates are in the same room with one or more interviewers.

H

handheld device An electronic device such as a smart phone or a PDA that allows the user to send and receive text messages on the go.

headhunter   A colloquial term for an "executive recruiter"; a member of a firm that tries to develop candidates for open positions, usually by phoning people with similar positions at competitor companies.

honorific   A title that "gives honor" to the recipient of mail, such as "Mr.," "Ms.," or "Dr."

hostile work environment   A legal term that refers to conditions in a workplace such that an employee fears for his or her physical or emotional well-being at work.

I

inform, persuade, or remind   The three possible purposes of any business communication.

Instant Messaging (IM)   A form of e-mail communication in which two or more people are online on the same service at the same time. It typically involves short comments without a greeting or closing, so may be referred to as "chatting online."

J

job description   An exact statement of the duties of a position and the skills required to perform it successfully.

job sample interview   An interview style in which a candidate is presented with a real-world business task and asked how she or he would handle it.

L

letter of transmittal   A simple letter describing something such as a brochure or contract that is being sent (transmitted) from one person to another.

letterhead   The preprinted firm name, logo, and address that appear on formal correspondence outside a company. Different divisions or departments may have their own letterheads and some senior executives may have individual letterheads.

level of formality   In both written and spoken language, a dimension concerning the type of language used. Informal language has contractions, colloquialisms, and simple structure. Most formal language avoids these in favor of strict grammar and style.

M

mail code, mail drop   A notation (such as "Mail Code: 1550") that helps postal mail get to the right desk in a large company. The mail code is invariably assigned to a department, not a building, so that if the offices are rearranged, the mail code remains the same. Some firms use the term "mail drop."

medium (singular), media (plural)   The channel of communication a businessperson chooses to communicate with the intended recipient of a message. For example, a decision could be announced by a phone call, letter, or e-mail—these are three different media.

mitbringsel   A small gift for a host and hostess brought with (*mitbringen* in German) a guest to express thanks.

moderator   The person responsible for beginning and ending a teleconference, watching the timing, and keeping to the planned agenda.

mute button   On a business phone, a button that silences the microphone at your end so you can avoid the person at the other end hearing coughs or paper shuffling.

N

need to know   A standard to determine what information should be shared with which staff members (e.g., not everyone in a work group needs to know the specific reason the personal assistant is out on leave for a month).

networking   Developing acquaintances with the hope of possible mutually beneficial business relationships later. The process of networking involves developing contacts (people you know well enough to phone) at many companies.

New Golden Rule   In business, you have but one job: to make it easy for other people to do their jobs. This is different from the traditional Golden Rule: Treat other people as you would wish to be treated yourself.

nonverbal communication   Interactions between people by other than words. Often called "body language." Might include stance (how you stand), interpersonal distance, facial expression, and hand gestures.

O

offer letter   The formal communication from a firm to a successful candidate specifying the terms of employment proposed.

on-campus recruiting   The process of formally announcing hiring for a firm using the career center of a college or university. Large firms like on-campus recruiting because they can interview a large pool of candidates in one or two days.

one-way communication   A form of communication in which a message is sent without any interaction with the recipient.

orientation   The process of educating a new employee about a firm. It can be a formal, structured program or a process that a new hire must self-manage.

outline   The skeleton of a communication; some notes that allow you to set out your ideas in the correct order before beginning to write.

outplacement   Job counseling offered to employees whose work has been terminated. It's almost always paid for by the firm.

Oxford cloth   A type of textile for shirts in which strands of thread are doubled so that the weave is visible and the fabric is quite thick. The opposite is *broadcloth.*

P

passive voice   The passive voice is a literary form of speech or writing in which the object of an action becomes the subject of a sentence. "The boy hit the ball" is active voice. "The ball was hit by the boy" is passive. Avoid this form in *Plain English.* See also *active voice.*

peer   A coworker of the same rank and status.

permanent record   A way to keep track of communication sent.

persuasive reasoning Using language that specifically supports one idea rather than another; comparing and contrasting concepts to achieve a change in attitude or belief.

phone interview An interview conducted over the phone, usually in the first round of interviews.

placeholder In speaking, nonword sounds such as "um" and "err."

place shifting The process of sending a message while in a different place from the recipient.

Plain English An approach to business writing that avoids bureaucratic language and forms. The key elements are short, direct sentences, using the most common words that express meaning and avoiding the passive voice.

politically correct Concept that certain turns of phrase are unacceptable in American public discourse. It is considered offensive to make disparaging generalized comments about any social group (national origin, gender, ethnicity, sexual orientation), even if that is your personal opinion. In addition, carefully choose forms of address that show respect—for example, "women," not "girls" for adult females. See also *significant other.*

portfolio A folder made of leather or imitation leather, about 12 × 9 inches; useful for keeping documents clean and flat and for carrying a notepad.

postal mail Communication that is written down on paper and sent through the company's internal mail, the U.S. Post Office, or couriers such as FedEx or UPS.

potluck A informal social gathering at which everyone invited brings a dish to share with the other guests.

professional Showing the highest standards of personal and interpersonal behavior in one's occupation.

prop In theater and film, a "property" (object), anything carried on stage by a performer (example: "Sarah enters holding a book," where the book is the prop). In public speaking, an object held up for the audience to see to engage its attention.

protocol   Unspoken rules of conduct that determine how people expect one another to behave.

Q

questions and answers (Q&A)   An expected part of almost all speeches and presentations, in which members of the audience are invited to ask questions of the speaker.

R

rate of speech   How fast a presenter speaks (that is, number of words per minute).

recipient   The person who will receive a communication.

reduction in force, "riffed"   When firms "downsize" (reduce the overall size of their workforce), some employees have their employment terminated. They are "riffed."

regrets   Shorthand for saying that a person cannot attend an event. A contraction of the form "I regret I am unable to accept your kind invitation."

reneging   Withdrawing from a position after it has been accepted in writing.

RSVP   An abbreviation for a courtly French phrase, "Repondez, s'il vous plait," literally, "Reply, if you please." In American usage, it means "Please let us know whether you are going to attend or not." The phrase "Please RSVP" is a tautology and shows that you don't know what the phrase means, so it's better to say, "RSVP," or in Plain English, "Please reply."

S

salutation   The beginning of a letter (most commonly "Dear [name]").

shadow an employee   The process in which a job candidate follows an existing employee around (like a shadow) for all or part of a workday to learn about the job.

Short Message Service (SMS) A form of sending messages in short form (usually no more than 160 words at a time); most famous form is text messaging.

sick leave Part of all employment agreements that allows a worker to stay at home while ill and yet still be paid.

signature file A block of text that can be appended to each e-mail that a person sends; most e-mail programs permit one routine signature file (for example, containing full personal name, mailing address, and telephone numbers) and several other optional signature files (for example, for e-mails within the firm where the mailing address would be replaced by an internal company mail code).

significant other A politically correct term to refer to the spouse, partner, or live-in boyfriend or girlfriend of someone else. For example, if two unmarried people have been living together but no one in an office is sure whether they are married, an invitation might read "and please bring your significant other."

signposting Announcing the structure of a talk at the beginning, so that audience members can follow the line of argument.

spam An e-mail term meaning a message that is sent to a very broad group of people, such as a company-wide message. "Spam" is usually used in the disparaging sense to indicate that the message was sent to many more people than cared to know about the subject.

split the bill, split the tab The process of two or more diners agreeing to divide payment for a bill at the end of a meal. Although people sometimes pay more or less depending on the cost of the items they themselves consumed, it's more usual for people to make a simple mathematical calculation: "$42—that's $14 each" (among three people).

stance In public speaking, where and how the speaker stands.

stress interview An interview format in which endless challenges and arguments are directed at the candidate to see if the candidate gets nervous under pressure and if she or he can think clearly.

suffix For a personal name, an addition after the family name to indicate the difference between family members who share the same name. Example: Lee Jacobsen, Sr., and Lee Jacobsen, Jr. Pronounced "Senior" and "Junior" but abbreviated "Sr." and "Jr." in the written form.

T

taking up references   The process by which a firm interested in hiring someone calls an associate, a former employer, or a teacher of a candidate and asks for input on the suitability of the person for a specific position.

tchotchke   A small gift of little monetary value, often a souvenir from another country.

technical skills interview   An interview with questions designed to test knowledge and problem-solving abilities.

"thank you" note   A routine part of polite social behavior. A short letter expressing thanks for hospitality or any other kindness.

time shifting   The ability to send a message at one time and have it read at another.

"to do" list   A list of action items, probably in order of priority or due date. Part of effective time management. Many computer programs (such as MS Outlook) provide ways to manage "to do" lists.

tone   The third dimension of written or spoken language. In general, it stretches from warm and friendly to cold and officious. It is independent of level of formality (that is, you can have a formal but friendly letter).

too much information   Extraneous details that obscure the actual information you are trying to convey.

transition   The process of moving from one topic to another topic in a speech.

transmittal   A letter that accompanies documents or other information that explains what is being sent and why.

twin set   For women, a matching fully fashioned thin sweater and over-cardigan suitable for business attire.

two-way communication   A form of communication in which messages are sent from the initiator and also from the recipient in the form of a conversation or discussion.

U

universal term of reference   A way of referring to another person without using her or his personal name—for example, calling another person at a dinner table "my friend" rather than "Sheila."

V

vesting   The processes by which employees are considered eligible for a benefit (such as pension) that accumulates over time. In the first years of employment, employees may be paying into a pension plan but would lose all contributions if they were not "vested." Benefit packages will explain how many years of service are required for vesting.

videoconferencing   A way to arrange meetings without being present in person. A videoconference is a phone call with video images of the participants.

visual aid   Any display that is visible to audience members during a presentation. Examples include props, handouts, and projected Power-Point slides.

voice mail   A system that is a routine part of almost all business telephone systems. It will play an announcement or greeting and then record messages if the owner of that phone number is unable to take a call in person.

voice-mail greeting   The announcement played to callers who reach a voice-mail system identifying the person whose phone it is and instructions for leaving a message or contacting someone else.

W

Web meeting   Short name for a "Web-enhanced meeting," which combines a telephone conference call (or voice-over Internet protocol, VOIP sound) and the ability for participants to see the same material on their computer screens, even if they are geographically separated by thousands of miles.

wordsmithing   Craftsmanship involved in smoothing and finishing a prepared speech or written work to avoid repetitions, vary vocabulary, clarify meaning, and add rhetorical effects such as taking two ideas and making them into a similar parallel form.